The Two Gospels of Mark

The Two Gospels of Mark

performance and text

Danila Oder

Domus Press
Los Angeles, California

Copyright © 2019 by Danila Oder

All rights reserved. No part of this book may be reproduced in any form or by any electronic or mechanical means, including information storage and retrieval systems, without permission in writing from the publisher, except by reviewers, who may quote brief passages in a review.

ISBN: 978-0-578-50531-2

Library of Congress Control Number: 2019905667

Unless otherwise attributed, all Bible quotations in this book are from the New Revised Standard Version Bible, copyright © 1989 National Council of the Churches of Christ in the United States of America. Used by permission. All rights reserved worldwide. http://nrsvbibles.org/

Photograph of the illustration of the Theater of Dionysus by Duncan1890, www.istockphoto.com

Cover design by Tim Barber, www.dissectdesigns.com

Printed and bound in the United States of America

First printing June 2019

Published by Domus Press
Los Angeles, California

Visit www.thetwogospelsofmark.com

To the memory of my father, Irwin Oder

It is important never to forget
that the plot must stand as a logical unity
quite independently of the ideas or concepts the play exhibits.

– Bernard Grebanier, *Playwriting*

Domitian slew, along with many others, Flavius Clemens the consul,
although he was a cousin and married to Flavia Domitilla,
who was also a relative of the emperor's.
The charge brought against them both was that of atheism,
a charge on which many others
who drifted into Jewish ways were condemned.

– *Epitome of Cassius Dio*

Truly I tell you,
wherever the good news is proclaimed in the whole world,
what she has done
will be told in remembrance of her.

– Mark (14:9 NRSV)

Contents

Preface	**xiii**
Introduction	**xv**
Major influences	xvi
Approach	xvii
My assumptions about Mark and his works	xvii
The limitations of my discussion of Jesus	xvii
Why I do not discuss doctrine	xviii
Envisioning the play	xix
Method	xx
Induction and uncertainty	xx
Judeans or Jews?	xxi
The Bible version used	xxi
Endnotes and footnotes	xxi
Notes on style	xxi
Definitions	xxii
Overview	xxiii

Part I: The Play and the Text

1 Performed Play and Polished Text	**25**
The discovery of a performed play under the received text	25
The genre of the polished text	27
Others' proposals	27
My proposal: Preserved play and myth	28
Literary features of the polished text	29
Narration of speech and action	29
Names of characters and places	30
Times of day and time lapses	30
Pointers to sources	30
Scene-level and larger structures	31
Key lines	32
Miscellaneous literary features	33
Features of the performed play	34
The genre of the performed play: Mime	35
The Gospel play within the mime universe	36

2	**The Structure of the Play**	**37**
	The Proposition	37
	Proposition of the plot of *Hamlet*	38
	The plot of the Gospel	39
	Proposition of the plot	40
	The subplot of the Gospel	42
	Proposition of the subplot	42
	The Passion	44
	Proposition of the Passion	44
	Foreshadowing of the Passion and narrowing of focus	45
	Reversals	45
	Does the Gospel have a five-act structure?	46
	The emotional power of the structure of the Gospel	46
3	**Features of the Play in Performance**	**49**
	The venue of performance	49
	Locations and permanent set	50
	a. The play's locations in the theater	51
	b. Indoor scenes	53
	c. Water and boat scenes	55
	d. The way	56
	e. Exposition of location names	57
	f. The Temple	57
	g. The villages	58
	h. The wilderness/deserted places	59
	i. Mountain scenes	60
	j. The tomb	61
	k. The courtyard with a fire	61
	Lighting	61
	Sound	63
	Costumes	63
	Healing prop	64
	Stage technologies	64
	Scent	64
	Party favors	65
	Roles	65
	The actors	65
	The Chorus	65
	Jesus	66

Satan	66
The disciples	67
The demoniac of Gerasa	72
The dancer	72
The enemies of Jesus	73
Judas Iscariot	74
The naked young man	74
Barabbas	75
The actors who mock Jesus	76
Simon of Cyrene	76
Mary Magdalene	77
Roman soldiers	78
Joseph of Arimathea	78
Acting and tone of the play	80
Characterization	81
Exposition of characters' names	81
Audience participation in the performance	82
4 Some Reconstruction of the Performance, and Editors in Rome	**85**
The Performability Criterion and the Dramaturgical Criterion	85
Analysis of edited scenes and sequences	86
The Herod material	86
Mark 6–8 (Bethsaida Plus)	89
Boat trip to Bethsaida (now missing)	98
The Second Feeding Miracle	98
The stilling-of-the-storm and water-walk scenes	99
Healings of the deaf-mute, the blind man of Bethsaida, and blind Bartimaeus	100
The original scene in Jericho	102
Other scenes	102
The calling of Levi	103
The Temptation	103
The Recognition	105
The Olivet Discourse	106
Jesus's cry from the cross	109
The empty tomb scene	110
My proposal for the performed ascension scene	111
The empty-tomb scene as a replacement for the ascension scene	113
Jesus's entry to the stage	114
The entry of the Chorus, and reconstruction of Mk 1	114
Conclusions about reconstruction	117

	The genre of the performed play, redux	120
	Pre-Matthean editors of the Gospel	122

PART II: CONTEXT AND AFTERMATH

5 Mark and the Roman Congregation — 125
- Mark's biography — 125
  - Honored playwright — 125
  - Possibly estranged from some of his family — 126
  - Of Judean heritage — 126
- The name "Mark" — 127
- Dates — 127
- Characteristics of the congregation — 128

6 The Occasion of Performance — 129
- The benefactor of the congregation — 129
  - The dinner in Bethany — 129
  - Flavia Domitilla, the benefactor — 130
- The performance in the context of benefaction — 131
  - Dinner-party and evening-event entertainment — 131
  - Flavia's role in the entertainment — 133
  - The play in the sequence of evening events — 133
  - Implications of benefaction for Mark's compositional process — 134
  - Implications of benefaction for the performance — 134
  - Elements of the play compatible with Flavia Domitilla as benefactor — 135
- The bias of the play — 137
- Sequelae of the performance — 138

7 The Second Century — 141
- The Roman congregation — 141
  - A third place for ethnic Judeans — 141
  - Insights from decorations in the Catacombs of Domitilla — 142
  - The future headquarters of orthodoxy and the Pope — 142
- Jesus the Nazarene becomes Jesus of Nazareth — 144
  - The Gospel story enters the mythos — 145
  - The usefulness of Jesus of Nazareth to the orthodox — 145
- "Mark" in the second century — 146
  - The orthodox creation of a link between "Mark" and a human Peter — 146
  - "Mark" outside Rome — 147
  - Summary — 148

APPENDICES

A	*The Gospel According to Seneca*	150
B	"Paul" and Acts	152
C	Times of Day in the Received Text	153
D	Model of the Two-Level Miniature Theater	158
E	A Partial Reconstruction of the Action of the Performed Play	161

Notes 187
Selected Bibliography 199
Index 205

List of Illustrations

Figures

Figure 1. The Theater of Dionysus in Athens in the late first century CE — 83

Figure 2. The stage of the two-level miniature theater, with locations of the play — 84

Tables

Table 1.	Sequence of scenes in Mk 6–8	90–91
Table 1a.	Scenes I deleted from the received text	92
Table 1b.	Parts of scenes I deleted from the received text	95
Table 2.	Healings of deaf-mute and blind men	100
Table 3.	Healings in the received text	118
Table 4.	Times of day specified in the received text	153–57
Table 5.	Proportions of the stage and wings of the Greek theater at Hadrian's Villa and the Theater of Dionysus at Athens	158
Table 6.	Measurements of the two-level miniature theater	159–60

Preface

This book began when I decided to inquire into how Christianity developed out of Judaism. I read a number of early Christian texts, including the Letters of Paul. I was surprised to find out they had essentially no information about the life of the founder of the religion, Jesus of Nazareth. So I decided to read the earliest story of Jesus's life, the Gospel of Mark. Like ancient readers, I read aloud. I noticed immediately that the Gospel was a play. But why was there a Narrator? Why were the scenes so short?

I delved into the Gospel of Mark. I found the story of Jesus of Nazareth—in a stage play. I found that the performance of the play was preserved in the received text. I reconstructed much of the staging of the play. And I found a plausible life-circumstance for Mark, and a plausible occasion for which he wrote.

I approach the Gospel of Mark from a unique perspective. When I started, I had never read it before, and had beginner's mind. I had studied in relevant fields: history, ancient and modern Judaism, playwriting, and acting. I am a native speaker of English at a time when English is the international language of scholarship. I live in a secular society. I have access to the internet for research. And in the last two decades, scholars have made a persuasive case that no human Jesus of Nazareth existed, and Mark's Jesus was a heavenly figure. As I did not need to reconcile my insights with the assumption that the Gospel of Mark was the record of a historical Jesus of Nazareth, I followed their inductive logic—which went very far indeed.

I ask the reader's forgiveness for my oversimplification of the complex landscape of proto-Christianity. In addition, I have done my best to read "around" my topic, but I expect that I have taken some things for granted that I should not have. I welcome corrections of errors of fact.

In this book, I have tried to imagine the staging of a play. Imagination goes only so far. Experiment with real actors on a real stage will test my theories. It will also yield additional insights into the performance and very likely reveal additional editing of the received text.

Kim Trimiew has been a reviewer, a sounding board, and a fellow enthusiast of antiquity. Thank you so much, Kim. The Los Feliz Writer's Block weekly Meetup group has been since 2014 a place to work, share, and support each other. Your dedication and professionalism have inspired me. Norman Oder reviewed an earlier version of the manuscript and offered useful advice on design, publishing, and marketing. Thank you for sharing your expertise. I acknowledge those friends and acquaintances who, on hearing the subject of my work-in-progress, expressed sincere interest in reading the finished product. Your trust that my book would be of general interest has meant a lot to me.

Dr. Hannah Platts answered my questions and kindly sent me the drawing of the ground plan of the Greek Theater at Hadrian's Villa. Dr. Marina De Franceschini and Jan Sammer responded helpfully to questions about their work. Russell Gmirkin provided editorial services with the right balance of skepticism and tolerance. Tim Barber of Dissect Designs patiently and skillfully responded to my specifications and produced a cover we are both proud of.

Introduction

IN THIS BOOK, I present a new scenario for the creation of the Gospel of Mark. I propose that the author wrote a play and staged it in a theater, in Rome, late one afternoon in the early 90s CE. The play was in the genre of mime. It incorporated as the Passion a previously written or outlined tragedy. The audience for the play was Mark's (very elite) congregation. The play was produced and hosted by the benefactor of the congregation. She was honored during the performance. To preserve the memory of the performance, Mark condensed it into a narrative. He left out much of the dialogue but kept many of the stage directions. He polished his narrative by adding (or making salient) literary features, such as chiasms and names of places not spoken during the performance. This text was edited at least twice in Rome before Matthew got a copy. After passing through many hands, Mark's "polished text" became the received text, the scholarly consensus versions of the Gospel of Mark that we have now.

I believe I am the first scholar to make the case that Mark wrote two gospels: a performed play and a narrative text. I believe I am also the first scholar to claim that Mark wrote his text in order to preserve the performance of the play. I believe I am also the first scholar to propose some reconstruction of the action of the play.

In this book, I ignore most scholarship on the Gospel of Mark (hereinafter "the Gospel"). I have two major reasons. Many scholars who write about the Gospel assume that it is a response to a historical Jesus of Nazareth, an assumption that makes their work almost unusable to me. Another reason is that many, if not most, scholars of the Gospel are interested in analyzing the Gospel as a literary text related to other literary texts. Such studies are largely irrelevant to my purpose. Instead, in this book I treat Mark's text as a record of a performance. I do cite scholars who have seen the Gospel as dramatic or performed, or offer observations germane to performance.

Initially, I thought that this book would contribute only to biblical studies. But I found it has implications for theater history and Roman history. This book concerns the only complete mime play to survive from antiquity, albeit at one remove from the performance script. I propose that the Gospel performance is an example of first-century Roman elite benefaction and private entertainment. And I propose an occasion of performance that illuminates the life-history of the benefactor.

This book is written for scholars and advanced amateurs who are already familiar with the Gospel of Mark. If you are not, prepare to be. I suggest that you refer to a version of the Gospel that is divided into "scenes" or episodes with descriptive titles.

Major influences

In *The Jesus Puzzle* and online articles, Earl Doherty has made a compelling case that the earliest Jesus-movement texts, including the canonical gospels and the letters of Paul, were written by people who knew only a heavenly Jesus.[1] I have read other scholars who have argued for a non-historical Jesus, but Doherty's case is the most comprehensive, and is directed at the general reader.

I often refer to Michael Turton's historical commentary on the Gospel of Mark from a skeptical point of view. Published online in 2004, the commentary is a little dated, but it remains an excellent introduction to observations at the verse and scene levels. Turton's extensive proposals for chiastic structures in the Gospel convinced me that Mark did make use of this literary feature in his polished text.

To understand the fate of Mark's preserved play in the century after his death, I have needed a basic understanding of second-century Christian politics and literature. I turned first to the works of Robert M. Price, the erudite dean of mythicist scholars.

The blog *Vridar* (owners Neil Godfrey and Tim Widowfield) presents high-quality, independent scholarly work and historical commentary, mainly on biblical topics. Much of my reading around the Gospel started with *Vridar*.

Early in my research, I read Livio Stecchini and Jan Sammer's book, *The Gospel According to Seneca*. The authors[*] argue that the Passion was a staged tragedy, and often refer to parallels in classical tragedy. Their work inspired me to ask if the *preceding* section of the Gospel of Mark was also a staged play.

Stecchini and Sammer's references led me to J. M. Robertson, who unequivocally asserted that the Passion had been performed. Robertson anticipated my observation that the Gospel is stageable and theatrical, but the scenes are dramatically static. Robertson's discussion of mystery-plays helped me to conceptualize the genre of Mark's play.

---

[*] Sammer put the book together from Stecchini's notes after his death. See Appendix A.

Richard Beacham's enjoyable history, *Spectacle Entertainments of Early Imperial Rome*, introduced me to Mark's aesthetic world. Even as the play repeatedly revealed itself as a theatrical masterpiece, an audience for such a lavish expenditure of talent on the entertainment of one evening remained possible.

"The Politics of Privatization: A Short History of the Privatization of Drama from Classical Athens to Early Imperial Rome," Chapter 6 of Eric Csapo's *Actors and Icons of the Ancient Theater*, supports my inductive conclusions about the genre of Mark's play and the occasion of its performance.

Approach

My assumptions about Mark and his works

The following assumptions underlie my work. I do not explain them later in the book.

- Mark wrote in Rome. From the mid-second century, orthodox tradition places Mark in Rome. The consensus of scholars is that Mark wrote in a major city.[2] The text of the Gospel contains several Latinisms and references to Rome.[3] My proposed occasion for the performance requires a location in Rome.
- In Mark's time, the Jesus movement was small and unorganized. Mark did not answer to church authority.
- Mark belonged to a congregation of the Jesus movement that included both born Judeans and born Gentiles.
- Mark wrote his play for a specific audience and a specific occasion.
- Mark was a skilled playwright. This is an inference from many features of the play, applied to the entire play. This means that if he knew about one theatrical convention, he knew about others.
- Mark wrote a play that was performed as a play. I discuss this below in the Introduction section "Envisioning the play."
- The performance consistently engaged the audience. This assumption is based on discovery after discovery of Mark's skill as a playwright.

The limitations of my discussion of Jesus

I assume that to Mark and his congregation, "Jesus" was a heavenly figure, an intermediary between YHWH and humankind. I make this assumption because in Mark's play, the heavenly Jesus comes to earth and is tested by another heavenly being, Satan. (Now on earth, Jesus engages with the Galilean/Judean multitudes and Council of Jerusalem.) I do not speculate on how Mark's congregation understood the "Jesus on earth" figure, or that figure's relationship to YHWH. Such speculation is extraneous to my discussion, which concerns "Jesus" as a character in a play.

I assume that Mark did not know the Letters of Paul. The Letters of Paul as we have them are second-century composites, as Robert M. Price argues in *The Amazing Colossal Apostle*. However, Mark may have known some of the texts that orthodox editors later excerpted in the (orthodox version of the) Letters of Paul. Mark and his congregation may have had beliefs about their heavenly Jesus that are *consistent* with elements of the Letters of Paul. But those beliefs are outside the scope of this book.

Why I do not discuss doctrine

By "doctrine," I mean teachings and positions on "religious" questions. During my discussion of the play, I came across statements and enactments of doctrine (for example, Jesus's statement that he must die and rise after three days [8:31]). Why do I not discuss these statements and enactments *as* doctrine? Didn't Mark want his audience to notice this doctrine?

There are several reasons. First, in a play, doctrine is conveyed in both action and dialogue. I cannot reconstruct the original dialogue of the play. Mark condensed the dialogue when he first wrote his polished text. Furthermore, dialogue can be seamlessly added, deleted, or changed by editors without disturbing the action of a scene. The received text has been through many hands. Some dialogue about doctrine that is now in the received text may not be original, and some original dialogue about doctrine may be missing.

Second, in this book, I imagine the play from the point of view of a playwright and stage manager. I am concerned with the who, what, where, when, and how. If I address the question "why?" I answer it only from the point of view of a playwright and stage manager. This relentlessly pragmatic approach may give the reader the impression that I believe that Mark was concerned only about entertaining his audience. I do think that was his first concern, and I think he also took a relentlessly pragmatic approach to his source texts: he used what was useful for his purpose. We have to first extract a performed play from the received text. We have to establish what happened onstage before we can discuss its meaning—to Mark, to the audience, to future readers of the secondary text in which he preserved the play. It just so happens that Mark was a writer of genius who gave many elements of the play double and triple meanings, some of which conveyed doctrine.

Third, the Gospel is not a didactic text. The play was built of and on beliefs the audience already had and texts and interpretations they already knew. (They could not have enjoyed a play that *challenged* their beliefs or presented new doctrine for the first time.) The doctrine expressed and enacted in the play is a *subset* of Mark's doctrine, including his doctrine about the Jesus figure. Also, the doctrine in the play does not necessarily map directly and evenly onto Mark's doctrine as he would have expressed it in a sermon or itemized it in a list. We must see the received Gospel text as based on a play that had been written for performance and followed the rules of effective performance. While Mark intended his text that preserved the play to be read and appreciated, it was first and foremost the record of a performance.

Envisioning the play

The received text is not necessarily a uniform condensation of the performance. Furthermore, some scenes are enacted in the text that in performance occurred offstage and were *reported*. The questions arise: If the text is not reliable in this way, is it a trustworthy guide to the performance? Did Mark write any scenes solely for the text? Did he add teachings that were not spoken onstage? I respond that such scenes and lines would be stylistically consistent with the rest of the text, and therefore probably impossible to identify. Still, I think it is extremely unlikely that Mark added new stageable material to the polished text. The occasion of performance that I propose implies that the performance was primary, and the text Mark wrote was secondary: he wrote to preserve the experience of performance.

Was a play actually performed? The question arises because some contemporary texts with theatrical features are not performable as plays.[*] I reply: The text of the Gospel has performable features that would not be present, or would not be present so consistently, in a text that was written only as a narrative. For example, almost every scene ends with stage directions that position the Jesus actor for his next scene. Such stage directions exist even in scenes that I later found were not original, or had been significantly edited. That is, the editors of Mark's original text provided stage directions to keep the edited scenes stageable *individually*. I infer that they knew the text was composed of theatrical scenes. Another performable feature of the received text is the stageability of almost all the scenes within a theater with a scene building and a permanent garden/tomb/mountain set. Another feature is the arrangement of the scenes in the received text—even

---

[*] For example, the Gospel of Peter reads like the account of a play, but the action unfolds too quickly for the text to have originally been a playscript. Some scenes in the Gospel of John are performable (e.g., the raising of Lazarus), but GJohn as a whole does not have a solid plot. The scenes in *Satyricon* unfold as though the reader is watching a play, but they are components of a narrative epic, not a play.

though it has been edited—in a sequence that requires few changes of the set. Compare GJohn, where scenes that require different sets succeed each other without intermission.

Another reason to think a play was performed is that in both the received and original texts of the Gospel, the plot spans the entire text, from Mk 1 to Mk 16 (see Chapter 2). There is no unstageable narrative material (such as the infancy material in the Gospel of Matthew). So, yes, I am convinced that a play was performed.

I recognize that there are two major obstacles to envisioning the pre-Jerusalem material as a performed play: The stagings of some of the healings and miracles lack dramatic interest. And the sequence of events before the entry to Jerusalem seems random. I address both of these problems at the end of Chapter 4.

Method

Induction and uncertainty

My method of reaching conclusions is inductive. I start with a fact and ask what could have caused it to exist. I review the possible explanations and identify the most plausible one. I review the relevant scholarship. If my provisional explanation is not contradicted, I consider the explanation a new provisional fact. I retain it in my scenario unless it is contradicted by new scholarship or other provisional facts.

I call these provisional facts "cantilevers." My conclusions in this book are cantilevers extended on cantilevers. Not infrequently I have extended a cantilever and found that it met a cantilever that originated from a different direction. I believe that the pattern I present here is internally consistent. It begins to fill in the Mark-shaped hole in the tapestry of history.

Still, the method of induction only provides a plausible explanation for facts that exist. Other explanations—structures made of different sets of cantilevers—remain possible.

And the facts themselves are not entirely stable. My inductive conclusions are based on the English received text of the Gospel, which is many steps removed from the Greek text that Mark left to his congregation's library. At each step, scribes made decisions about what to include and what to omit, and could have introduced errors and "corrections." I have not identified all of these changes and therefore may have unknowingly retained material that Mark did not write.

Judeans or Jews?
Historians disagree on the term they should use to refer to people of Judean ethnicity in the first century CE.[4] I have chosen to refer to Mark and his fellow congregants as "Judeans."* There is no distinction between ethnicity and belief—yet. The terms "Jew" and "Judaism" were used widely only after Mark's time.[5] But looking backward from the 21st century, I see Mark and his congregation as intentionally taking steps that would create a religion, a system of beliefs and practices independent of ethnicity.

The Bible version used
Quotations from the Bible are, unless otherwise specified, from the New Revised Standard Version (1989).

"Chapter" refers only to divisions of this book. When I refer to the divisions of the Gospel, I sometimes use "act" (Mk 2 = Act II). In that context, "act" does not imply anything about the structure of the underlying play.

Endnotes and footnotes
I cite ancient texts, under their English titles, inline. I cite other works in the endnotes. I place my comments and tangential material in the footnotes.

Notes on style
I follow *The Chicago Manual of Style* (17th edition) with one exception: I capitalize the chapters and appendices of this book (Chapter 1, Appendix B). For convenience, I capitalize the names of some well-known scenes (e.g., the Temptation, the Recognition).

Definitions
"The Gospel" means the Gospel of Mark.

---

* "Judean" is appropriate from my point of view. In Mark's context, I think the situation was complex. I think that Mark and his ethnic Judean congregants presented themselves to Gentile outsiders and to ethnic Judeans of other sects as "Judeans" (their religious practice was legitimate for an ethnic Judean). Gentile outsiders had no reason to dispute this. Judeans of other sects would have seen Mark and his ethnic Judean congregants as sectarians within the ethnic Judean cultural universe. Mark's Gentile-born congregants were in a different situation. Because "Judean" was an ethnic identity, I suspect that they said they were members of the sect, e.g., "member of the Church of X." Such an answer side-stepped the question of whether (if male) they had been circumcised, and which elements of the Law they observed. They could retain their born-Gentile ethnic identity and still be a member of the congregation. Outsiders could call these Gentiles "member of the Church of X" and not have to deal with the question of whether they were "Judeans" or not.

"God" means YHWH, the transcendent deity of the Judean *ethnos*.

"Scripture" means the set of texts accepted as authoritative/true by a Judean or a sect of Judeans. The core of the Judean canon was the Five Books of Moses/Torah, which Judeans believed contained their national history and laws. The Septuagint (LXX) was a Greek translation/version of the Torah and other Judean holy books. It was written/assembled in Alexandria before the first century CE. As Greek-speakers, Mark and his congregation used the LXX. Their "Scripture" may have included other texts, which are not relevant here.

The "Council" means the Judean authorities in Jerusalem. In the Gospel, the Council is comprised of scribes, chief priests, and elders. The scribes are affiliated with Pharisees.

The "Law" means the laws of the Torah. Every Judean sect, community, and congregation had to engage with the Law, interpret it, and decide how to observe it.

"Jesus of Nazareth" means a human being of flesh and blood who lived on earth and founded a religious movement, and whose life story is recorded in the canonical gospels. I believe that "Jesus of Nazareth" was created in the second century, as I briefly review in Chapter 7. It is possible that Mark thought his heavenly Jesus had "lived on earth" at some time or been "flesh and blood" in some sense, but I do not discuss these possibilities in this book.

The terms "Jesus" and the "Jesus figure" mean the "Jesus the Nazarene" character in Mark's play, or the doctrinal concept behind him. In the play, Jesus is a heavenly being who comes to earth on a mission, "dies" on a cross, then ascends to the heavens.

The term "Jesus movement" means all persons and congregations between c. 0 and c. 150 CE whose belief systems included a semi-divine intermediary/angel/son of God whom they called "Jesus." The term "Jesus movement" is for my convenience as a historian. Well into the second century, the persons in these congregations and sects would not have seen themselves as part of a "Christian" religious universe. They would have seen themselves as sectarians: Judeans, Judean philosophers, Judaizers, God-fearers, members of the Church of God or other sect, followers of Marcion, and so on. The earliest extant record of "Christian" comes from Syrian Antioch, in the second century (Acts 11:26).

"Proto-orthodox" refers to some first-century and early-to-mid-second-century members of the Jesus movement. They valued Scripture.

They rejected revelation as a method of perceiving the truth. They created an official history (the Acts of the Apostles) of their (supposed) founders. Orthodoxy evolved out of the Jesus movement into a church in the mid–second-century, when an orthodox person or committee compiled the first version of the orthodox New Testament canon. Several decades later, Irenaeus's work *Against Heresies* (c. 180) advocated the "unity of the faith of the Church throughout the whole world" (1.10), that is, catholic orthodoxy. (The orthodox sect later became the state religion of Rome, and the parent of the Catholic and Orthodox churches.)

For a first-century organized group of Jesus-movement members, I use "congregation" rather than "church." I use "church" only for the second-century orthodox institution that was headquartered in Rome and led by the Bishop of Rome/Pope.

The term "Passion" refers to events that begin with the Last Supper. This is because approximately 24 hours elapse from the Last Supper to the (proposed) ascension scene after Jesus's death.

The term "play" means a dramatic entertainment with a solidly structured plot (see "The Proposition" in Chapter 2), performed on a stage.

Overview

Part I concerns the play underlying the received text of the Gospel of Mark.

In Chapter 1, I argue that Mark wrote two versions of the Gospel: a performance script/performed play and a condensed, literary version that I call the "polished text." I differentiate between the *dramatic* genre of the performance script/performed play and the *literary* genre of the polished text.

In Chapter 2, I discuss the plot and the subplot of the play, and the Passion as an element of the entire play.

In Chapter 3, I analyze the received text of the Gospel to infer the theatrical elements of the play and the logistics of the performance. I discuss the performance from the point of view of a director or stage manager.

In Chapter 4, I suggest two criteria to identify nonoriginal material in the received text. I reconstruct speeches, individual scenes, and several sequences, including the (single) trip to Bethsaida. I suggest that two editors in Rome with distinct agendas revised Mark's polished text before Matthew made his own version.

Part II concerns Mark, his congregation, the occasion of performance, and the near-term fate of the Gospel.

Chapter 5 considers the biography of Mark, who was "not without honor." I discuss the date of the Gospel. I infer some characteristics of Mark's congregation from the performance and the fact of the performance.

Chapter 6 concerns the occasion of the performance. I argue that Mark wrote and directed the play on behalf of the benefactor of the congregation, who I propose was Flavia Domitilla, a niece of the emperor Domitian. I discuss implications of this scenario for the contents of the play and the polished text.

Chapter 7 skims Jesus-movement history over the next 100 years, with a focus on the uses of Mark's polished text. I suggest how the historical Jesus of Nazareth came into being. I suggest why the orthodox downplayed Mark's identity and biography.

Appendix A briefly reviews *The Gospel According to Seneca*, in which Livio C. Stecchini and Jan Sammer describe the production of a hypothesized first-century Passion play that tells the harmonized gospel story.

Appendix B concerns "Paul" and the Acts of the Apostles. I explain why I do not use Acts and the Letters of Paul as sources for the Jesus movement of the first century.

Appendix C provides a table of the lighting specified in the received text of the Gospel.

Appendix D provides the dimensions I used for the two-level miniature theater (Figure 2).

Appendix E is a condensed play script, a first attempt at reconstructing the blocking and other physical action of Mark's original play. The script incorporates my proposals from this book, presented mostly in Chapters 3 and 4.

Part I: The Play and the Text

CHAPTER 1

Performed Play and Polished Text

IN THIS CHAPTER, I review how I concluded that a performed play existed under the received text of the Gospel. I then review the received text for literary features that were not present or salient to the audience during the performance. I then propose that the genre for the text that Mark wrote is "preserved play."

Next, I turn to the genre of the performed play. I propose that its genre was mime. I propose that the Passion was a mini-tragedy, a component that Mark integrated into the overall mime play.

The discovery of a performed play under the received text

When I first read the received text of the Gospel, I intuited that it was the script of a play. I formatted the received text as a playscript to defamiliarize it. There was narration, so I provisionally assigned it to a Narrator. Here is the reformatted version of a simple, probably original scene. Note that I have not omitted or changed any words of the received text.

ACT III, SCENE 1 (3:1–6)
Capernaum.

NARRATOR: Again he entered the synagogue, and a man was there who had a withered hand. They watched him to see whether he would cure him on the sabbath, so that they might accuse him. And he said to the man who had the withered hand,

JESUS: Come forward.

NARRATOR: Then he said to them,

JESUS: Is it lawful to do good or to do harm on the sabbath, to save life or to kill?

NARRATOR: But they were silent. He looked around at them with anger; he was grieved at their hardness of heart and said to the man,

JESUS: Stretch out your hand.

NARRATOR: He stretched it out, and his hand was restored. The Pharisees went out and immediately conspired with the Herodians against him, how to destroy him.

(next scene, 3:7) NARRATOR: Jesus departed with his disciples to the sea, and a great multitude from Galilee followed him...

"Jesus" speaks and acts like an actor in a play. But what did the Narrator do in the play? At first I supposed that the Narrator *was* a role: an actor offstage who described the action, while the actors onstage silently gestured. But then I realized that later in the play, the Jesus actor spoke long teaching passages. When he taught, he addressed the audience as well as the other actors onstage, and therefore had to speak in his own voice. If the Jesus actor spoke his teachings, he spoke *all* his lines. Therefore, for the entire play, the audience would hear only the voices of the Jesus actor and the Narrator. The other actors would only gesture. That seemed extremely awkward. I concluded that every actor spoke their own lines and there was no Narrator at the performance; the Narrator was an artificial role created for the Gospel text *after* the performance.

Now let us return to the quoted passage above. It is one step away from a playscript. At scene end, the actors move between locations that are physically feasible in a theater or performance space—from the synagogue (a few benches) to the sea side (the edge of the stage). (In contrast, imagine a text without feasible transitions, in which the actors must move directly from the synagogue to a boat *in* the sea or from the synagogue to a high mountain.) The stage directions that precede and follow the scenes in the received text are feasible in a theater or performance space.

Next I unfolded the Narrator's part. In this scene, the narration seems to only refer to stage action/gestures. It does not seem to imply any dialogue by any other actors. But in other scenes, the narration does imply that dialogue spoken onstage has been omitted.[*]

I concluded that a staged play underlies the received text, but the received text is not the master performance script or an actor's "part." Rather, the received text *preserves* a condensed version of the performed play. The text

---

[*] The amount of dialogue Mark omitted in his polished text varies by scene. (I am assuming the following summations of dialogue are original and not edited.) Sometimes the narration conveys the *gist* of the omitted dialogue but not the details, e.g., the Gerasene demoniac proclaims "how much Jesus had done for him" (5:20). And sometimes not even the gist is preserved, e.g., in the trial scene, "many gave false testimony against him" (14:56), but only one false testimony is preserved (14:58). The duration of the trial scene is not knowable.

Mark wrote was a variation on the master performance script, but it was not for the use of an actor or a crew member. It was for the use of readers after the performance was over. In modern terms, it was the novelization of a screenplay.

The genre of the polished text
Others' proposals
The genre of the received text of GMark has been described variously.[*] A 2011 literature survey lists Hellenistic biography, Hellenistic novel, Homeric epic, "eschatological historical monograph," biblical narrative (Scripture or quasi-Scripture), Greek drama, and Greek tragedy.[6] These proposals are often entangled with assumptions about Mark's "community," the existence of Jesus of Nazareth, and the prior development of the gospel story that are not compatible with my assumptions. Here I will mention only proposals that see performance in the received text (or in part of the received text).

The first group argues that Mark's text was performed as dramatic or performative reading.[7] I agree that the received text is dramatic. However, it is not *optimized* for dramatic reading. Events occur too quickly to make an impression on the listener. The trial, for example, is over in less than a minute. In contrast, in texts optimized for dramatic reading, the action is drawn out (given dramatic extensivity). In addition, to involve the listener, words and phrases are repeated, and the text uses rhyme and other poetic devices. An example of a text written for performative reading is the Book of Esther, which is still read aloud (and still entertains the audience) on the Jewish holiday of Purim.

A variation on this proposal of dramatic reading is that Mark wrote a play that was intended to be read aloud rather than performed (a "closet drama").[8] The genre of closet drama is proposed based on the nine (or eight) authentic extant dramas of Seneca the Younger. The performability of those dramas is debated.[9] In any case, even if there *was* a recognized genre of closet drama in Mark's Rome, Mark's play does not belong to it. Seneca's dramas are in Latin and have "long declamatory, narrative accounts of action…obtrusive moralizing…bombastic rhetoric."[10] In contrast, Mark wrote in a terse, simple Greek. His text has few long speeches, no elaborate rhetoric, and almost no editorial comment.

---

[*] *In a discussion of literary genre*, I treat—and think it is valid for others to treat—the received text as equivalent to the text from Mark's hand (the "polished text").

The second group argues that the received text of GMark (or just the Passion) is a transcript or other secondary version of a performed play. For J. M. Robertson, the received text of GMark is a hybrid of transcribed play and narrative. He notes that the scenes in the Passion display the compression of time and other dramatic features of modern stage plays. He asserts that the (harmonized synoptic) Passion was a performed mystery-play that was added to another document. "The Mystery Play is an addition to a previously existing document....The transcriber has been able to add to the previous gospel the matter of the mystery-play; and there he loyally stops." Robertson says that some scenes prior to the Passion may have been presented dramatically but does not discuss them further.[11]

Building on Robertson's work, Livio C. Stecchini and Jan Sammer propose that the Passion was a performed play. They propose that Mark and Luke saw a performance of the play, Matthew worked from Mark's narrative, and John had a copy of the script of the play and wrote his own narrative.[12] While this scenario is hard to imagine, Stecchini and Sammer deserve credit for recognizing that the performed Passion play and the received texts of the Passion story are in different genres. And they do account for the different degrees of stageability among the four canonical gospels. (For the reader who intends to refer to Stecchini and Sammer's work, I offer some comments in Appendix A.)

Michael Bryant builds on Stecchini and Sammer's work. He proposes that an anonymous Christian translated the (Passion) tragedy into Greek, then Mark rewrote it to his needs.[13] Mark wanted to present the Passion story "as narrative, not drama, in accordance with the literary customs inherited from Judaism."[14] Bryant is correct in identifying the received text as a narrative that overlays a performed play.

Michael Turton has asserted that the *entire* gospel story was a staged play, but does not detail the performance or try to identify its theatrical genre. Nor does he explain why Mark wrote a literary text.[15]

My proposal: Preserved play and myth

I see the received text of the Gospel as secondary to the performed play. The received text is *functionally* a condensed, narrated version of the performed play, a "preserved play."

I believe that Mark always intended to preserve the play in a text, and as he wrote the play he simultaneously planned literary features of the text. They were not necessary if his goal was solely to preserve the audience's experience at the performance.* In plain terms, Mark wrote a myth—and a candidate for Scripture. I infer that Mark expected the polished text to have readers who could appreciate these literary features—and preserve it within his sect.

Literary features of the polished text

Now I turn to the polished text of the Gospel of Mark. (By "polished text" I mean the text from Mark's hand.) The polished text has been extensively edited. The version we have now—the "received text"—nevertheless retains the original literary features. Some of these features are expected in a literary genre (for example, proper names are given to characters and places that during the performance were not named to the audience). Other literary features tie the narrative together (chiasms at the scene-level and play-level), or direct the reader/listener to Mark's sources (emulations, quotations). Now I turn to some salient literary features of Mark's polished text.

Narration of speech and action

When Mark preserved his play, he converted the audience experience of performance into a text. The main tool that he used was narration.

Sometimes the narrated speech in the polished text seems to closely track the lines spoken onstage, for example, "As they were coming down the mountain, he ordered them to tell no one about what they had seen, until after the Son of Man had risen from the dead" (9:9). (There is no reason to think dialogue on any other topic was spoken in performance.) Other times, the narration implies additional (and now lost) dialogue, such as "And crowds again gathered around him; and, as was his custom, he again taught them" (10:1b). (What lines did the Jesus actor speak?)

Often narration closely tracks the physical actions onstage, for example, "Immediately, while he was still speaking, Judas, one of the twelve, arrived; and with him there was a crowd with swords and clubs, from the chief priests, the scribes, and the elders" (14:43). Mark has condensed physical action into narration.

Sometimes the physical action in the narration is vague. In those cases, I strongly suspect that the narration is not original. For example, "he did not speak to them except in parables, but he explained everything in private to his disciples" (4:34). (Where is "in private" located in the world of the play?)

---

* Compare the Gospel of Peter, where the writer speaks as though he is remembering and recounting the performance of a stage play. GPeter does not have the same literary features as GMark.

Names of characters and places
There are many small roles whose actors, during the performance, were not named to the audience (John the Baptist, Joseph of Arimathea, and Barabbas are the exceptions). The audience kept track of the other roles by sight. When Mark wrote the polished text, he gave names to some of these actors, for example, Jairus, Judas Iscariot, Mary Magdalene.

Similarly, during the performance the actors move from location to location in the performance space. But only one location name, "Jerusalem," is mentioned *in dialogue* in the received text. There is no dramatic need *during the performance* for the audience to hear "Capernaum," "Gerasa" and "the way to the villages of Caesarea Philippi." (Some names might have been spoken, but certainly not all of them.) When Mark wrote the polished text, he gave names to many locations. The polished text contains many more names of people and locations than the audience heard in speech.

Times of day and time lapses
During the play, the actors indicate early morning, evening, or a new day in dialogue or by gestures such as yawning, or by moving to a different part of the theater. Narration, however, requires time markers: "in the morning," "after some days," etc. These terms are artifacts of the polished text.

Pointers to sources
In the performed play, Mark frequently referenced Scripture in dialogue and in action. When he condensed the performance into the polished text, Mark made many references clear to the reader. He retained dialogue and described the action onstage, often in words that evoked his sources. Occasionally he added details that had not been staged, e.g., "*Six days later*, Jesus took with him Peter and James and John, and led them up a high mountain apart, by themselves" (emphasis added) (9:2). The detail comes from and is a pointer to Mark's source, "The glory of the LORD settled on Mount Sinai, and the cloud covered it for six days" (Ex 24:16a).* Another example is in the healing of the paralyzed man (Mk 2:1–12). The entire scene is performable except 2:4, the breaking of the roof and the lowering of the man through it. These details are literary pointers to Mark's source, which Robert M. Price identifies as 2 Kings 1:2–17.[16]

---

* Mark obviously used as sources Scripture, other Judean texts (e.g., the Enochian works), the works of Homer, and tragedy. He also may have referenced contemporary texts now lost.

Scene-level and larger structures

The term "chiasm" (from Greek *chi* "X") refers to an inverted parallel literary structure. In the polished text, Mark used chiasms to structure sentences in dialogue, descriptions of scenes, and the arrangement of scenes in the play as a whole.

Examples of chiasms at the sentence and paragraph level are "Whoever welcomes one such child in my name welcomes me, and whoever welcomes me welcomes not me but the one who sent me" (9:37) and "The wedding guests cannot fast while the bridegroom is with them, can they? As long as they have the bridegroom with them, they cannot fast" (2:19).

Michael Turton is an independent scholar of GMark who believes that Mark structured the (polished) text of each scene with inverted parallel events or concepts. Turton calls this arrangement of a scene a "chiasm," but acknowledges that another term is needed.[17] For convenience, I use "chiasm."

Here is a simple chiasm proposed by Turton for the received text of Mk 3:1–7 (RSV)[18]:

> A Again he entered the synagogue, and a man was there who had a withered hand.
>> B And they watched him, to see whether he would heal him on the sabbath, so that they might accuse him.
>>> C And he said to the man who had the withered hand, "Come here."
>>>> D And he said to them, "Is it lawful on the sabbath to do good or to do harm, to save life or to kill?"
>>>>> E But they were silent.
>>>>> E′ And he looked around at them with anger, grieved at their hardness of heart,
>>>> D′ and said to the man, "Stretch out your hand."
>>> C′ He stretched it out, and his hand was restored.
>> B′ The Pharisees went out, and immediately held counsel with the Hero′di-ans against him, how to destroy him.
> A′ Jesus withdrew with his disciples to the sea, and a great multitude from Galilee followed;

The A brackets have what Turton calls "geographical movements"[19] (i.e., stage directions). The B brackets concern action by the Pharisees. The C and D brackets frame the healing in the E brackets. The E brackets form what Turton calls a typically Markan "prolix/pithy" center.[20]

It is logical that if Mark wrote *any* scenes in the polished text as chiasms—and as it appears from this exercise, he did—he wrote *all* the scenes as chiasms. (Why would he apply this format to such a simple scene, but not to more important and complex scenes?) I use this insight when I reconstruct Mark's original Olivet Discourse, p. 106. If a scene-level chiasm is structurally defective, we should assume that an editor has intervened.

Scene-level chiasms are a literary device. We cannot infer that they *evenly* condense the action and dialogue that occurred during the performance. They are not an *average* of the scene in performance. (These cautions are particularly apropos for scenes that are mostly action, like the entry to Jerusalem and the Temple Incident.)

I note that the audience did not perceive the structure of scene-level chiasms during the performance. In fact, I suspect that although Mark had structures in the back of his mind while he wrote the performance script, and those structures helped him construct each scene, the chiasms only came into existence when he wrote the polished text.*

I end my discussion of scene-level chiasms here. I leave the reconstruction of Mark's original chiasms to others.

Mark created larger parallel structures within the play as a whole. For example, Simon (Peter) is the first disciple to be introduced, and the last disciple to leave the stage. During the prologue of the play, the heavens (curtains) separate when God acknowledges Jesus as his son; they separate again (the Temple veil rips) when Jesus dies, shortly before the end of the play. As with chiasms at the scene level, these parallel events would be more salient to the attentive reader/listener of the polished text, who could stop and reflect, than to an audience member at the performance, who might be focused on other elements of the performance.

Key lines

The dialogue that Mark chose to preserve I call "key lines." Key lines are usually spoken by Jesus, or, sometimes, by another character in a conversation with Jesus. Sometimes the key lines are wise sayings or teachings.

---

* How would a mental plan for a chiasm help Mark construct a scene? The scene needs an introduction to an action/event, the event, and the end of the action/event. For example, Jesus and disciples enter. They interact with the Chorus. Jesus teaches/debates. Something unique about the scene occurs (or is described). The Chorus reacts. Jesus and disciples leave. As long as Mark kept those elements in mind, he could enact them in the performance script in many ways—and the performance could include much material that he omitted from the polished text.

Sometimes the key lines quote or reference Scripture. Because key lines are part of scene-level chiasms, Mark must have planned the dialogue in each scene around its key line(s).

Miscellaneous literary features

1. Pigs rush down a mountain into the sea and drown (5:13). Live pigs cannot be used, and stuffed pigs would be ridiculous. I propose that in performance, the audience saw Roman soldiers drown (p. 61), and never heard the word "pigs" spoken. There are several possible explanations of why, in the polished text, Mark chose to describe the stage action in code ("pigs").* The point here is that Mark expected his readers to assimilate this term to their imagining of a staged play.

2. The Recognition scene takes place on the way to the villages of Caesarea Philippi (8:27). But Caesarea Philippi was a city, not a district. This impossible piece of geography catches the reader/listener's attention and suggests the staging of this scene was unusual.

3. Joseph of Arimathea is described, impossibly, as a member of the ruling (*boulē*) council (15:43) (p. 79). This anomaly alerts the reader that there is something unusual about the description of the character.

4. The play has *four* characters named Simon (Simon Peter, Simon the Cananaean, Simon the Leper, Simon of Cyrene). A playwright must give characters distinct names, and four Simons in a performance is three too many. I propose that the name "Simon the Cananaean" is by the editor who changed Mark's Three at the mountain into Twelve at the mountain (p. 68). For the other three Simons, I suggest that Mark uses "Simon" as a placeholder "John Doe" name for Judean characters whose names are not spoken in performance and whose characterization is conveyed in their second name (see pp. 76, 80n, and 136).†

---

* These possibilities include: 1) in a Judean context, "pigs" indicate Gentiles and could refer to the Roman legion occupying Jerusalem; 2) a drove of pigs that drown emulates the (Gentile) Egyptian soldiers who drown in the Red Sea in Exodus 14:27–28; 3) a transformation that involves pigs emulates Circe's transformation of Odysseus's men in *Odyssey* 10; 4) "pigs" who throw themselves off a mountain emulate the mysteries of Demeter, among whose rituals was throwing piglets into a pit.

† Approximate modern equivalents would be a chauvinistic actor, unnamed in the performance, who in the narratization is named "John Bully," and a drunken actor, unnamed in the performance, who in the narratization is named "John Barelycon" (close to "John Barleycorn"). The reader would infer the characteristics of these actors from their names alone.

So, here we have a coded term, impossible geography, an impossible characterization, and a conspicuous flouting of basic playwriting technique. These literary features tell the reader to not take the text at face value.

The Judean theater of Alexandria

Mark must have known about the Judean theater of Alexandria. Ezekiel the Tragedian wrote in Alexandria, probably in the second century BCE. Scholars have usually seen his extant text, "The Exodus," as a single play.[21] However, a theory published in 2003 holds that his text comprises fragments of *four* plays.[22] If this is true (I find it plausible), Ezekiel wrote a tetralogy, like the early playwrights of Greece. Ezekiel treated a Judean subject in a traditional Greek format.

Such syncretism must have increased over the next several centuries. We know that Judeans in Alexandria attended public performances. "Philo was a regular spectator at the theatre (Ebr. 177)....Aristeas (284) approves attendance at the theatre for performances done with respectability and moderation."[23] And other theatrical forms of the era have left traces in the Jewish canon.*

With the considerable Judean population in Alexandria well into the imperial period, for *centuries* audiences there must have seen plays with Judean characters, and dramatizations of Judean stories and themes. Judean playwrights other than Ezekiel must have learned Greek and Egyptian theatrical techniques. They could read playscripts in the Library. So it is reasonable to assume that Mark used contemporary theatrical forms for a story based mainly on Judean Scripture and meaningful only within a Judean religious context.

Features of the performed play

The received text of the Gospel reveals a play with a plot and subplot. The play has the following features:

- An episodic/journey structure;
- A section that is stylistically distinct (the Passion);
- Many speaking parts;
- Actors who do not wear masks;
- Female actors;
- A foolish second character (Peter).

---

* The Book of Job is easily imagined as poetry spoken by virtuoso actors on a stage, and the Song of Songs is easily imagined as the libretto for a pantomime performance at a wedding banquet.

The play is not tragedy, Old Comedy, or New Comedy. The play is written in Greek; therefore, it is not a *fabula palliata* or a *fabula togata*. The play is obviously not an Atellan farce.

The only remaining contemporary theatrical genre is mime. All the features listed above were acceptable in a mime play, and the foolish second character was standard. I note that mime (and the ballet-like pantomime) were living genres in Mark's time, with centuries of popularity still to come.[24]

The genre of the performed play: Mime

In Mark's time, the term "mime" had several meanings.* It referred to both the performers and the performances. Originally, mimes were street performers who set up a small stage in the town square, and offered entertainments such as songs, music, dance, animal acts, skits, sexually explicit repartee, and insults to the audience. These variety shows were also called "mimes." The free-spoken performers and their bawdy and vulgar shows were the shadow side of Roman propriety. Naturally, mime performances were extremely popular. The mime genre of entertainment suited dinner parties, as we see in the variety-show entertainments presented at Trimalchio's dinner in *Satyricon*. (That work was influenced throughout by mime.[25])

In Mark's time, the term "mime" was also used for full plays performed in theaters. Mime plays had been presented in Rome at the annual spring festival, the *Floralia,* since 173 BCE. R. Elaine Fantham points out, "From that time the sponsored plays must have been subject to rehearsal for approval before purchase; thus they will have assimilated towards the regular structure of comedies and their dialogue will have abandoned improvisation for a formal script."[26] Two centuries later, "in Rome there were performed mimes with 'multiple actors' and 'dramatic plots'...while mimes in general—here reference is made to Greece—were divided into *paignia* (short plays that were nothing more than burlesque scenes) and *hypotheses*, which are further defined as costly and lengthy dramas (i.e. stage plays), presumably indicating an elaborate plot ([Plutarch,] *Symposiaca* VII 8.712A)."[27] So, in Mark's time, the performance genre of "mime" included coarse street performers, variety shows for dinner parties, and rehearsed, full plays with formal scripts (the *hypotheses* mentioned by Plutarch).

The extant references to "mime" in antiquity occur over more than eight centuries and a substantial portion of the Mediterranean world.[28] Little of the actual texts or quotations from mime (at least identified as such) are

---

* Modern mime is an entirely different performance genre.

extant.[29] The only extant texts of literary mimes are two partial texts, in Greek, from Oxyrhynchus in Egypt. The texts were written down in the second century CE, possibly based on earlier originals. The plays, *Charition* and the *Moicheutria* ("The Adulteress"), are farces, "easily digestible products intended for mass consumption."[30] But they are two bits of data in an opaque sea. We cannot infer that all mime plays were farces.

Recognizing the scarcity of data, modern scholars define the mime genre broadly. Fantham writes that mime "is best defined negatively. Whatever did not fit the generic categories of tragedy or comedy, Atellane or the Italian togate comedy was mime: a narrative entertainment in the *media* of speech, song and dance."[31] Stavros Tsitsiridis adds "imitation of life": "As opposed to comedy, mime tradition did not possess a fixed structure and strict stock characters (its only basic ingredient was the 'imitation of life', even when its themes were not everyday per se)."[32]

The Gospel play within the mime universe

If we look at the Gospel play within the genre of mime, it was an unusually decorous example. Mark nods to several mime conventions: He checks off nudity, with the flight of the naked young man, but his nudity is not gratuitous (p. 75). Mark uses female actors, but without any sexual overtones. Mime performances, including mime plays, often ended with a "raucous mêlée,"[33] and the ascension scene I have proposed includes the precipitous exit of the shocked Council and multitudes. If the audience perceived the performed play as a sort of variety show, they would accept the mini-tragedy (the Passion) as a component of a play that *overall*, was in the genre of mime. We can now understand why Mark wrote the polished text in "rough, crude prose that has more in common with low class colloquial speech than ancient high class classical language."[34] Mark was *signaling* the mime genre of the performed play to the readers of the polished text.

CHAPTER 2

The Structure of the Play

IN THIS CHAPTER, I analyze the structure of Mark's performed play. In the plot, Jesus is a heavenly being who comes to earth on a mission. Satan, the antagonist, tries to prevent him from completing his mission. Because both the protagonist and the antagonist are heavenly beings, I call the plot the "heavenly story." I propose that the play has a subplot. In the subplot, Jesus deliberately challenges the authority of the Council over the multitudes. The Council eventually decides to eliminate Jesus—as he always intended. Because the subplot concerns Jesus's activities on earth, I call it the "earthly story." The Passion is then discussed as a distinct component of the play.

The Proposition

The Proposition is a series of statements that make explicit the logic of a dramatic plot. The Proposition was created in the late 19th century by the American drama critic and play doctor William T. Price. Price's Proposition was clarified and improved by playwriting teacher Bernard Grebanier. Grebanier explains the Proposition in his classic 1961 textbook, *Playwriting: How to Write for the Theater*. Grebanier calls Price's Proposition "the one significant contribution to the science of playwriting since Aristotle's *Poetics*. This was the judgment of many of his students, among whom were the most successful American dramatists of their generation. It is a large remark, but…we do not dispute it."[35]

The Proposition is "an analysis of the *main action* only.…It has reference *only to action*, not to motives, psychological states, moral issues, or the theme, for plot is entirely a matter of action" (emphasis in original).[36]

I recognize that modern playwrights and critics use other tools to analyze plots. These other tools may be valid, but I do not discuss them. I do not seek to provide an exhaustive analysis of the structure of the Gospel as a performed play. I only want to see if the Gospel has a solid plot (and subplot).

In this book, "Proposition" means Grebanier's improved version of Price's Proposition. Because in this chapter I frequently quote from *Playwriting*, I place the page numbers for these quotations in parentheses, preceded by the letter "P," inline, not in the endnotes. In these quotations from *Playwriting*, italics are in the original.

Proposition of the plot of Hamlet

Here, to familiarize you with the Proposition, I present Grebanier's analysis of the plot of *Hamlet*.

"In applying the Proposition to any given play…ask first; *What is this play about?* By which we mean: *What is this play's action about?*" Answer: The play's action is about Hamlet's quest to kill the King.

"What raises the question: Will Hamlet kill the King? This event: Hamlet, by presenting a little play before the King, proves to himself that the King is unquestionably guilty of the murder of Hamlet's father."

Why does Hamlet decide to present the little play before the King? "Hamlet is told by the Ghost…that the King has murdered Hamlet's father, and is enjoined to avenge that murder" (P86–88).

With the above in mind, Grebanier reverses course and begins at the beginning of the play. Here is Grebanier's statement of the Proposition of *Hamlet*:

1. "Hamlet is told by the Ghost that the King has murdered Hamlet's father, and is enjoined to avenge that murder.
2. Because Hamlet is unsure of the reliability of the Ghost's revelations, he presents a little play before the King, and through it proves that the King is really guilty of the murder.
3. Will Hamlet now kill the King?" (P94)

Answer to the question of the play: Hamlet kills the King.

"*The Proposition always deals with events in which both the central and second characters are concerned*" (P91). In *Hamlet*, the central and second characters are Hamlet and the King. They appear in all three steps of the Proposition.

A play must have a climax. At the climax, "*the most violent dislocation occurs in the relationship between the central and second characters*" (P109). The climax is a deed done by the central character; a third character (or symbolic object) is involved. In *Hamlet*, the third character is Polonius. At the climax, Hamlet does a deed: he kills Polonius. That moment is the climax because "Hamlet and the King exchange roles: the King becomes the pursuer of Hamlet, murderer of Polonius and now the pursued" (P112). Hamlet still wants to kill the King, but now he must kill the King before the King kills him!

In summary, the plot is about the relationship between the central and second characters. They appear in steps 1, 2, and 3 of the Proposition of the plot. The climax is a deed done by the central character that involves a third character or "*some dramatic object...with the catalytic force of a third personality*" (P123). That deed has consequences for the relationship of the central and second characters which lead to the answer to the question of the play.[*]

The plot of the Gospel

When I thought about Mark's play, I initially assumed that the plot concerned Jesus's conflict with the Council. After all, that is the "Gospel story" that we all know. But I changed my mind. My train of thought began when I tried to reconstruct the Temptation scene.

The Temptation scene in the received text (1:12–13) is not stageable (p. 103). But GMatthew (Mt 4:1–11) has a stageable, theatrical Temptation scene that could have originated in GMark, and been summarized by an editor of GMark as Mk 1:12–13. So I assumed for the moment that Mt 4:1–11 *was* approximately Mark's original Temptation scene. If that is the case, the Satan actor is onstage just after the prologue to the play (the Voice of God and the baptisms). The audience sees Satan test Jesus's commitment to his Father and to his mission (and in the process, hears important exposition).

In the received text of GMark, the Satan actor is not onstage again, but there are traces of his presence. Jesus repeatedly exorcises Satanic spirits.[†] As they are agents of Satan, they try to make Jesus's mission more difficult by revealing his true identity to the multitudes. Later, in the Recognition scene (8:27–33), Jesus says (apparently to Peter), "Get behind me, Satan!" The blocking of the scene in the received text does not work. However, the blocking *does* work if the Satan actor is onstage, and Jesus sees him and addresses *him* as the agent responsible for Peter's behavior (p. 106).

If the Satan actor was onstage at the beginning of the play, tried to derail Jesus's mission via the Satanic spirits, and was again onstage at a critical moment near the midpoint of the play (the Recognition), then the relationship between Satan and Jesus was very likely a major structure of the play. And therefore the Satan actor was probably also onstage near the end of the play. I had already concluded that the last scene of the play was not the dramatically dull empty-tomb scene, but rather, a spectacular ascension

---

[*] Grebanier should have clarified that the "question of the play" is actually the "question of the *plot*." A play can have subplots, each with its own Proposition.

[†] In the Gospel of Mark, Satan, the heavenly adversary, is conflated with Beelzebul, the prince of demons. Why Mark conflated them is outside the scope of this book.

scene. If the Satan actor were present there, his conflict with Jesus would be resolved: he would see for himself that Jesus had passed all of the tests and had completed his mission on earth.*

Was the relationship between Satan and Jesus the plot or the subplot? The Temptation answers that question. Satan and Jesus are both heavenly beings. A conflict between two heavenly beings must be the frame story for any conflict that takes place on earth. Therefore, the conflict between Jesus and Satan is the plot: I call it the "heavenly story." The plot frames the subplot of the Gospel, the conflict between Jesus and the Council: the "earthly story."

Proposition of the plot
1. Jesus, a heavenly being who is sent by God to earth on a mission to die, is offered earthly power by Satan, the heavenly adversary.
2. Because Jesus refuses his offer of earthly power, Satan places in the multitudes demonic spirits that, when exorcised, reveal Jesus's identity. (The demonic spirits' statements that Jesus is the Son of God and the possessor of divine healing power give the multitudes a reason to keep him alive.)
3. Question of the plot: Will Jesus resist Satan and complete his mission on earth?

Climax: Peter rebukes Jesus for predicting his Passion. Now Jesus knows that Satan has entranced Peter. Jesus responds with a rebuke to Peter for "setting your mind not on divine things but on human things" (8:33). At that moment, the audience hears that Jesus will not trust his chief disciple to support him. This scene also tells the audience—and the reader/listener—that Jesus knows that Satan is responsible for Peter's entrancement.

Answer to the question of the plot: Jesus does complete his mission on earth. He is arrested, tried, and sentenced to death. He dies. In the last scene of the play, he ascends to heaven.

I recognize that my explanation of the *climax* of the plot may seem strained, because the received text does not tell us why Jesus cares if his disciples want

---

* Was the Satan actor onstage at any other time? I think not. If the actor were visible to the audience *throughout* the play, e.g., on a balcony, the audience would be constantly wondering if they had missed his gestures or reactions while their attention was elsewhere. And in the received text, there are no other scenes where his presence is implied. Still, it is possible the audience receives some sort of visual reminder when Jesus teaches "How can Satan cast out Satan?" (3:23) and "Satan immediately comes and takes away the word" (4:15).

to keep him alive. Why does he need their support? And what can Peter do (when entranced) to derail his mission? I suspect that the climax sets up the inner disciples' failure to watch in Gethsemane, and thereby somehow weakens Jesus's resolve to complete his mission. But the entranced Peter character may have originally displayed overt opposition to Jesus's mission that has been edited out.

Prior to the Recognition scene in Mk 8, the disciples do not understand Jesus's mission, so we can assume that he has not explained it to them. How has the audience remained interested in Jesus's apparently arbitrary itinerary, and apparently random activities as a teacher and healer? My response is, Jesus has told the audience about his mission—*when the disciples were not present*. I think that the Jesus actor says the equivalent of "Here's my plan. I am going to do X and Y to make the Judean authorities kill me. I ask my Father for the strength to carry out the mission on which he has sent me." The logical occasion for this speech is just after the Temptation scene, *before* Jesus has acquired disciples. I propose that this speech/prayer is narratized in the text as Jesus's solitary prayer (1:35) (p. 115).

Mark, I believe, used a second method to keep the audience interested in the plot. The parable of the sower could have alerted the audience that Satan would interfere with the disciples. Imagine the Jesus actor speaking the following, as he looks directly at the inner disciples, "The sower sows the word. These are the ones on the path where the word is sown: when they hear, Satan immediately comes and takes away the word that is sown in them" (4:14–15). The disciples do not understand this, because they were not present for the Temptation or Jesus's solitary prayer. But the audience was. Now the audience anticipates that Satan will show up onstage again—and interfere with the inner disciples.

In the received text, the conflict between Satan and Jesus is blurred, almost erased. The received text does not tell us how the Jesus actor periodically reminded the audience that he remained committed to his mission. Perhaps the Jesus actor stared at Satan's "perch" on the scene building. Perhaps Jesus's dialogue referred to his contest with Satan (in words that the audience understood but the disciples did not). Remember that we have only the key lines of the polished text, and it has been edited.

Why does God send Jesus to earth on a mission? Jesus probably addresses this question in that early prayer. I note that, just before the climax of the plot, Peter recognizes that Jesus is the Christ. Obviously the identification of "Jesus" as "Christ" was important doctrine. Several scenes, taken together, suggest that Jesus is sent to earth to be tested to see if he is worthy to become the high priest in the heavenly Temple. This suggestion is supported by the Recognition, the anointing at Bethany, the opposition of the *earthly* high priest, and Jesus's ascent to the heavens. See also endnote 49.

The subplot of the Gospel

Subplots are structured like plots, says Grebanier. The one difference is that because subplots depend on the plot, the locations of the various steps of the Proposition and the climax are "much more fluid" (P334–35). Subplots, in other words, are subordinate to the plot and must adapt to its structure. In the Gospel, we find the subplot nestled inside the plot.

I call the subplot of Mark's play "the earthly story." The subplot is about the heavenly Jesus's quest to be killed on earth. Mark chose the Council to be the agent of Jesus's death. This choice brings with it a mutual interest in the Temple. Mark could have chosen to make the antagonist of the subplot a king, a Gentile administrator, or the high priest. And Mark could have set the subplot at a time *other* than the time of Pontius Pilate.

In the subplot, Jesus comes into Galilee, where he impresses the Chorus with his miracles, wisdom, and interpretations of Scripture. Jesus's popularity* worries the Council, which sees him as a competitor. When Jesus interferes with the operations of the Temple, the Council decides to arrest and kill him. Aided by its agent, Judas, the Council does arrest Jesus. The Council tries him and he is killed (as he had intended).

Proposition of the subplot

1. Jesus, a healer and charismatic teacher who teaches "as one having authority, and not as the scribes" (1:22) impresses the Judean and Galilean multitudes and thereby challenges the Council's authority as interpreter of Scripture.

2. Because Jesus steadily acquires followers from the Judean and Galilean multitudes, the Council worries that they will lose their authority.

3. Question of the subplot: Will Jesus be allowed by the Council to continue to teach and heal the multitudes?

---

* It is fair to say that Jesus acquires followers mainly because of his miracles. From the received text, it is impossible to tell how much Jesus's preaching has convinced the multitudes to grant him authority to interpret Scripture. But some of them are at least intrigued, which is sufficient to alarm the Council.

Climax: Jesus interferes with the operations of the Temple. His disrespect for the Temple convinces the scribes and chief priests on the Council that he must be killed (11:18).

Answer to the question of the subplot: Jesus is not allowed to continue teaching and healing. The Council and high priest conduct an illegal trial, then the chief priests manipulate the multitudes into demanding from Pilate the release of a different prisoner. This sequence of events condemns Jesus to death. Jesus dies on a cross.

In the climax of the subplot, the Temple is the third character/dramatic object. The Temple is important to both the central character and the second character. When Jesus interferes with the operations of the Temple, he provokes the Council to take action.

I have always found the Temple Incident awkward and unconvincing. Jesus's behavior seems unmotivated. But in the main plot, the heavenly story, Jesus's goal is to be killed on earth. In this context, his interference with the Temple operations makes the Council decide to arrest and kill him. The Temple Incident is a *success*.*

The Temple Incident has a second function in the play. The inner disciples (and possibly the outer disciples) participate in the Temple Incident: they block or restrain the Temple attendants while Jesus overturns the tables. Later, when the arrest party comes to Gethsemane, the disciples present know that they are just as guilty as Jesus of having interfered with the Temple's operations. Therefore, they flee. The Temple Incident provides the disciples present at Gethsemane (except Peter and Judas) with their motivation to exit from the stage.

Exegetes have long wondered why the Council does not arrest Jesus immediately after the Temple Incident. I suggest that in the world of the play, his interference with the Temple operations was fairly innocuous from a ritual point of view. The disciples block or restrain fewer than a dozen Temple attendants from carrying objects across the stage. (Those objects could have been ritually innocuous, e.g., used bowls.) Meanwhile, Jesus overturns two tables in the public-area Temple Court. After insulting the Council, and allotting time for the audience to chase after the coins and birds, he signals the disciples to release the attendants. In real life, the Temple Incident would have taken less than 10 minutes. In the play, the Council certainly

---

* I note that Jesus *plans* the Temple Incident when he "looks around" the Temple after he enters Jerusalem (11:11). His "looking around" alerts the audience that he will return.

saw Jesus as a provocateur who had to be stopped, but his actions need not have polluted the Temple or seriously interfered with its operations. His arrest could be delayed.

Another point about the subplot: Jesus's goal is to continue teaching wisdom and healing the multitudes. That goal makes for a boring play, because it is open-ended. This goal has dramatic value only within the context of the plot: Jesus's mission to die on earth.

The Passion

As many people have noted, the Passion has much in common with tragedy. The Passion obeys the Aristotelian unities of time, place, and action; it has a sympathetic protagonist with a fatal flaw (hubris); it has a Chorus.

What is the Passion's structural relationship to the entire performed play? Technically, the Passion is a subplot. Within the entire performed play, the Passion is a mini-tragedy, a component of a literary mime play.* Mark integrated the Passion into the entire play; both the subplot and plot resolve near the end of the Passion (Jesus dies—and ascends).

Proposition of the Passion

1. Jesus, a healer and charismatic teacher who has antagonized the Council of Jerusalem, holds a last supper with his 12 disciples, including Judas, during which Jesus predicts his death.
2. Because Judas has notified the Council of Jesus's whereabouts, Jesus is arrested by the Council and put on trial.
3. Question of the Passion: Will Jesus be killed by the Council?

Climax: The high priest, on behalf of the Council, asks Jesus if he is the son of God. Jesus's answer contains statements that the Council interprets as blasphemy. The Council condemns him to death.

Answer to the question of the Passion: Jesus is brought by the Council to Pilate, to carry out the sentence of death. Despite several potential reversals, Jesus eventually dies.

I believe that when Mark decided to write the entire mime play, he already had in hand the play that he used as the Passion. I suspect that that Passion

---

* That is, Mark took advantage of the "variety show" format of mime to include a nonmimic component within his literary mime play. Until the approximately 24-hour period of tragedy begins at the Last Supper, the acting style of the inner disciples and some other characters is humorous, and the tone of the play is often light.

play, or the original from which Mark adapted the Passion we know, was the third play of a trilogy: the audience at these first two plays was introduced to the characters and the protagonist's mission. (Centuries later, directors of Passion plays added material prior to the entry to Jerusalem.[37])

Could Mark have used a Passion play written by someone else? Outside the four canonical gospels and the Gospel of Peter, there are no known versions of an earlier Passion play.* We have to ask about the Jesus-movement *community* for which it would have been written. That community would have considered drama an appropriate treatment of the Passion story. That means that the Passion story was either devotional/ritual, or entertainment. There is no evidence of a first-century Jesus-movement community with a ritual Passion play. If, alternatively, the community saw the Passion story as entertainment, then they had to have an allegorical approach to the Jesus figure. In that case, the Passion story was a secondary work, an *illustration* of their beliefs in a nondevotional setting. That is exactly what I propose for Mark in Rome in the late first century.

Foreshadowing of the Passion and narrowing of focus

Mark has prepared the audience for some of the Passion's tragic features. The three Passion predictions (8:31, 9:31, 10:33–34) inform the audience about the protagonist's future. Once Jesus arrives in Jerusalem, the action is restricted to Bethany and Jerusalem, in a defined sequence of time. The focus zooms in from "all of Galilee" to "Bethany and Jerusalem" to Jerusalem. Then it zooms in to a specific part of Jerusalem. Jesus no longer interacts with the Chorus: it has assumed its traditional tragic function as the general population of the locality—here, Jerusalem.

Reversals

Mark creates several potential reversals in the Passion. These potential reversals create dramatic tension, because Jesus *wants* to be executed. I offer the following; there may be others.

First, the trial is staged at night and during a festival. (The disciples have asked, "Where do you want us to go and make the preparations for you to eat the Passover?" [14:12].) The trial is illegal and impossible in a number of ways.[38] A Council member who noticed any of these violations—some of which must have been salient to the audience—could have stopped the trial.

Second, Pilate is not eager to condemn Jesus, and even asks, "Why, what evil has he done?" (15:14).

---

* The gospel used by Marcion was ultimately based on GMark.

Third, Pilate offers the Judean multitudes the opportunity to free a prisoner. If they choose to free Jesus, he will not complete his mission.

Fourth, while the soldiers are marching Jesus to Golgotha, they impress a passerby, Simon of Cyrene, to carry the cross. I suggest that Jesus, weakened by the beatings, stumbles and falls. Will he die *before* he is crucified?

Does the Gospel have a five-act structure?

The play as a whole does seem to have five acts. But the duration of each act is impossible to determine. The text we have has been edited by many hands. Also, every performance of a play is unique and can be only partially captured by a text, even the original performance script. I propose the following divisions for Mark's original play:

Prologue: Introduction of the protagonist, baptisms by John the Baptist.

1. Introduction of the antagonist (Satan) and establishment of the plot conflict. Introduction of Chorus and inner disciples. Beginning of Jesus's mission on earth (healings and teachings) to Galileans.
2. Continuation of Jesus's mission on earth in Galilee. Interference by the antagonist via agents (Satanic spirits). Establishment of the subplot conflict (with the Council).
3. Expansion of mission on earth to Gentiles (Gerasa and Bethsaida). Jesus rebukes Satan for having overcome Peter—climax of the plot.
4. Jerusalem/Bethany section. Entry to Jerusalem. Continued conflict with the Council. Jesus provokes the Council at the Temple Incident—climax of the subplot. Activities in Jerusalem and Bethany: teachings, Last Words, anointing prior to death.
5. The Passion. Last Supper, Gethsemane scene, arrest, trial, and condemnation of protagonist. Death of protagonist—resolution of the subplot and Passion. Ascension of protagonist—resolution of the plot.

Epilogue: Exit of Peter and the Chorus, singing.

The emotional power of the structure of the Gospel

Here I treat the received text, the polished text, and the performed play as the same, because their *structures* are the same. The plot and subplot both begin in Act I. They unfold simultaneously throughout the play. The subplot ends when Jesus dies. The plot ends shortly thereafter when Jesus, having completed his mission on earth, ascends to heaven.

If we think of Jesus's career on earth, we are angry that a wise teacher and compassionate healer has been unjustly killed because he asserted his authority to interpret Scripture in a new way. If we focus on Jesus as a heavenly being, we are gratified that the Son of God has fulfilled Scripture and successfully resisted the testing by the heavenly adversary. If we think of Jesus as the protagonist of a tragedy, the logic of the tragic structure makes us sympathetic to him even though we know that he wants to be condemned to death and die on the cross. No wonder the Gospel Jesus seems multidimensional and beyond human experience. Mark wrote him that way.

CHAPTER 3

Features of the Play in Performance

IN THIS CHAPTER, I first discuss the possible venues of performance. I conclude that the play was performed in a Greek theater. I map the locations named in the received text onto the stage and other areas of the theater. I then focus on the technical elements of the play. I discuss many of the characters in the play. Finally, I discuss several miscellaneous issues, including the actors' contributions to the performance.

The venue of performance

The question of the venue of performance came up very early in my research. I had identified the Gospel as a performed play, and assumed that it was performed in Rome. I asked, Which Romans outside Mark's congregation would have attended a performance of the Gospel play in the 70s–90s? I had no reason to think that there was more than one congregation of the Jesus movement in Rome. (We cannot infer their presence from the story that the emperor Nero had martyred Christians several decades earlier; the story of that martyrdom was invented in the second century.[39]) Samaritans would not have been interested in a play about Jesus's conflict with the *Jerusalem* authorities. The Roman public would not have been interested in a theatrically unspectacular play whose entertainment value often depended on the audience's recognition of emulations of Scripture. Therefore, the audience for the play was almost certainly Mark's fellow congregants, and their slaves and guests. The performance was private.

Was the play performed in a *triclinium* (dining room), atrium, auditorium, or private theater? Private entertainment was associated with dinner. But Mark's play could not be performed at a dinner party.* An ordinary triclinium was too small to accommodate the audience, the stage, and an

---

* In this book, I find it useful to distinguish between a dinner party and an evening event (my term). At a dinner party, the guests recline, and the entertainment is presented during the meal or the drinking party afterwards. An evening event is a more general term that includes the service of food and wine at some point, but also includes activities that are not accompanied by food and wine, and which occur in spaces other than a triclinium.

"orchestra" area. A large triclinium (in a villa or palace)—even if it could accommodate a stage and small orchestra—would have had poor acoustics, lighting, and sightlines. The atrium—the large reception room in the public area of the house—also had poor acoustics and a pool in the center of the floor. A small stage could be built, but there was no room for a scene building. The houses of some wealthy people contained auditoria, for private use or for rent. These auditoria had daises for poetry readings, musical performances, etc.[40] But even if such a room was large enough and had a stage, it did not have the orchestra Mark needed for the boat trips. A private theater would be ideal. It would include a stage, an orchestra, and a scene building. But private theaters must have been rare. I put that problem to the side for quite some time. Eventually I discovered a situation in which Mark could have had access to a private theater.

Locations and permanent set

Before I begin, let me clarify some terms. In theater productions today, the terms "Stage Right" and "Stage Left" are used *from the actors' point of view*. (That makes sense, since the terms are used mainly during rehearsal.) This convention dates to antiquity.[41] I follow it in this book.

Stage Right	Stage Left
	Audience

There was another convention associated with these directions. "The location of the Dionysiac theater at Athens on the south slope of the Acropolis was such that a character coming from the city, marketplace, or harbor, would naturally enter on the spectator's right, while persons coming from the open country would enter on the left."[42]

Stage Right	Stage Left
← Country	City, Marketplace, Harbor →
	Audience

In a 1911 article, Kelley Rees reviews the extant classical Greek plays to see if they observed this convention. He concludes that tragedies and comedies departed from it, but New Comedy used it.[43] So, given the popularity of New Comedy in Mark's world, we can assume that Mark knew this convention. It is plausible that he used it; he had to use *some* convention for the actors' entrances and exits, in a journey story that included travel to and from cities, and boat trips across the Sea of Galilee. And this convention produces a stageable play.

I suggest that you write down these directions on a piece of paper, as I will refer to them frequently in my discussions of the staging of the play.

a. The play's locations in the theater

I assume that the play was performed in a Greek theater. Here, I propose where the locations of the polished text mapped onto the parts of the theater. I began my research as follows:

In their reconstruction of a Passion play, Stecchini and Sammer note that, by convention, the way to the country was on the left side of the stage from the audience's point of view (Stage Right). Therefore, the "country" set—the Gethsemane garden, with potted plants and trees, and a rock wall with the tomb door—was Stage Right.[44] I assumed that Stecchini and Sammer were correct. I asked if *earlier* scenes in the Gospel used this garden/tomb set. They did. In Act V, in Gerasa, the demoniac emerges from the "tombs." This means that the actor enters the stage from behind the rock wall.

The scene in Gerasa provides another detail of the set: "Now there on the hillside a great herd of swine was feeding" (5:11). If a hillside/mountain is "there," i.e., near the tomb, the mountain and the tomb are on the same side of the stage. That side is Stage Right. The mountain had been used earlier: Jesus had called the disciples from a mountain (3:13). Therefore, the play must have begun with a permanent set of a garden/tomb and a mountain placed Stage Right. That part of the stage was now occupied.

During the (full) play, where were the multitudes (the Chorus) stationed when not involved in a scene? They cannot be Stage Right or Stage Center. Therefore, they waited Stage Left.

I note that a permanent set Stage Right and a waiting area Stage Left imply that these areas are a bit separated from the empty area (presumably for major scenes) Stage Center. So I assumed that this separation meant wings: an area on each side of the stage that extended forward into the orchestra and was therefore visually separate from Stage Center.

Where was the boat stationed? The first boat trip ends at Gerasa, where the demoniac emerges from the tombs. The presence of the tomb and the mountain in Gerasa mean that it is Stage Right. Therefore, the boat must have traveled from Stage Left, where it had been used earlier by the fishermen. (Recall that Stage Left represented "the way to the harbor.")

We can now infer other features of the theater. As the boat was in the orchestra, the actors had to use stairs to enter the stage from the boat. So stairs existed on each wing, probably on their outer sides. Another set of stairs Stage Center was needed to provide access from the Way to Jerusalem (in the orchestra) to the Temple Court Stage Center. Side entrances (*parodoi*) were needed for stagehands to bring in and remove the boat. An exit door behind the audience area was needed for the re-entry of the Blind Man of Bethsaida. Several scenes require a "house" set. Jesus is "in a house" or "reclining at dinner." In several scenes an actor lies on a bed. This means that a part of the stage was designated as the "house," with at least one bed/couch visible. In addition, several scenes are set in a synagogue, which was another location onstage.

Initially, I assumed that the stage had one level. I constructed a miniature theater to test the blocking of the play. I placed the garden/tomb and the mountain Stage Right. I placed the Chorus on the wing Stage Left. I placed the house set next to the Chorus, between Stage Left and Stage Center. The couch(es) that signified "house" had to remain onstage through the dinner at Bethany (14:3–9). Therefore, the Temple Incident had to be staged Stage Center, between the couches and the garden/mountain. But when I blocked the Temple Incident, the stage was too crowded. Mark would not have squashed the choreographed action of the Temple Incident between the garden/tomb set and the house set!

A single-level stage had another problem. The Last Supper requires an "upper room." (I assume this detail is original.) Therefore, the theater needed an architectural feature above the stage large enough to hold 13 seated actors and a table. A balcony was not large enough.

I looked at the design of Greek theaters. What features did they have? Early Greek theaters had a flat-roofed scene building. But the Last Supper was staged in an upper room, not on a roof. Then I happened upon an artist's drawing of the Theater of Dionysus (TD) at Athens in the first century CE (Figure 1). TD had a two-level stage, with exterior stairs between levels. TD is what I sought.

The artist of the drawing in Figure 1 is not credited, and his or her sources are not known. Still, the architecture shown is plausible for the following reasons:

- The proportions of the ground plan of TD as shown in Figure 1 are similar to the proportions of the ground plan of the Greek theater at Hadrian's Villa (Appendix D). And the foundations of the stage are still extant in Athens. The artist could have referred to measurements of these theaters.
- Greek theaters in the Hellenistic period typically had two stage levels linked by exterior stairs: a wide lower level, and an upper

level that was backed by the scene building.⁴⁵ TD had been used in the Hellenistic period. In addition, in Mark's time TD had recently been renovated: "major revisions, probably including the introduction of a raised stage, were carried out in *c.* AD 61 under the Roman emperor Nero."⁴⁶

- Nero, an actor and Grecophile, would have spared no expense. The elaborate decoration of the theater in the drawing is plausible.

I will assume from now on that Mark used a two-level theater similar in layout and proportions to TD.* In Mark's theater, the scene building was on the upper level. The "house" set was in front of one of the smaller doors. The Last Supper was staged in front of the large central "royal" door. That space could serve earlier as the synagogue, and later as the *praetorium*. On the wide lower level, Stage Center was large enough to serve as the Temple Court and host the Temple Incident. The wings on the lower level extended a few feet forward into the orchestra and hosted the mountain Stage Right and the mooring for the boat Stage Left.

I then constructed a new, *two*-level miniature theater (Figure 2). I blocked the play in this theater. I imagined and reimagined the play. I revisited the blocking. Sometimes experiment revealed that a scene was staged not on the stage or in the orchestra, but in another part of the theater. Sometimes experiment revealed that a scene was unstageable, and therefore out of order, edited, or reported. These experiments contribute to my discussion in this chapter and Chapter 4, and underlie the reconstruction in Appendix E.

b. Indoor scenes

The received text contains a number of scenes that take place inside a house. How were these scenes staged? The doors of scene buildings allowed the audience to see only a few feet inside. For an "indoor" scene, playwrights had two options: the scene could be performed in front of a door, or reported by a messenger.

Let us look at an "indoor" scene in GMark, the dinner with outcasts (2:15–17):

> ¹⁵ And as he sat at dinner in Levi's house, many tax collectors and sinners were also sitting with Jesus and his disciples—for there were many who followed him. ¹⁶ When the scribes of the Pharisees saw that he was eating with sinners and tax collectors, they said to his disciples, "Why does he eat

---

* I note that every theater was different, as the architect was expected to modify his design "to suit the nature of the site or the size of the work" (Vitruvius, *On Architecture* 5.6.7).

with tax collectors and sinners?" [17] When Jesus heard this, he said to them, "Those who are well have no need of a physician, but those who are sick; I have come to call not the righteous but sinners."

Let us assume that this scene was performed as narrated. In front of one of the small doors on the upper stage, Jesus and the disciples recline on three couches. Tax collectors and outcasts join them. The actors dip their bread, they chew. The scribes approach and ask the disciples about Jesus. The other guests stop and listen. Jesus responds with a wise saying. The actors stand up and leave.

This staging makes for poor theater. The audience has to wait while the actors recline, eat, and stand up. Stagehands have to clean up the food. And the audience below can't see all the diners.

What is the purpose of this scene? Only this: Mark wants the audience to know that Jesus has eaten with tax collectors and outcasts (and, perhaps, to *see* one or two of these actors). A different staging more efficiently accomplishes those purposes. Jesus, the actor who plays the tax collector, and one or two recognizable "outcasts" from the multitudes enter the "house" door of the scene building. One or two disciples follow them inside. Scribes walk over from the synagogue area and ask the other disciples, "Why does he eat with tax collectors and sinners?" *The scribes' question tells the audience the identity of the actors who have entered the door, and the fact that Jesus is dining with them.* The disciples open the house door and call to Jesus. He emerges and responds to the scribes. The scene is over. The fact of the dinner has been reported. Jesus and the disciples are free to move into the next scene. (The tax collector and the outcasts will quietly rejoin the Chorus.)

The healing of the paralytic (2:1–12) was also embellished in the narrative. Most of the scene (2:1–3, 2:5–12) is stageable as an ordinary healing in front of the house door. As for 2:4, a roof could not be built onto the scene building. And the scene is not important enough for the audience to wait while the "bearers" lowered the paralytic from above onto the stage.

I discuss the other "house" scenes at various places in the text. See Appendix E for the enactment of my conclusions.

I note that the received text contains three "private" teachings/explanations by Jesus to his disciples (7:17–23, 9:28–29, 10:10–12) that are set "in the house" but are not compatible with the blocking of the adjacent scenes. I suspect that these didactic passages were added by an editor who was not thinking of the Gospel as a preserved play.

Now I consider the uses of the area in front of the royal door on the upper level. That area is successively the synagogue in Capernaum, the sacred area of the Temple, the upper room of the Last Supper, and the praetorium. I suggest that the Pharisees and scribes were based in this area during the Galilee section, and the Council was based there during the Jerusalem section.

The staging of the Last Supper on the upper level means that if the actors reclined, some would be hidden from the audience. Therefore, I suggest that the actors sat behind a long table, with Jesus in the center. That made for a tableau that mapped onto other 12+1 groupings in the world of the audience, such as the signs of the zodiac plus the sun. This area of the stage had earlier represented the sacred area of the Temple. At the Last Supper, the audience *sees* Jesus offer his body and blood in the same location where, implicitly, the high priest in the earthly temple had performed his service!

c. Water and boat scenes

When the John the Baptist actor baptizes the multitudes, the actor stands on the central stairs to the orchestra (the "Jordan River") or in the orchestra itself. In the world of the audience, the Jordan River flowed into the Sea of Galilee. So a few scenes later, when the audience sees a boat in the orchestra, and actors with nets, the audience assumes that the actors are fishermen and the boat is in the Sea of Galilee (the Jordan is too shallow for fishing with nets from boats). The orchestra will represent the Sea of Galilee into Act VIII.

In the received text of the Gospel, the boat crosses the Sea of Galilee six times. In the performed play, I believe, the boat makes only four trips: to and from Gerasa, and to and from Bethsaida (see Chapter 4).

How many disciples accompanied Jesus in the boat? Three, I suggest (p. 68). A boat with three disciples conveys the same meaning ("Jesus is accompanied by disciples") as a boat with twelve disciples, and is much easier to stage. I note that the scenes set in Gerasa and Bethsaida involve "disciples," not "twelve disciples."

The stilling-of-the-storm scene is preceded by the verse, "Other boats were with him" (4:36b). But the received text does not state which actors are in these boats. There is no stage direction to introduce or remove these boats. I conclude that this verse was added by an editor.

In 3:9, Jesus "told his disciples to have a boat ready for him because of the crowd, so that they would not crush him." Shortly thereafter, Jesus teaches several parables from the boat (4:1–32). The staging of this scene is not clear: How does Jesus face simultaneously both the audience and the multitudes on the stage? Is Jesus elevated within the boat? Was "teaching from a boat" only a literary term, with the actual staging something else?*

d. The way

Once the boat has made its fourth trip, the return from Bethsaida Stage Right to Stage Left (which may have been named "Dalmanutha" in the polished text), it is removed and the orchestra is no longer the Sea of Galilee. It is now a place to walk, "the way."

Here are three stagings in the orchestra: "Jesus went on with his disciples to the villages of Caesarea Philippi; and on the way (*hodō*) he asked his disciples…" (8:27). After Jesus heals the epileptic boy, "They went on from there and passed through Galilee. He did not want anyone to know it" (9:30). The stage is too crowded for secrecy, so they must walk through the orchestra. Later, Jesus refers to that walk: "What were you arguing about on the way (*hodō*)?" (9:33). Another passion prediction is, "They were on the road (*hodō*), going up to Jerusalem…" (10:32). Jerusalem at this time is synonymous with the Temple, Stage Center (on both levels). Therefore, the *hodō* going up to Jerusalem is in the orchestra.

Jesus's entry to Jerusalem—the parade—occurs on the Way to Jerusalem and therefore begins in the orchestra. Was the parade confined to the orchestra, or did it continue through the audience area, or even outside the theater? I believe the parade traveled only through the audience area. Here are my reasons: I see three major functions for the scene. First, it shows Jesus fulfilling the Scriptural prediction of a messiah who rides on a colt/foal (Zec 9:9). Second, it shows Jesus entering Jerusalem in a parade, like an earthly ruler entering his city. Both of these can be accomplished with a parade that is staged entirely in the orchestra. But, third, *the audience's attention must be diverted from the stage while the stage crew brings out the Temple set*. The parade must therefore either leave the theater, or continue in the audience area. I considered whether the parade left the theater and circled around it, from Stage Right (country) to Stage Left (city). But Jesus is a poor philosopher and the theatricality of the parade as described in the received text was simple *and consistent with the world of the play*: an animal for Jesus to ride on, cloaks on the ground, foliage, and shouts of acclaim. With these limitations, an exterior parade would not add dramatic value

---

* "Teaching from a boat" *might* have been a topical allusion to "speaking from the Rostra," the main speaking platform in the Forum. (The Rostra was decorated with *rostra* [rams] from ships captured in battle by the Romans.)

to the play. Therefore, I propose that the parade began in the orchestra, continued in the audience area, then returned to the orchestra.*

e. Exposition of location names
How many places that are named in the polished text were named to the audience?

"Jerusalem" is specified in a key line: Jesus says, "See, we are going up to Jerusalem" (10:33). This line also tells the audience that the mountain onstage is near Jerusalem, possibly the Mount of Olives.

The boat's presence identifies the orchestra as the Sea of Galilee. That name does not have to be spoken. The locations on the stage are therefore, implicitly, in Galilee. Once the boat is removed, the Sea no longer exists and the stage and other physical features of the theater no longer represent Galilee.†

Jericho, I suspect, was not named but the audience recognized the location as Jericho by the action that occurred there.

Bethsaida ("house of fishing") was an important place in the world of the audience, and I suspect that its name was spoken in performance.

Otherwise, it is impossible to tell how many location names in the polished text were spoken in performance because a) sometimes Mark converts dialogue into narrative (i.e., the name *was* spoken); b) sometimes Mark gave names to locations only in the polished text; and c) the polished text has been edited. I can only say that the audience knows, from the boat trips that imply the Sea of Galilee, that Jesus and the disciples have come from Galilee.‡ The audience does not need to know the names of the locations ("Jerusalem" excepted) to follow the action.

f. The Temple
For the Temple, Mark used both levels of the stage. The lower stage represented the Temple Court, where visitors—Judeans and Gentiles—exchanged their coins and purchased animals for sacrifice. On the upper stage, the

---

* Mark could have had a wooden theater constructed for the occasion (Chapter 6), and specified extra space between sections of seats for the parade and other scenes that used the audience area.

† In the received text, 9:30–32 and 9:33–50 are set in Galilee and Capernaum respectively—*after* the orchestra has been redefined as "the way." If these scenes are original, an editor has added these location names.

‡ Mark elegantly confirms the audience's inference that the early part of the play had taken place in Galilee when he has the slaves of the high priest state that Peter speaks with a Galilean accent (14:70).

royal door represented the entry to the Holy of Holies. The upper stage in front of this door was therefore a part of the Temple restricted to "Judeans." I suggest that Council members and Pharisees are stationed here from Jesus's entry to Jerusalem until the arrest scene.

In the earthly Temple, the door to the Holy of Holies was covered with an embroidered curtain. I suggest that Mark used a similarly decorated curtain *above* the stage: the dove descends through it in Act I of the play, and it rips apart when Jesus dies.*

g. The villages

The received text uses the term "villages" several times. Where in the theater are the villages? My analysis started with 6:6: "Then he went about (*periēgen*) among the villages (*kōmas*) teaching." At this time, the orchestra is still the Sea of Galilee. The upper level of the stage represents only one village at a time. The Jesus actor would look silly if he repeatedly exits and enters the stage in order to visit different "villages." So the villages must be elsewhere. I propose that 6:6 means that Jesus walked in the audience seating area of the theater.

The Jesus actor has just stated that he has been honored, but not by his family and or in his hometown (6:4). Now he walks through the audience "teaching": that is, speaking wisdom appropriate to the audience members he visits.†

With the audience seating area now designated as "villages," I could block other scenes in the play:

- After the scene in Jericho, Jesus tells the disciples, "Go to the village (*kōmēn*) ahead of you" (11:2) and obtain a colt. I propose this staging: the disciples descend the stairs on the outer side of the wing. They face the parodos. There or nearby, they obtain the

---

* The real Temple curtain was embroidered with "all that was mystical in the heavens, excepting that of the [twelve] signs, representing living creatures" (Josephus, *Jewish War* 5.5.4). This design was ideal to indicate "the heavens" in the staging of Mark's play. In the decades after the Jewish War, the Temple treasures were on public display in Rome. If the curtain was among them, Mark's crew could copy its design.

† I think that the actor stays in character and does not interact with the audience. Although audience interaction was permitted in mime, I realized that interactive scenes could easily go on too long and lose dramatic momentum. The longer I lived with the play, the more it revealed itself as an entertainment *in front of* the audience, with minimal, clearly defined, and rehearsed audience participation.

animal* from a stagehand. After the parade, Jesus returns the animal to the disciples. Then he ascends the stairs to the stage.

- (Not original: Jesus heals at Gennesaret, "And wherever he went, into villages [*kōmas*] or cities or farms, they laid the sick in the marketplaces, and begged him that they might touch even the fringe of his cloak; and all who touched it were healed" [6:56]. These stage directions mean that the Jesus actor walks around in the audience area and/or parodoi, and heals the Chorus members stationed there. But all this movement takes time and adds nothing new to the play—Jesus has already healed people in various places. And if it is reported, the report adds nothing new to the play. I conclude that this verse was added by an editor.)
- Jesus heals the blind man of Bethsaida after they go "out of the village (*kōmēs*)" (8:23). This scene occurs in the parodos or audience area.
- The healed demoniac "went away and began to proclaim in the Decapolis how much Jesus had done for him" (5:20). The (Gentile) Decapolis was a group of cities; therefore, the stage direction refers to an area larger than the stage. The demoniac walked out of the theater, "proclaiming," through the seating area of the partly Gentile audience.

h. The wilderness/deserted places
Several scenes take place in the wilderness/desert/solitary place:

- John the Baptist appears in the wilderness (*erēmō*) (1:4).
- The Temptation is staged in the wilderness (*erēmō*) (1:13).
- "In the morning, while it was still very dark, he got up and went out to a deserted place (*erēmon topon*), and there he prayed" (1:35).
- "Jesus could no longer go into a town openly, but stayed out in the country (*erēmois topois*); and people came to him from every quarter" (1:45).
- (Not original: I think an editor added both the First Feeding Miracle and the stage direction to move the actors there: "And they went away in the boat to a deserted place (*erēmon topon*) by themselves" [6:32].)
- The Second Feeding Miracle occurs in the desert (*erēmias*) (8:4).

---

* From the non-fantastic style of the play, I infer that the "colt" was not an artificial animal (hobbyhorse, costumed actor) but a live animal, perhaps a donkey.

Where in the theater is the wilderness located? All of these scenes occur prior to the journey to Jerusalem. During this part of the play, the upper level of the stage represents a town, with two "house" doors and a synagogue in front of the royal door. The orchestra is the Jordan River, then the Sea of Galilee. The audience area is "villages." The wing Stage Left is occupied by the multitudes/Chorus. The wing Stage Right is occupied by the garden/tomb and mountain. The only location available for the wilderness is the lower stage, Stage Center.*

With this location fixed, I was able to block the entire play. When the received text required actors to make impossible movements between locations, I assumed editing had occurred: the scene had been revised, moved, or added in its entirety. In Chapter 4 I discuss several scenes with impossible movements by the actors.

The reader might ask if irregularities in the entrance/exit stage directions could be Mark's attempt to tell the reader/listener to look deeper. The answer is no. If Mark wanted to catch the reader/listener's attention, he would have made the anomalies more obvious, as he did with the presence of several characters named "Simon."

i. Mountain scenes

The received text contains six scenes that take place on a mountain:

- Jesus calls the Twelve from a mountain (3:13).
- Jesus prays alone on a mountain (6:46).
- Jesus gives the Olivet Discourse from the Mount of Olives (13:3).
- After the Last Supper, Jesus and the disciples go to the Mount of Olives (14:26).
- Jesus leads Peter up a mountain (Transfiguration) (9:2).
- The herd of pigs rushes down a mountain (5:13).

In the first four scenes listed, Jesus sits "on" the mountain and speaks to the disciples and the audience. I suggest that steps are cut into the side of the mountain, and the Jesus actor sits or poses on a step a few feet above the stage.

In the staging of the Transfiguration, Jesus leads the disciples up these steps. He disappears behind the mountain, so the steps must continue on the back

---

* The center of the lower stage continues to represent the *erēmō* and undefined space until Act XI, when it becomes the Temple Court. After that, it is used for the house of the high priest.

of the mountain. Peter, who remains visible to the audience, reports that he sees Jesus speaking with Moses and Elijah. A cloud descends. Still behind the mountain, the Jesus actor exchanges his ordinary clothes for white clothes. Then he follows the three disciples down the mountain (9:2–9).

The drowning of the pigs in Gerasa, as written, is not stageable: "The herd, numbering about two thousand, rushed down the steep bank into the sea, and were drowned in the sea" (5:13b). Some exegetes have proposed that "pigs" referred to the *Legio X Fretensis*, the Roman legion that occupied Jerusalem after the Jewish War. (A boar was one of the legion's emblems.) Let us assume that in the play, the "herd" was actually several Roman soldiers. The soldiers become possessed by the demons exorcised from the demoniac of Gerasa. The soldiers are already near the mountain. They climb the back of the mountain, then acrobatically dive/somersault into the orchestra, where they flounder and "drown." This action is good theater. And the drowning of the Roman soldiers in the Sea of Galilee emulates the drowning of Egyptian soldiers in the Red Sea. More on this scene later.

j. The tomb
The door to the tomb "rolls away." I suggest that the door was a disc, not a boulder. Though rare, disc-shaped doors were used for tombs of the Jerusalem elite in the Second-Temple period.[47] If audience members did not recognize the rock disc in front of the wall as a tomb door, they saw the inside of the tomb when the disciples of John the Baptist rolled the disc away and entombed his body (6:29). (Joseph of Arimathea later uses the same tomb.)

k. The courtyard with a fire
The early Greek theaters had in the orchestra a *thymele*, a permanent structure several feet tall. It was used as a funeral monument or an altar.[48] In Mark's venue, there was no *thymele* because the orchestra was used as the Sea of Galilee. But I suggest that in the Passion, Mark nods to the traditional *thymele* when Peter is in the orchestra, "sitting with the guards, warming himself at the fire" (14:54). The fire was in a small brazier, probably carried in by the slaves of the high priest after the arrest scene.

Lighting
I asked if "darkness at noon" was real, and Mark used ambient darkness for a light show. Also, did he coordinate the play's lighting in other scenes with the ambient light? To answer these questions, I listed (Appendix C) the times of day that are specified for the scenes in the received text.

Table 4 in Appendix C shows that, before the Last Supper, every scene is compatible with ambient daylight. A few scenes take place in the "evening" (for example, the stilling-of-the-storm scene, the exit after the Temple Incident), but none *require* ambient evening. (In these scenes, "evening" can be indicated by yawns, gestures, or dialogue. The storm can be indicated by physical action.) The water walk occurs during the fourth watch of the night (which ended at dawn) (6:48) and therefore is compatible with ambient daylight. So prior to the Last Supper, every scene can be staged in ambient daylight without any contradiction to the action.

Let us assume that the play was performed at Passover, which occurs in late March–mid-April. On a representative date, April 1, 2018, sunset in Rome occurred at 6:35 p.m. Astronomical twilight ended with full darkness at 8:11 p.m., for a total elapsed time of 1½ hours. Based on my run-through in the miniature theater, I assume the duration of the entire play was approximately 1 hour 40 minutes. So, if we require real ambient darkness in Act XV, the play must start just before sunset—or later. In this case, the entire play—including the pre–Last Supper scenes in daylight—occurs during the failing light after sunset. Artificial light is required for all scenes. Alternatively, the play starts after 8:00 p.m., in real ambient darkness. Again, artificial light is required for the entire play. If we start the play before sunset, there will never be real ambient darkness in Act XV. In short, the benefit to realism of real ambient darkness for the "darkness at noon" scene is always offset by the loss in realism caused by the need for artificial lighting for most or all of the pre-Passion "daytime" scenes in the play.

Given the inconvenience and expense of artificial light, and the custom that plays were almost always staged outdoors during the daytime, I conclude that it is much more likely that the entire play was staged during daylight than it was staged during partial or full darkness. Therefore, I believe that the performance started at 5:00 p.m. or earlier. "Darkness at noon" is not a literal stage direction.

It is clear from the received text that Jesus's death is marked by several special effects: The audience hears a loud sound. The Temple veil above the stage shakes and tears (15:38). (The shaking fulfills Jesus's prediction in the Olivet Discourse: "the powers in the heavens will be shaken" [13:25].) Perhaps these events are accompanied by flashes of lightning (produced with mirrors?) or sparklers, fulfilling Jesus's prediction that "the stars will be falling from heaven" (13:25). Such lighting effects must have already been developed for theatrical performances staged during daylight. There might also have been an earthquake, as in GMatthew (Mt 27:51).

Sound

Sound effects are implied in some scenes in the play: the Voice of God, the storm, the cock crows, the (possible) earthquake at Jesus's death. Music must have been used in the performance, at least in the entry to Jerusalem. The Temple Incident could have had musical "punctuation."

Costumes

John the Baptist wears a leather belt and a garment of camel's hair (1:6).

The young man who flees naked (14:51–52) wears a *sindona*, an inexpensive piece of linen. Joseph of Arimathea uses a *sindona* to wrap Jesus's body (15:46). Presumably the body of John the Baptist (6:29) was also wrapped in a *sindona*.

The young man in the tomb wears a white *stolēn* (robe) (16:5). As a robe was not ordinary garb, I suggest that it identified him as an angel/heavenly being.* The Satan character, also a heavenly being, probably also wore a robe.

The tunic was the basic body garment for both men and women. Jesus tells the disciples not to wear two tunics (6:9). (Perhaps the disciples then discard their second tunics, which provided warmth.) The Jesus actor wears a tunic and cloak. The multitudes and most of the bit-part characters wear tunics, with or without cloaks.

The *himation* was a large rectangular cloth used as a shawl or cloak. The woman with the issue of blood (5:27) and the multitudes (6:56) are healed when they touch Jesus's himation. Jesus's himation has "contagious holiness" (an attribute of the high priest, and one of the several ways Mark portrays Jesus as the high priest).[49]

In the Transfiguration, the Jesus actor changes his ordinary tunic and himation for a brilliantly white tunic and himation (9:3). Thereafter, these white garments distinguish the Jesus actor visually among the other actors. After the trial, Jesus is flogged, stripped, dressed in a purple himation, re-clothed in his (blood-stained) white himation, then taken offstage to be crucified (15:17–20). The soldiers return to the stage with the blood-stained white tunic and himation, and gamble for them (15:24), ignorant of their history in the world of the play, and their significance in the world of the audience.

---

* According to the received text, the actor is a young man, yet his costume is unlike the tunics and cloaks worn by the multitudes. This anomaly is one of several reasons to think that the empty-tomb scene in its current form is not original (p. 110).

Healing prop

Jesus heals by touch, authoritative speech, and incantation. The diseases/disorders he heals—paralysis, blindness, leprosy, fever, bleeding, epilepsy—are conditions that people believed were caused by possession. The demons worked by "overwhelming or 'seizing'" the victim.[50] The action in these scenes is theatrically simple. The actors convey their conditions of sickness and health by acting. The only prop needed is a "diseased skin" (or makeup) for the leper.

Stage technologies

Stage cranes carried actors between the heavens and the stage, and enabled actors to "fly." I believe that Mark employed a stage crane in his original Temptation and ascension scenes.

In GMatthew (Mt 27:51), an earthquake occurs while the Temple veil splits. The bodies of the saints come out of their graves (Mt 27:52–53). This stage direction cannot come from GMark—there are no "saints" and no graves. But Mark might have used an earthquake at Jesus's death—a combination of acting and physical shaking of the stage.

Scent

In Mark's world, scent was sometimes used in theatrical presentations.[51] In the Gospel play, a woman anoints Jesus with nard (14:3). Jesus says, "she has anointed my body beforehand for its burial" (14:8). Spikenard was used to anoint dead bodies before burial or cremation. It was also a component of the incense offered in the Jerusalem Temple, so the anointing makes Jesus's body like the offerings there. Because of its expense, nard may have *also* been used in the anointing oil for the high priest in the Temple. If so, at 14:3 the anointing simultaneously prepares Jesus for his death as an earthly being, for his sacrifice on earth as a heavenly being, *and* for his future service as the high priest in the heavenly Temple!

I think that real nard was used in the play. The high praise Jesus gives to the anointing woman (14:9) is anomalous if *no* scent is used. And the audience would experience cognitive dissonance if they smelled a *different* scent but heard it described as expensive nard. I note that the Jesus actor remains aromatic for the rest of the play; he is irrevocably different from the other actors.

Party favors

During the Temple Incident, Jesus overturns the tables of the money-changers Stage Center. Coins fall onto the stage. Coins fall into the orchestra (which is now "Jerusalem outside the Temple"). I suggest that children in the audience left their seats and picked up the coins. Jesus addresses both the actors onstage and the children in a line preserved in 11:17, "Is it not written, 'My house shall be called a house of prayer for all the nations'? [beat] But *you* [wink, wink] have made it a den of robbers."

Roles

The actors

The Gospel, like other mime performances, used female actors. The twelve-year-old girl must have been played by a female. Therefore, other female parts were played by females: Mary Magdalene, the woman with hemorrhage, the poor widow, the anointing woman at Bethany. The woman with hemorrhage spoke lines.

I suggest that two audience members were honored with small roles in the play (the blind man of Bethsaida, the anointing woman at Bethany). In Chapter 6 I discuss these honors.

The Chorus

In the subplot of the play—the earthly story—Jesus competes with the Council (and its allies, the Pharisees) for authority to interpret Scripture for the multitudes. Therefore, the audience must see the Chorus's reactions. But the received text provides little information on how the Chorus behaves throughout the performance. It is not clear if the Chorus's loyalties are always divided, or if the Chorus acts as a unit but is easily swayed (by Jesus and the Pharisees/Council). And there is no information about *which* Chorus members are onstage at any given time.

The play contains many small roles (some speaking) that, in early Greek drama, would have been played by the Chorus Leader. That raises the question if any Chorus actors doubled (played more than one part). I note that as the actors were not masked, if an actor played two different roles in two different scenes, the earlier role would transfer resonances into the later role. I do not see any added theatrical value if, for example, the actor who played Levi or the questioning scribe later played Pilate. Furthermore, on the occasion of performance I propose in Chapter 6, Mark had a large budget and did not need to have actors double. However, possibly the actors of some of the small roles in Galilee later became "follower" disciples of Jesus.

Jesus

The Jesus character does not behave like an ordinary human being prior to the Passion. If the received text accurately presents his character, he behaves compassionately toward the Chorus, but not toward the disciples. He tells them to disregard their natural human reactions (their fear during the storm). He remonstrates them when they take his teachings seriously (they protest that the money spent on the anointing oil could have been given to the poor). He never changes: he is the same in Act XIV as he is in Act I. As permissible in a heavenly being, his eyes are on the clouds although his feet are on the earth.

The audience first identifies with Jesus when he makes his Passion predictions in Acts VIII-X. In Gethsemane, he displays more emotion, as the play transitions into the mini-tragedy. Possibly his distress and agitation (14:33) foreshadow a more sympathetic character during the rest of the Passion. But perhaps not. The received text does not tell us how Jesus *acts* after Gethsemane.

The Jesus actor is the star: he is onstage in every scene until the crucifixion. He must have been an experienced actor.

The Jesus actor presents the congregation's doctrine to the audience, and performs the Eucharist. To be credible in this role, the actor must have been an ethnic Judean, and a committed congregant.

The Jesus actor goes "about among the villages teaching" (6:6). If this line is original, it means that he walks through the audience area and speaks to the audience. I believe the actor stays in character, but his teachings are meaningful in both the world of the play and the world of the audience.

Now to the identity of the actor. I suggest that *Mark* played the role of Jesus. Playwrights had long played leading roles in their own plays. Furthermore, the Jesus actor is onstage in almost every scene. Mark could direct the play from the stage, and improvise as needed. No other actor could be trusted with that responsibility.

What are the implications for the staging if Mark, the playwright, played the role of Jesus? I can only say that Mark must have been a mature man at the time. He probably played the role as a wise, bearded philosopher, not a gentle young teacher.

Satan

Editors have replaced Mark's original Temptation and ascension scenes with shorter scenes. An editor has excised Satan's entrancement of Peter just before the Recognition scene, which has also been edited. With these changes, Satan is almost erased from the received text. The missing material might tell us about Mark's doctrine. Is Satan a dutiful agent of God? Is he a malevolent being who wants to see Jesus fail? Is he pleased or disappointed that Jesus completes his mission? What is his relationship to Beelzebul?

The disciples

In the received text of the Gospel, the disciples are present approximately as follows: Jesus calls 4 fishermen. They leave their work and follow him. Jesus calls 12 disciples at the mountain, and also renames 3 of the original 4 (3:13–19). Jesus travels through Galilee accompanied by 3 or 4 disciples.* The Twelve are established as a group in Act IX: they surround Jesus when he displays the little child, and remain with him during the Jerusalem scenes. Only 4 are at the Olivet Discourse. Some disciples are at the Bethany dinner. There are 12 again at the Last Supper. Only the inner 3 go to Gethsemane. Some disciples flee when Jesus is arrested by a group that includes Judas. Peter reappears in the courtyard of the house of the high priest and remains there for the rest of the play.

When I blocked these scenes in the two-level miniature theater, I realized that the staged play was somewhat different. In this section on "the disciples," I will address four questions:

- The number of disciples at various points in the play.
- When these actors were introduced to the audience *as disciples*.
- Which names of disciples were spoken during the play.
- The implications of the answer to the first question for the current sequence of scenes in Mk 13 and 14.

Inner disciples

My discussion starts with the boat. A boat that holds 13 actors is quite large and cumbersome. A boat that holds 4 or 5 actors (Jesus plus the Four) is adequate for the boat scenes. Therefore I assume that only 3 or 4 disciples accompanied Jesus while the boat was in use, that is, in Galilee and through the return from Bethsaida (Act VIII).

---

* In the received text, Andrew is present through the calling at the mountain, but then is not mentioned until the Olivet Discourse. *In this section* on "the disciples," I acknowledge the uncertainty of Andrew's presence prior to the Olivet Discourse by using "three or four" for the inner disciples, and "eight or nine" for the remaining "follower" disciples.

If only 3 or 4 "inner" disciples accompany Jesus in Galilee, why does Jesus call 12 actors at the mountain earlier, in Act III, and give them the power to preach and exorcise demons (3:14)? The audience may have already seen some of the 8 or 9 "outer" disciples as characters sympathetic to Jesus (e.g., the healed leper), but there has not been time for the audience to have seen them *all*. In addition, there is no reason in the play why Jesus gives *them* the power to preach and to exorcise demons. They haven't earned these powers—some are onstage for the first time! Then, once they've "joined," they go offstage or mingle with the Chorus until Act IX, at the healing of the epileptic boy (the first time that Jesus definitely has 12 disciples with him). If the outer disciples remain onstage in the Chorus, then the Chorus's loyalties are heavily imbalanced in favor of Jesus. If the new outer disciples go offstage and remain there until Act IX, the calling in Act III wasted the audience's attention. I conclude therefore that in the performance, in Act III at the mountain, Jesus calls only the actors he had called at the boat, and appoints only them as disciples, without any special powers.* The outer, "follower" disciples are introduced later.

Andrew

Let me review the Andrew character in GMark. Andrew is present:

- At the seaside at 1:16 "Simon and his brother Andrew";
- By inference, in the next scene, the healing of the possessed man (1:21–28);
- In the next scene, the healing of Simon's mother-in-law: "they entered the house of Simon and Andrew" (1:29);
- At the calling on the mountain (3:18);
- At the Olivet Discourse (13:3).

Later in this book (p. 115) I reconstruct Mk 1 and find that the healings of the possessed man and Simon's mother-in-law are probably not original. That leaves references to Andrew in 1:16, 3:18, and 13:3.

---

* The anachronistic term "apostles" in some ancient texts of Mk 3:14–15 makes those verses highly suspect: "And he appointed twelve, whom he also named apostles, to be with him, and to be sent out to proclaim the message, and to have authority to cast out demons." Another sign of an editor is that there is no stage direction after the calling of the Twelve that places the eight outer disciples into their next scene. I also note that "to have authority to cast out demons" duplicates 6:7, where Jesus "gave them [the inner disciples] authority over the unclean spirits."

At the calling on the mountain, the Andrew character is not named to the audience. He then disappears from the narrative until the Olivet Discourse. Why would Mark show the audience this actor casting nets, bring him to the mountain with the three named inner disciples, not name him, then keep him offstage for a large part of the play? That is poor dramaturgy.

Furthermore, if Andrew is present at the Olivet Discourse, he hears Jesus warn the disciples to be watchful (13:32–37), which obviously foreshadows their failure to watch in Gethsemane. But Andrew is not present in Gethsemane! I must conclude that an editor added Andrew's presence at the Olivet Discourse.* I believe that a fourth fisherman was never part of Mark's play or polished text.

Reconstruction of the roles and names of the disciples

Now without Andrew, the following is a first step to reconstructing the roles of the disciples in the performed play:

1. In Act I, Jesus calls three unnamed fishermen (one casting a net, two mending nets) and they follow him. At the mountain, Jesus addresses the fishermen, and speaks their names ("Peter" and "Boanerges"). Jesus does not give them the power to preach or exorcise.

2. The Three accompany Jesus throughout Galilee. They accompany him in the boat to and from Gerasa and Bethsaida.

3. At least once, the audience sees the Judas actor conspiring with Pharisees† and/or scribes. (Judas has not yet been appointed as a disciple.)

4. Jesus tells the Three how to be disciples, and gives them power over demonic spirits (6:7–11).‡

---

* I suggest that possibly "Andrew" is a creation of Matthew, as acknowledgment of the brother Gentiles/God-fearers in Matthew's congregation; an editor of GMark added Andrew to the disciples in GMark to conform to GMatthew.

† The Pharisees are the Council's allies and are present in locations outside Jerusalem.

‡ Why do I think 6:7–11 is original? Three reasons. First, Jesus's grant to the disciples of power over Satanic spirits is chiastically parallel within the play to their failure to exorcise Satanic spirits (9:18). Second, their failure is prefigured by the line, "How can Satan cast out Satan?" (3:23). (The disciples cannot cast out Satanic spirits in 9:18 because they—Peter, certainly, and possibly James and John—are entranced by Satan!) Third, Jesus's admonition in 6:8–9 to live like a Cynic sets up the disciples' protest against expensive oil later at the dinner in Bethany. Although 6:7–11 is probably original, 6:12–13 is not original because it requires a lapse of time and does not contribute to the unfolding of the plot/subplot.

5. Peter is "taken over" by Satan before 8:29 (Peter's Recognition of Jesus as the Christ). James and John may also be "taken over."
6. Immediately thereafter, Jesus invites the multitudes to become "follower" disciples. "He called the crowd with his disciples, and said to them, 'If any want to become my followers, let them deny themselves and take up their cross and follow me'" (8:34). Nine members of the multitudes, including Judas, "join" his entourage (separate themselves from the main body of the multitudes?).
7. The Three accompany Jesus up the mountain for the Transfiguration. The new follower disciples remain onstage.
8. When Jesus and the Three descend, a man runs toward them. He tells Jesus that his son is possessed by a spirit, and says, "I asked your disciples to cast it out, but they could not do so" (9:18). The man's speech refers to the new follower disciples. This group may include men that the audience has seen Jesus heal or help, such as Levi and the healed leper—and Judas. However, the logic of the play requires that the Three *also* try (and fail) to exorcise the spirit.*
9. The group of twelve disciples stays with Jesus—on and off—until he leaves for Gethsemane. Note that the names of the nine new disciples are never spoken. At the Last Supper, Jesus does not address the Twelve as "disciples" or "followers"; he says, "One of the twelve" (14:20). Their names are unnecessary information to the audience—even the name "Judas."

But wait! What is that "on and off" in item 9? Therein lies a problem. Here, I address the sequence of events in Mk 13:3–14:42 (the Olivet Discourse through Gethsemane). The *number* of disciples present in these scenes varies, as stated at the beginning of this section. This variation may be a hint that the order of these scenes has been disrupted. What are the themes of the main scenes in Mk 13:1–14:42? The Olivet Discourse is Jesus's Last Words. The Bethany dinner is his anointing before his death. The Last Supper is his last meal. Wouldn't it make more sense for the Last Words to *follow* the Last Meal? The order would then be: Anointing for Death—Last Meal—Last Words. That

---

* I suspect that after the man complains about the followers' inability to heal the boy, the Three also try and fail. After all, Jesus has given the Three power over Satanic spirits, and this is their only opportunity to use that power and for the audience to see their failure. (Remember that Peter is possessed, and possibly James and John are possessed.) I propose that an editor erased the Three's participation as part of a campaign to rehabilitate them; that is why, in the received text, the disciples who fail are left unnamed.

change would *also* make the number of disciples present in this sequence and its precursor scenes more rational: 12 for the display of the little child, the entry to Jerusalem, and the Jerusalem scenes; an unknown number (12 is possible) at the Bethany dinner; 12 at the Last Supper; 3 at the Olivet Discourse on the mountain afterwards; then 3 at Gethsemane. (Jesus would dismiss the other 9 after the Last Supper.*) This proposal *also* has the virtue of placing Jesus's admonition in the Olivet Discourse to "watch" immediately before the inner disciples' failure to watch in Gethsemane. And it makes Jesus's Last Words really his Last Words—they *are* the last words the (sleeping at Gethsemane) inner disciples ever hear him speak!

However, the sequence of scenes in the received text of Mk 13:3–14:42 is stageable. There is apparently original material (e.g., 14:29–31) whose original position I cannot reconstruct. Therefore, I do not alter the received sequence in my reconstruction of the action of the performed play (Appendix E).

The names of the inner disciples

Now back to the introduction of the three inner disciples. What names does the audience hear, and when? Let's review the action of 1:16–20. An actor is onstage, casting a net into the "sea." Jesus says to him, "Follow me." He does. Jesus then calls two actors who are in the boat. They also follow him. Jesus heals several people. He has a reported dinner with tax collectors and outcasts. The scribes question his actions; Jesus responds. The subplot is now established: Jesus is a healer and teacher who has followers and impresses the multitudes. He has intellectual competitors, the scribes. During these scenes, Jesus is accompanied by the three fishermen. Their names are not important to the audience and therefore are not spoken.

Then Jesus formally calls followers to him (3:13–19) and addresses them. Jesus gives names to three disciples ("Peter" and "Boanerges"). I infer that the actor named in the received text as "Simon Peter" was never called "Simon" onstage. The "Boanerges" (Sons of Thunder) were never called "James" and "John" onstage. The audience knew these actors only as "Peter" (Rock) and "Boanerges."†

---

* This raises the question of what the other nine disciples (Judas excepted) do for the rest of the play. Do they exit after the Last Supper, or are they among the multitudes of Jerusalem who choose to spare Barabbas instead of Jesus?

† Jesus does address the first disciple as "Simon" at 14:37. I suggest that there, "Simon" is an editor's contribution: in the corresponding verse in GMatthew, Mt 26:40, Jesus does not address Peter by name.

Inner and follower disciples

This discussion of the disciples has been difficult to think through and write. A major source of confusion is that the received text uses *mathētais* for both the three inner "called" disciples who accompany Jesus in Galilee and the nine outer "follower" disciples who join up at 8:34. In fact, the text does not say that this second group thinks of themselves as disciples at all—the term is used by the man who complains about them at 9:18! Their status never formally changes from followers to disciples. But once the second group has been introduced to the audience as "disciples," the two groups appear to be equivalent in Jesus's eyes. Both groups hear Passion predictions, surround Jesus in Jerusalem, and attend the Last Supper.

Then Jesus takes only the Three to Gethsemane. This is not because they have displayed any superiority to the other nine disciples! But the stage is less crowded for the scene, which is about Jesus's prayer. Also, the exit of the Three is approximately parallel to the Calling of the Three (p. 116).

The demoniac of Gerasa

The demoniac is naked and cuts himself. He is possessed: he writhes, gestures, and speaks in voices. The voices say, "Send us into the swine; let us enter them" (5:12). The role is clearly a comic one. When the demoniac is cured, he asks if he can follow Jesus. Jesus tells him to go home and tell others what has happened. So the actor "went away and began to proclaim in the Decapolis how much Jesus had done for him; and everyone was amazed" (5:20). The Decapolis (Ten Towns) is a district—it is larger than the stage. I propose that the healed demoniac walks out through the audience, proclaiming (speaking loudly).

This walk through the audience is superfluous if the point of the healing scene is to demonstrate Jesus's power over Satanic spirits. I suggest that this exit gives a comic actor extra stage time. And therefore he must have been a known entertainer, a guest star. ("How much Jesus had done for him" in the world of the play might *also* have referred to how much his colleague Mark had done for him in the world of the audience.)

The dancer

In the received text, the daughter of Herodias dances before the king and his guests at a banquet. This is the only scene where the Jesus actor is not onstage, so we expect this elaborate scene to make an important contribution to the plot or subplot. But the purpose of the girl's dance is merely to illustrate that Herod is decadent. To characterize Herod, I cannot believe that Mark would engage a dancer. I also cannot believe that Mark would stage an entire banquet scene simply to inform the audience that Herod's wife had manipulated him into ordering the execution of John the Baptist, a minor character in the play! The story of John's execution can be *reported*.

The received text contains a flashback. The flashback explains that John the Baptist is dead because he had criticized Herod (6:17–19). I suggest that this flashback preserves most of the original scene: in performance, a *messenger* reported to the Chorus that John the Baptist was dead, and explained why Herod had had him killed (p. 87). I conclude that there was no dancer or Herod banquet scene in the performance.

The enemies of Jesus

In the play, Jesus's enemies comprise Pharisees, Herodians, scribes, chief priests, and elders. Most have distinct interests and actions:

- The Pharisees are interested in behavior: observance of the Sabbath (2:24), eating with ritually clean hands (7:5), and divorce (10:2). The Pharisees are allied with the scribes. The Pharisees are not members of the Council.
- The Herodians are attached to the Pharisees (3:6, 12:13). The Herodians are not members of the Council. They have no distinct qualities, and therefore may have been added by an editor.
- The scribes teach without authority (1:22) and argue (9:14). The scribes join the Pharisees to point out that the disciples eat with defiled hands (7:5). Presumably the scribes are exegetes, like the rabbis of the Talmud. The scribes are members of the Council.
- When Jesus is in the Temple Court, the chief priests, scribes, and elders ask, "By what authority are you doing these things? Who gave you this authority to do them?" (11:28). Later, these three groups are named as the members of the Council (14:43, 14:53, and 15:1). The chief priests, presumably, have the largest role in the Council. (Possibly, they are the "Sadducees" who ask Jesus a question in the Temple.)
- The elders do not act independently. But on the other hand, they do not participate when the chief priests and the scribes mock Jesus (15:31). They have more dignity than the others.

Even if the audience perceives differences between Jesus's opponents only subconsciously, the Council seems to have support from several social groups. Against it, Jesus has only the questionable support of his disciples and the wavering support of some of the multitudes.

Judas Iscariot

Judas is a pro-Pharisee spy. I do not know when Judas receives his assignment to infiltrate the disciples, but an appropriate time is after a synagogue scene: "The Pharisees went out and immediately conspired with the Herodians against him, how to destroy him" (3:6). Later, when the Judas actor goes to the chief priests and offers to betray Jesus, they promise him money, which implies that this is their first encounter with him (14:10–11). I note that Judas can testify to Jesus's unorthodox teachings even if Judas has observed Jesus only in the synagogue and the Temple.

What did "Iscariot" mean? It is an artifact of the polished text—at the performance, the audience did not need to know the name(s) of the spy who conspired against Jesus. "Iscariot" is similar to Greek *eschariotes*. Independent scholar Michael Bryant says, "The bearer of a charcoal burner (ἐσχαριωτης, thurifer in modern liturgical parlance) is a junior priest who leads a procession of Roman high priests: this ceremony would provide a basis for a dramatic rendering of the arrest in Gethsemane....An incense-burner was a stock property, which identified a character as a priest in Roman theatre."[52] I suggest that the original author (Mark or an editor) of the calling of the Twelve used the name "Judas Iscariot" in the polished text to inform the reader that the spy was a Judean *priest*. The name "Iscariot" referred to a Roman practice because the readers/listeners of Mark's polished text were in Rome, and were more familiar with Roman liturgical practice than with the Temple service, which had last been conducted more than 20 years before. We cannot be sure that the Judas actor in performance actually carried incense, although that would certainly add to the dramatic effect. If not, Judas's priestly status could have been conveyed by his costume or his behavior in the arrest party.

The naked young man

When Jesus is arrested in Gethsemane, "A certain young man was following him, wearing nothing but a linen cloth. They caught hold of him, but he left the linen cloth and ran off naked" (14:51–52). When and how did this actor *enter* the stage?

He is not one of the Twelve. He is not one of the Judean multitudes—they are not present during the arrest scene. He does not enter *behind* the arrest party, which crosses the stage from Stage Left to Stage Right. He is not hiding behind the trees in the Gethsemane set. Therefore, he must enter from "the country" via the parodos Stage Right. Perhaps he is entering as the Three flee, and that is how he realizes that Jesus is nearby. He advances onto the stage, where he encounters the arrest party.

Is this actor already known to the audience? He must be, because there is no time in the scene for him to be introduced to the audience, and they need to know why he tries to follow Jesus.

I propose that this actor is the healed Gerasene demoniac. Here are my reasons: First, the audience has seen the healed demoniac proclaim "how much Jesus had done for him" (5:20). The healed demoniac is now pro-Jesus, and we may assume he will want to see Jesus again. Second, the scene set in Gerasa begins with the demoniac less than fully clothed. We know this because after Jesus heals him, he is "clothed and in his right mind" (5:15). It is at least possible that "clothed" means that he is now wearing a loincloth and wrapped in a himation. If so, the healed demoniac's *loss* of his loincloth (and himation) during the arrest scene chiastically returns him to his original condition. Third, the audience has already seen the demoniac actor naked, or nearly naked. So his sudden nakedness does not seem gratuitous, as it might for a new actor. Fourth, his scuffle and flight in Act XIV is physical comedy. I have proposed that the actor who played the Gerasene demoniac was a "guest star" comic actor. The arrest scene gives him a second appearance onstage. Fifth, the actor who plays the naked young man should be, like the demoniac, an uncircumcised Gentile. (We know he is not circumcised because Gethsemane is Stage Right, as is Gentile Gerasa and Bethsaida. Only Gentile characters have entered from the parodos Stage Right.)

Why does Mark create the seizure, stripping, and flight of a minor character during the arrest scene? I will answer here only from the point of view of a playwright. First, the scuffle and subsequent flight add dramatic value to the arrest scene. Second, the actor's sudden nakedness and comedic flight hold the audience's attention while the set is changed to the house of the high priest (lower stage) and the praetorium (upper stage). Third, if I am correct that this actor was the healed demoniac guest star, this scene gives him a second appearance before the audience.

Barabbas

Here is the staging: Pilate questions Jesus, who is restrained by guards, as is a second actor. The Chorus approaches and asks Pilate to release a prisoner. The chief priests point to the second actor and tell the Chorus to demand *his* release. The name of this second actor need not be spoken: he is the alternative to Jesus.

But, on the other hand, his name in the polished text—"Barabbas"—has dramatic value if spoken. "Barabbas" is not a personal name: it is Aramaic for "father's son." The Chorus does not know what the audience knows: in Gethsemane, Jesus had addressed *his* Father as "*Abba*" (14:36). Jesus is also a "*bar-Abba*"! The Chorus ignorantly chooses the son of an earthly father instead of the son of the heavenly Father. The audience perceives the Chorus's ignorance only if the name "Barabbas" is spoken in performance.

The actors who mock Jesus

Several groups of actors mock Jesus: the soldiers in the praetorium, passersby, the chief priests and scribes, and the two other crucified men. Justin Martyr (c. 150) describes a few elements of the gestural vocabulary of mocking, which must have been used on the mimic stage, "For when He was crucified, they did shoot out the lip, and wagged their heads" (*First Apology* 38) and "For they that saw Him crucified shook their heads each one of them, and distorted their lips, and twisting their noses to each other …" (*Dialogue with Trypho* 101).

Simon of Cyrene

I will not review scholars' proposals for the meaning of the name "Simon of Cyrene." Instead, I will offer the one I find most plausible. I have said that I believe that Mark used "Simon" as a placeholder name. Michael Bryant has a plausible explanation for "Cyrene": *Kyrēnaios* sounds like *aquarinus,* and *aquarinus* was acceptable Latin for "water bearer."[53] Bryant proposes that the actor who carried the cross had already been onstage: he had carried a pitcher of water to the location of the Last Supper.* Bryant also proposes that the *aquarinus* provided the water in which Pilate washed his hands.[54] In the received text of GMark, Pilate does not wash his hands (but he does in Mt 27:24, an action that may have come from GMark). Bryant's two proposals are stageable and provide a reason for the *aquarinus* to be onstage during the Passion.

Now I imagine the action of the march to the cross and the involvement of the "Simon of Cyrene" character. Soldiers lead the Jesus actor across the orchestra towards the garden/mountain Stage Right. Jesus carries the cross beam. He staggers and falls. (Will he die now?) The *aquarinus* is nearby. The soldiers force *him* to carry the cross beam. The soldiers kick Jesus. He stands and walks. The procession exits through the parodos Stage Right.

---

* The *aquarinus* leads the disciples to the upper room and shows the audience what the pitcher contains—water—by pouring it into a bowl. Then Jesus and the disciples wash their hands.

When Mark wrote the polished text, I suggest, he wanted the reader to know that the actor who carried the cross beam was the same actor who had carried the pitcher of water at the Last Supper. The actor's name was not pronounced onstage in either scene. So Mark gave the actor who carried the cross beam the placeholder name "Simon," and a second name, *Kyrēnaios,* that reminded the reader of "*aquarinus.*"

Mary Magdalene

The character Mary Magdalene is first mentioned by name at 15:40. She has been a follower of Jesus since his time in Galilee. Scholars have proposed several explanations of "Magdalene." The most common is that Mary is "of/from Magdala." The Talmud refers to a Magdala on the Sea of Galilee. However, there is no record of this town in the first century CE. And there is no obvious reason for Mark to mention it. Michael Bryant again has a suggestion that is dramatically plausible in the world of the play. Bryant suggests that Mark's "Magdalene" points to "*amygdalene.*" That Greek word means "*to do with almonds or almond-blossom*" (italics in original).[55] Bryant suggests that Mary was a dealer in almonds, and she provided cyanide for Jesus to drink.[56] Poison allows Jesus to die quickly rather than suffer an (unstageably) slow death on the cross.

What happened onstage? The received text states at 15:36 that a man soaks a sponge in *oxous* (vinegar or sour wine) and gives it to Jesus (who is, by convention, offstage). I suggest that the audience saw a woman onstage add a small amount of liquid or powder to the *oxous*. But how are they informed that this substance is poison? Possibly the actor was one of the outcasts at the dinner in Galilee, and wears a costume that designates a dealer in almonds. Or perhaps she resembled the professional poisoner Locusta (d. 69) or the Emperor Nero's infamous mother Agrippina the

---

* Why did Mark choose the *aquarinus*, of all the characters available in the play, to carry the cross? I suggest that the scene enacts astrological symbolism concerning Jesus. I suggest that Mark and his congregation identified their Jesus figure with the new astrological age, the Age of Pisces, which had just begun or would soon begin. (An astrological age, which lasts about 2,100 years, is named for the constellation of the zodiac in which the sun rises at the spring equinox. In the first century CE, the turnover from the Age of Aries to the Age of Pisces had recently occurred [within a century or so], or would soon occur.) In the march to the (solar) cross, Jesus is followed by an *aquarinus*, a water carrier. A water carrier is the astrological symbol of the *next* age, the Age of Aquarius. Mark is dramatizing the succession of the ages. But why he does so and what he wanted the audience to experience is beyond the scope of this book.

Younger.* Alternatively, the presence of poison could have been conveyed in dialogue. I note that the woman helps Jesus. She shortens his agony and hastens the completion of his mission.

During the performance, the audience does not need to know the woman's name. Her identity is shown by her action. But when Mark created the polished text, he needed to give her a name. He used "Mary," which I believe was his placeholder name for female Judeans. To indicate that this woman had provided the poison, Mark gave her a second name similar to "*amygdalene.*" A Greek-speaking reader/listener who encountered this character near a dying person would understand.

Roman soldiers

In Gerasa, Roman soldiers are possessed by Satanic spirits and throw themselves into the sea. Later, Roman soldiers appear in the praetorium. It is logical that the soldiers in both scenes were played by the same actors. If so, the Roman soldiers in the praetorium have never been exorcised!

After Jesus dies, one of these possessed soldiers says, "Truly this man was God's Son!" (15:39). As earlier in the play, only possessed characters recognize Jesus's true identity. Mark here forces the audience to identify with the ultimate outsider in Jesus's world, a Roman soldier! Jesus's identity has transcended its ethnic origin and is now comprehensible by all. This is a skilled playwright at work.

Joseph of Arimathea

In performance, the body of the dead Jesus is requested by an actor. The actor must convince the guard and Pilate to release the body. Therefore, the actor must identify himself and provide credentials. According to the received text, he is "a respected member of the council" (15:43) and named "Joseph *apo Harimathaias.*"

What does "*apo Harimathaias*" mean (if these are the original words)? Most exegetes translate these words as "of/from Arimathea." Joseph therefore introduces himself as "of Arimathea." Many exegetes identify "Arimathea" with the town Ramathaim-Zophim in Ephraim, mentioned in 1 Sm 1:1. This explanation, however, provides no obvious dramatic value to the play. (But maybe there is a lost topical allusion or pun.)

I mention another proposal that does have dramatic value. This is that "*Harimathaias*" in the polished text sounds similar to (and is a pointer to) *Bar Matthias* (Aramaic for "son of Matthias"). That is, Mark expected

---

* Both women were involved in the murder by poison of the emperor Claudius.

the reader of "*Harimathaias*" to pronounce it and understand it as "Bar Matthias." Possibly the actor onstage in the performance spoke the words "*Bar Matthias*." Mark thereby intended the audience to conflate the actor onstage with Flavius Josephus.

Josephus was a Judean aristocrat and priest, born Joseph son of Matthias.* (He used the Latin name "Flavius Josephus" because he was a client of the Flavians, the imperial family.) Josephus was still alive in Rome at the time of performance. He had been a commander of the Galilean forces in the Jewish War and had surrendered to the Roman general Vespasian. Josephus writes that he predicted to Vespasian that he would become emperor (*Jewish War* 3.8.9 399–408). Vespasian did become emperor. He died in 79 CE and was deified after his death. In the world of the play, Joseph *Harimathaias* who was "waiting expectantly for the kingdom of God" (15:43) mapped, in the world of the audience, onto Joseph Bar Matthias who, one could cynically argue, had waited expectantly for (his opportunity in) the kingdom of Vespasian (a future god)!

This scene contains a second detail that, I suggest, insulted Josephus. The Joseph actor *personally* handles Jesus's body: "Then Joseph bought a linen cloth, and taking down the body, wrapped it in the linen cloth, and laid it in a tomb" (15:46). Josephus was by descent a *priest*. Leviticus 21:1 mandates that priests shall not be defiled for dead persons. Priests should not "make bald spots upon their heads, or shave off the edges of their beards, or make any gashes in their flesh" (Lv 21:5). Talmudic rabbis added that priests should not touch dead bodies. Perhaps this concept was already current among the Pharisees in Mark's time, and known to Mark and his audience. If it was, in the play, Joseph (Josephus) touches a dead body—and defiles himself!

Mark gives another hint to the reader of the polished text that Joseph of Arimathea is Josephus. John W. Crossan points out that "Joseph is described not as a member of the *synedrion*-council but as a member of the *boulē*-council, as if there were two councils in charge of Jerusalem, a civil council and a religious council."[57] Josephus was an advisor to the emperor, and thus a sort of member of a "civil council."

How did the Joseph actor play the role? I think he played it straight. He was proud that he had done a good deed on behalf of his people. The audience, which I propose identified the actor with Josephus, perceived the actor as a pompous fool. Touché, Josephus!

---

* Josephus introduces himself as "the son of Matthias" in the Greek version of his *Jewish War*, pref. 1.2.

Acting and tone of the play

Prior to the Passion, many scenes are evidently comic. Among them:

- Demon spirits are exorcised.
- The disciples try to wake Jesus during the storm.
- The demoniac of Gerasa speaks in several voices, then proclaims what Jesus has done for him (an opportunity for double meanings).
- "Pigs" jump off the mountain into the sea, flounder, and drown.
- The disciples are afraid when they see Jesus walk on water.
- The epileptic boy convulses.
- Jesus overturns tables and the disciples block attendants during the Temple Incident.

The major clue to the tone of the play prior to the Passion is the well-known dimness of the disciples. The fool ("*stupidus*") was the standard second actor in mime, and Peter, the second actor, is Jesus's chief disciple and present at the climax of the plot. Mark tells the audience what to expect when Jesus speaks the names "Petros" ("Rock") and "Boanerges" (Sons of Thunder) at the calling on the mountain.* Markan scholar Whitney Shiner, who gave many dramatic readings of the Gospel, observed, "Once the audience has decided that the disciples are comic, the other scenes of misunderstanding tend to be perceived that way as well."[58] I add that Quintilian, Mark's contemporary, includes fishermen, along with the standard comic characters of slaves and parasites, as roles whose movements onstage are rapid (*On Oratory* 11.3.112). Does this mean that Mark's audience understood "fishermen" as inherently comic?

The Pharisees and Council can be villainous, or mock-villainous. The same is true for Satan. When Jesus teaches in the Temple, he seems to "take on all comers" in the manner of a modern professional wrestler.

The Last Supper, in which there is no humor, sets the tone for the Passion. The Gethsemane scene is entirely serious. (For this reason I think the arrest scene, though lively, is also serious.) Thereafter, the Jesus and Peter characters, as well as the other characters in the Passion, are imprisoned in the format of tragedy. I believe that they conformed their style of acting there to the expectations of the audience.

---

* Greek-speakers may have taunted boys and men named *Petros* for being "dumb as a rock" or the equivalent. The Jesus actor may have reminded the audience about Peter's character by indicating him when speaking about "rocky ground" (4:5).

Characterization

Grebanier states, "*the quintessence of drama is conflict or opposition*" (italics in original).[59] The dramatist must create conflicts to keep the audience interested throughout the play. Because Mark's first job was to write an entertaining play, he had to stylize the characters of the disciples, the Pharisees, and the Council. We cannot trust the Gospel to present objectively true information about any historical persons behind the characters in the play.

Exposition of characters' names

The audience does not need to know the names of all the actors onstage. Names are exposition—background information that the playwright wants the audience to know. Grebanier says that exposition should be brought in "when it can be of maximum dramatic service to the action itself."[60]

Mark skillfully manages the exposition of the characters' names and identities: most are introduced by others during an action. Here are some examples:

- The Voice of Heaven identifies an actor as the Son of God. That actor's name is first pronounced in the course of an action, by a Satanic spirit affected by his power, "What have you to do with us, Jesus of Nazareth?" (1:24).[*]

- Initially, the audience does not need to know the name of the John the Baptist actor or the Satan actor. The audience can infer their identities from their costumes and behavior. When the Chorus asks, "Why do John's disciples and the disciples of the Pharisees fast, but your disciples do not fast?" (2:18), the audience sees actors who had earlier been associated with the baptizer. The audience infers that the name of that actor was "John." I will propose that at the end of Mark's original performed Temptation scene (preserved in the Gospel of Matthew), Jesus introduces Satan with "Away with you, Satan!" (Mt 4:10) (p. 104). This line informs the audience of the name of the tempter, in the course of an action.

- The audience first hears the names of the three fishermen when Jesus formally makes them disciples (3:16–17).

- The scribes introduce the "outcasts" (2:16).

- At 9:18, the father of the epileptic boy introduces as "disciples" the actors who have "taken up the cross" after 8:34.

---

[*] "Nazareth" is by an editor, who has inserted it into the polished text just once: here, when Jesus is introduced. Elsewhere, Jesus is "Jesus the Nazarene."

I note that my reconstruction of the play reveals that the play could be performed with only the following names spoken onstage: Jesus, John (the Baptist), Satan, Peter, Boanerges, (Pontius) Pilate, Barabbas, and Joseph (possibly also *Bar Matthias*). The polished text contains proper names for many characters whom the audience knew only visually during the performance.

Audience participation in the performance

In street mime, the performers interacted with the audience. Possibly that freedom also carried over into literary mime. The Jesus actor certainly *addressed* both other actors and the audience simultaneously in a number of scenes. Did the audience ever respond verbally or with applause?

It is impossible to know how much the audience participated in the performance. Here, I note only those instances that seem very likely to me:

- Small children from the audience come onstage to be blessed (10:13–16). (This must have been arranged in advance.)
- Children from the audience retrieve coins that have fallen from the tables of the moneychangers on the lower level of the stage into the orchestra. When Jesus "would not allow anyone to carry anything through the temple" (11:16), the disciples assisting him prevent the children from climbing onto the stage, where there are more coins. (The children's participation here must also have been arranged in advance.)
- One or more (selected) congregants donated money at 12:41.
- The roles of the blind man of Bethsaida and the anointing woman at Bethany were probably played by congregants.

The question arises whether the Last Supper was interactive, i.e., bread and wine were distributed to the audience. I think that food (as gifts) *was* distributed to the audience at the Second Feeding Miracle. A second distribution within the half hour would have been excessive. Furthermore, as I have studied the Gospel, I have come to the conclusion that the play was an entertainment, and not at all a ritual or devotional experience. More on that later.

Figure 1. An artist's impression of the Theater of Dionysus at Athens in the late first century CE. From A. D. Innes, Arthur Mee, and J. A. Hammerton, *Harmsworth History of the World*, rev. ed. (London: Educational Book Co., 1914).

Figure 2. The stage of the two-level miniature theater, with locations of the play. Design, construction, and photograph by author.

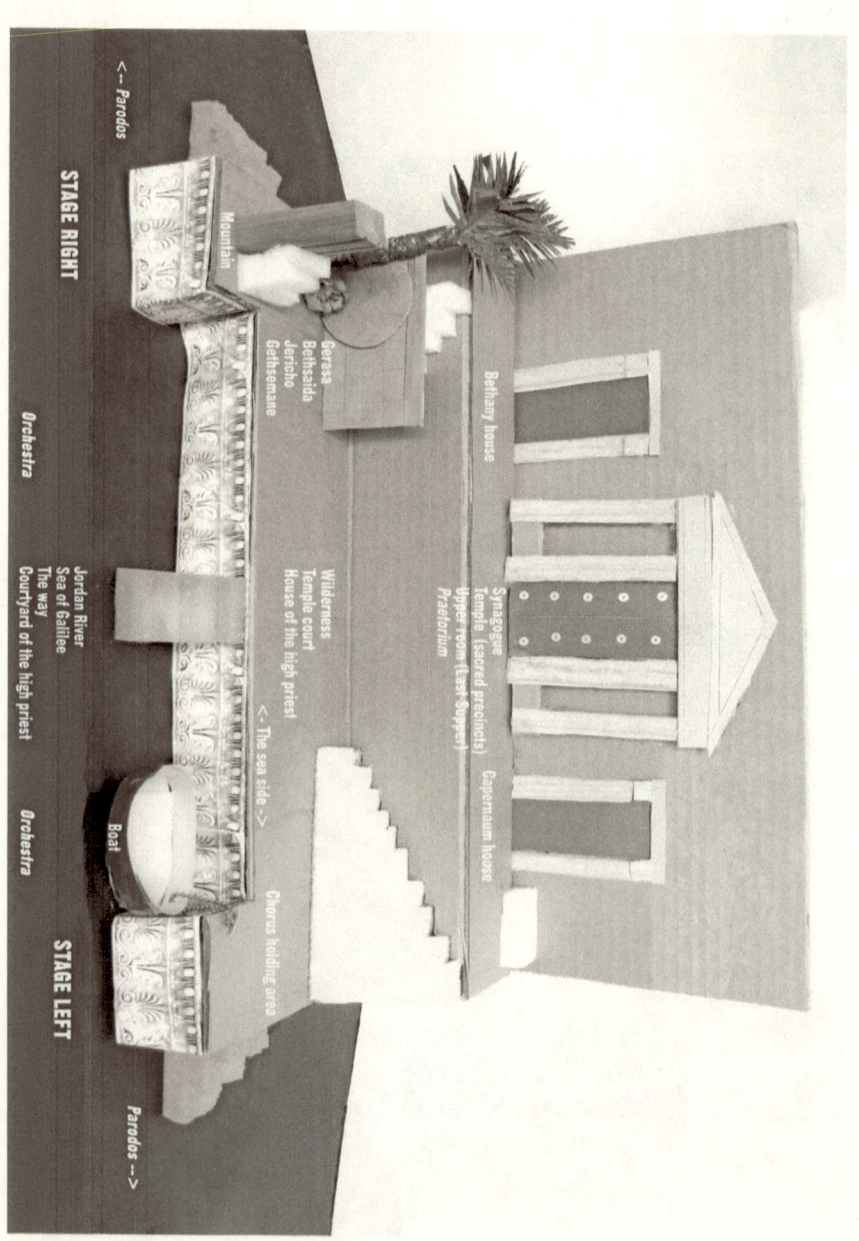

CHAPTER 4

Some Reconstruction of the Performance, and Editors in Rome

I HAVE ESTABLISHED, I hope, that the play was performed on a two-level stage in a Greek theater, and that Mark was a competent playwright. In this chapter, I extend those cantilevers and assume that nonperformable and dramaturgically weak elements of the received text imply that editing has occurred. Then I review scenes in the received text in which I have identified editing. For most of these scenes, I propose a reconstruction of the action. Figure 2 will help you follow my discussion. I then discuss some of the factors that limit reconstruction of the performance. Finally, I suggest that two editors with distinct agendas changed Mark's polished text before Matthew obtained a copy.

This chapter is dense but modular. If you are more interested in Mark's social context and the occasion of the performance, you can skip ahead at any time to Chapter 5.

The Performability Criterion and the Dramaturgical Criterion

I propose two criteria to identify editing of the polished text. One is the "Performability Criterion" (PC). It is based on the assumptions that a play was performed and that Mark intended the polished text to be a record of the performance. This is the PC: "Every scene and action in the play preserved in the polished text of the Gospel is performable in a theater with the same plan as the theater shown in Figure 2, unless the verse(s) can be explained as a coded reference to an alternative staging." If a scene or action in the *received* text fails the PC, it is not original, or it has been edited away from Mark's polished text. A scene that fails the PC is the received Temptation scene (1:13): "[Jesus] was in the wilderness forty days, tempted by Satan; and he was with the wild beasts; and the angels waited on him." The time period of forty days cannot be shown, and there are no other actors onstage to whom the lapse of time can be reported. There are no stage directions for the angels to enter or exit the stage. Wild beasts cannot be brought onstage; substitutions such as costumed actors or domestic beasts would be ridiculous.

The second criterion is the "Dramaturgical Criterion" (DC). ("Dramaturgy" means "the art or technique of dramatic composition and theatrical representation."[61]) This is the DC: "The scenes in the received text—when performed in a theater as written (or, rarely, as unpacked from Markan wordplay)—should evidence the author's competence at dramaturgy. If the performance of a scene does not—even if the scene is stageable—editing has occurred." A scene that fails the DC is 16:1–8, the empty tomb scene. Three women approach the tomb and a young man in the tomb speaks to them. The women flee. The play ends with many actors still onstage. But the Passion is a mini-tragedy, and tragedies ended with the exit of the Chorus. The scene's failure to clear the stage at the end of the play is evidence that Mark's polished text has been edited.

I note that the PC and DC cannot identify all edits in the received text. Lines of dialogue and narrative details such as names of locations and characters could have been added or changed. And the PC and DC cannot identify all places where material has been deleted. Entire scenes could have been seamlessly deleted or reordered prior to the Passion.

Analysis of edited scenes and sequences

Now I will discuss scenes in which I have identified editing. I will start with the Herod material, which precedes the Bethsaida section.[*]

The Herod material (6:14–28)

Here is the beginning of the Herod material in the received text. First there is a flashback (6:14–20), then a stageable scene (6:21–28).

> [14] King Herod heard of it, for Jesus' name had become known. Some were saying, "John the baptizer has been raised from the dead; and for this reason these powers are at work in him." [15] But others said, "It is Elijah." And others said, "It is a prophet, like one of the prophets of old." [16] But when Herod heard of it, he said, "John, whom I beheaded, has been raised."
>
> [17] For Herod himself had sent men who arrested John, bound him, and put him in prison on account of Herodias, his brother Philip's wife, because Herod had married her. [18] For John had been telling Herod, "It is not lawful for you to have your brother's wife." [19] And Herodias had a grudge against him, and wanted to kill him. But she could not, [20] for Herod feared John, knowing that he was a righteous and holy man, and he protected him. When he heard him, he was greatly perplexed; and yet he liked to

---

[*] The Bethsaida section (6:45–8:26) is so-called because Jesus and disciples take a boat trip to Bethsaida in 6:45 and also "came to Bethsaida" for another scene at 8:22.

4 - Some Reconstruction of the Performance, and Editors in Rome

listen to him. ²¹ But an opportunity came when Herod on his birthday gave a banquet for his courtiers and officers and for the leaders of Galilee. ²² When his daughter Herodias came in and danced, she pleased Herod and his guests; and the king said to the girl...

Let us assume the banquet at 6:21 was staged. Herod and his officials recline on couches. A girl enters and dances. Herod asks her what she wants. She goes to the side and speaks to her mother, then speaks to Herod. One of Herod's soldiers brings in the head of John the Baptist (6:28) and the girl gives it to her mother. The background material about Jesus and John in 6:14–20 has not been spoken—the actors have been watching the dancer. When is this material conveyed to the audience?

The banquet scene in the received text has other problems: It is the only scene in the play where the Jesus actor is not onstage, yet the scene has no consequences later in the play. This is a strong indication that the scene is not original. Also, the scene is tedious to set up and break down, yet it must be brief, as it is tangential to the plot and subplot, which are about Jesus. In these ways, the banquet scene displays poor dramaturgy. It fails the DC.

To reconstruct the action of the performed scene, we can look at the next scene and infer what led up to it. Here is 6:29: "When [John's] disciples heard about it, they came and took his body, and laid it in a tomb." This verse preserves this stage action: John's disciples (whom the audience recognizes because they were identified while fasting at 2:18) enter, carrying a headless body wrapped in a cloth. They put the body in the tomb. They exit and the stage is ready for the next scene.

Let us assume that the Herod banquet scene did not exist. The flashback remains. What information in the flashback does the audience need to know? Two things: the multitudes speak about John as a precursor to Jesus, and Herod has had John killed. The audience does not have to *see* Herod at the banquet. They do not have to see the dancer request John's death. They do not have to know about Herod's reluctance to kill John (which has no consequences later in the play). The information in the flashback about John's death can be *conveyed to the multitudes by a messenger*. The information can be *reported*.

I propose the following as an approximation of how the Herod material was staged in performance:

Enter MESSENGER FROM HEROD.

MESSENGER: I come from King Herod. John the Baptist is dead!

CHORUS: What happened to that holy man?

MESSENGER: He insulted King Herod and his wife. John told King Herod, "It is not lawful for you to have your brother's wife." King Herod was angry. He ordered John's head cut off. It was done.

CHORUS: Woe is us!

MESSENGER: If you want his body, come with me now.

JOHN'S DISCIPLES step forward, and exit Stage Left with MESSENGER.

CHORUS: *(variously, pointing at JESUS, who has stayed to the side)* "John the baptizer has been raised from the dead; and for this reason these powers are at work in him." "It is Elijah!" "It is a prophet, like one of the prophets of old."*

JOHN'S DISCIPLES re-enter, carrying a bloody, headless body. They go to the tomb Stage Right, roll the disc to the side, put the body on a shelf inside, then roll the disc back in place. They exit. The stage is now ready for the next scene, with JESUS adjacent to the CHORUS.

This simple scene tells the audience why John the Baptist was killed, and shows them his distinctive corpse. Some members of the Chorus speculate on the identity and relationship of John and Jesus. That is all Mark needs for his play.

John the Baptist compared to Jesus

John the Baptist was a respected holy man of Judea (Josephus, *Antiquities* 18:5.2). John was executed c. 36 CE by Herod Antipas, the ruler of Galilee and Perea.

The actor who plays John appears onstage only at the beginning (prologue) of the play, when he baptizes the Galilean/Judean multitudes and Jesus (1:4–9). But John is referred to *throughout* the performance: John's disciples are fasting (2:18). The Chorus says that Jesus has miraculous powers because John rose from the dead (6:14). John's disciples carry his headless body to the tomb (6:29). Jesus's disciples report that people say that Jesus is John, Elijah, or one of the prophets (8:28). Jesus asks the Pharisees if John's baptism was from heaven or of human origin (11:30). The Pharisees fear the people "for all regarded John as truly a prophet" (11:32). These lines of dialogue and stage actions remind the audience of John the Baptist's holiness. He was the holiest human being possible.

---

* The Chorus's speeches (and Jesus's reactions?) engage the audience while John's disciples are offstage, obtaining his body.

Mark utilizes the John the Baptist character as contrast for the Jesus character. In Act VI, the audience sees John's disciples carry and entomb John's headless corpse, which we may assume is bloody at the neck. The corpse is still in the tomb when Joseph of Arimathea opens the tomb and places Jesus's body inside. When the tomb is opened again at the end of the play, John's distinctive corpse is still inside, but Jesus's body is not. The audience has been told that John was the holiest human being possible. Yet *his* body remains on earth. At the end of the play, the audience is reminded of what they had learned in the prologue: Jesus is different from John: *Jesus is not (only) a human being.*

Why did an editor condense Mark's original Herod scene into a flashback, and add the banquet scene to the polished text? Here is one, very speculative, explanation; there may be others. The play was performed 90–95 CE in Rome. Herod Agrippa II was living in Rome (or had recently died). He had been a friend and client of the Emperor Titus and may have remained a client of the current emperor, Domitian. Perhaps the editor of GMark was concerned that a reader who saw "Herod" in the polished text as the executioner of John the Baptist would associate "Herod" with Herod Agrippa II. So the editor wrote a new scene, the Herod banquet scene. It was an obvious emulation of the Judean folktale of Esther, set in Persia. In addition, the editor makes it clear that Herod had been manipulated by his wife into imprisoning and killing John. The name "Herod" remains but has nothing to do with Herod Agrippa II.

Mark 6–8 (Bethsaida Plus)

With the Herod material sorted out, I can continue forward and take on the Bethsaida section of the received text (6:45–8:26). I will try to figure out which scenes and actions are original, and I will propose their original sequence. Needless to say, my proposals are very speculative.

Table 1 shows the current sequence of scenes compared to my proposed original sequence of scenes. I begin just before the original Herod scene.

Table 1. Sequence of scenes in Mark 6–8

Sequence of scenes in the received text of GMark	My proposed original sequence in the polished text
1. Jesus instructs his disciples on behavior and gives them power over Satanic spirits, then sends them out (6:7–13)	**partial 1.** Jesus instructs his disciples on behavior and gives them power over Satanic spirits (6:7–11)
2. Herod flashback and banquet scene (6:14–28)	**original 2.** Original Herod scene (messenger from Herod tells Chorus that John the Baptist is dead)
3. John's disciples entomb his body (6:29)	**3.** John's disciples entomb his body (6:29)
4. Jesus's disciples report to him (6:30)	**partial 9.** Jesus defends his position on defilement/ritual purity/the Law to the Pharisees and disciples (7:1–15) **A.** As a follow-up, Jesus warns the disciples about the yeast of the Pharisees (and of Herod/the Herodians?) (8:15)
5. Jesus and disciples travel to a deserted place by boat (6:31–32)	*Bethsaida section begins*
6. Feeding of the 5,000 Judeans (5 loaves, 2 fish, 12 baskets leftovers) (First Feeding Miracle) (6:33–44)	**original 15.** Boat trip *to* Bethsaida. Possibly, Jesus teaches about bread.
Bethsaida section begins	**12.** Feeding of the 4,000 Gentiles (7 loaves, a few small fish, 7 baskets leftovers) (Second Feeding Miracle) (8:1–9). Feeding is reported.
7. (first trip to Bethsaida) Disciples cross orchestra in boat, Jesus walks on water (6:45–52)	**16.** Healing of blind man who sees people "like trees, walking" (8:22–26)

4 - Some Reconstruction of the Performance, and Editors in Rome

Sequence of scenes in the received text of GMark	My proposed original sequence in the polished text
8. Healings at Gennesaret (6:53–56)	**original 7.** Boat trip *from* Bethsaida. Disciples cross orchestra in boat, Jesus walks on water (6:47–52)
9. Jesus defends his position on defilement/ritual purity/the Law to the Pharisees and disciples (7:1–23)	*Bethsaida section ends*
10. Healing of Syrophoenician woman's daughter (7:24–30)	14. Pharisees meet Jesus and demand a sign (8:11–12)
11. Healing of deaf-mute of Decapolis (7:31–37)	17. "Who do people say that I am?", Recognition by Peter, and joining of "follower" disciples (8:27–9:1)
12. Feeding of the 4,000 Gentiles (7 loaves, a few small fish, 7 baskets leftovers) (Second Feeding Miracle) (8:1–9)	
13. Boat trip to Dalmanutha (8:10) (no details given in text)	
14. Pharisees meet Jesus and demand a sign (8:11–12)	
15. Boat trip from Dalmanutha. Conversation about "we have no bread," warning about leaven (8:13–21)	
16. (in Bethsaida) Healing of blind man who sees people "like trees, walking" (8:22–26)	
Bethsaida section ends	
17. "Who do people say that I am?", Recognition by Peter, and joining of "follower" disciples (8:27–9:1)	

Here is my proposal for the order of the scenes in and adjacent to the original Bethsaida section of the play and polished text:

- A In Judean territory, Jesus tells the Pharisees that they abandon God's commandments and replace them with their human traditions. Jesus tells the multitudes and the disciples that they cannot be defiled by eating.
    - B Jesus and disciples travel in a boat from Judean territory to Bethsaida (in Gentile territory). Possibly, during the trip, Jesus teaches about bread.
        - C Gentiles are fed with fish and bread (Second Feeding Miracle)/Distribution of gifts to the audience.
        - C' Healing of blind man (a Gentile).
    - B' Jesus and disciples travel in a boat from Gentile Bethsaida to Judean territory. During the trip, Jesus walks on water.
- A' In Judean territory, Pharisees demand a sign from heaven that Jesus is extraordinary.

In this chiasm, the A and A' brackets have Jesus encounter Pharisees in Judean territory. The B and B' brackets are boat trips to and from Gentile Bethsaida. The C and C' brackets are events that take place in Bethsaida. (I use this sequence in Appendix E.)

This sequence gives theatrical value to the Pharisees' demand for a sign from heaven that Jesus is extraordinary. The audience has just seen Jesus walk on water! *They* know that Jesus is extraordinary. The Pharisees, who have not seen Jesus walk on water, seem ridiculous.

Now I will review the scenes that I deleted from the Bethsaida section of the received text.

TABLE 1A. SCENES I DELETED FROM THE RECEIVED TEXT

4. Jesus's disciples report to him (6:30)
5. Jesus and disciples travel to a deserted place by boat (6:31–32)
6. Feeding the 5,000 Judeans (5 loaves, 2 fish, 12 baskets leftovers) (6:33–44) (First Feeding Miracle)
8. Healings at Gennesaret (6:53–56)
10. Healing of Syrophoenician woman's daughter (7:24–30)
11. Healing of deaf-mute of Decapolis (7:31–37)

Jesus's disciples report to him (6:30)

I argue below that Jesus does not send out his inner disciples on a mission trip (6:12–13). Instead, they remain onstage with him during the report of Herod's death and the entombment of John the Baptist's body. As the disciples have not left the stage, they cannot report to Jesus in 6:30. The mission trip and its report were added by an editor.

Travel to a deserted place (6:31-32) and the First Feeding Miracle (6:33-44)

The boat trip to a deserted place (6:31–32) is necessary because the First Feeding Miracle (6:33–44) must occur in a location different from the holding area for the Chorus. But the description of the miracle has staging problems. I have already assigned "the wilderness" or "a deserted place" to Stage Center, but that is adjacent to the Chorus area Stage Left. There is no mooring for the boat Stage Center. The boat trip is not described. Together, these observations suggest that the boat trip is not original. But let us return to it after discussion of the First Feeding Miracle.

In the First Feeding Miracle, the diners lie down "on the green grass" in groups of hundreds and fifties. This staging is impossible. The Chorus is much smaller. And they would look ridiculous if they lie down on the stage Stage Center. This stage direction does not appear to hide an alternative staging. Therefore, the First Feeding Miracle fails the PC.

Could the miracle be reported by a messenger? Yes. But the scene has several problems that, taken together, imply that it was written and added by an editor. First, the scene-level chiasm has problems. Turton says, "The center of the major chiastic structure is very unMarkan, and the brackets do not speak to each other like typical Markan brackets."[62] Second, one of the two early editors of the polished text had a pro-Judean agenda (p. 123). The First Feeding Miracle is consistent with that agenda (Jesus feeds Judeans *before* he feeds Gentiles at Bethsaida). And third, the First Feeding Miracle is structurally a duplicate of the Second Feeding Miracle, a scene that I believe is original and that fits into my reconstructed Bethsaida sequence. In drama, a duplicate scene must have something *dramatically* interesting and unique in it, but the First Feeding Miracle does not. And a *report* of the miracle would be a near-duplicate of the report of the Second Feeding Miracle, only with different quantities. The First Feeding Miracle in the received text fails the DC. And therefore, we can discard the prelude to the miracle, the boat trip at 6:31–32.

If we eliminate the First Feeding Miracle and its preceding boat trip, the play needs only four boat trips, not six. My partial reconstruction of the play, in Appendix E, includes only four boat trips: to and from Gerasa, and to and from Bethsaida.

Healings at Gennesaret (6:53–56)
These verses (6:53–56) refer to action in multiple locations: "And wherever he went, into villages or cities or farms, they laid the sick in the marketplaces" (6:56). At this time, the orchestra is still the Sea of Galilee. Therefore, to stage this scene, the Jesus actor must leave the stage, and visit the "sick" actors, who are lying down in the audience seating area and/or parodoi.

The scene is performable but tedious to stage. It does not have any interesting theatricality. And it does not add any new information to the play (Jesus has already healed several people, including a woman who touched his cloak). Therefore the scene fails the DC. Also, the chiasm does not have a Markan structure.[63] I conclude that the scene is not by Mark.

The Syrophoenician-woman scene (7:24–30)
In this scene (7:24–30), Jesus enters a house. A Gentile woman enters and begs him to heal her daughter. The woman and Jesus speak. Then she goes to another house, and finds the girl on a bed, healed.

There are several staging problems here. First, Jesus and the woman are in a house, then the woman goes into another house. This would be the only scene in which the actors cross the upper stage (in front of the synagogue) from one small door to the other. Second, the disciples are not present, and their absence is not explained. Third, the scene is dramatically boring; it adds nothing to the play. Fourth, the audience has to be shown that the daughter is healed, or the woman has to report it, but there are no stage directions for those actions and no other actors present on the upper stage for the woman to speak to. And fifth, the scene leaves the Jesus actor waiting without anything to do while the audience's attention shifts to the woman.

The scene as written is performable but shows poor dramaturgy because it adds nothing new and it does not place the Jesus actor in position for the next scene. The scene fails the DC. Furthermore, the interesting part of the scene is the dialogue. The Gentile woman refers to herself as a dog: "even the dogs under the table eat the children's crumbs" (7:28). This line cannot be by Mark, who is pro-Gentile. I believe that the entire scene was written by an editor.

TABLE 1B. PARTS OF SCENES I DELETED FROM THE RECEIVED TEXT

Jesus's disciples exit, preach and cast out demons (6:12–13)
Jesus privately explains what defiles a person (7:17–23)
Boat trips to and from Dalmanutha (8:10, 8:13)
The boat conversation "we have no bread" (8:14–21)
Jesus prays on a mountain (6:45–46)

Jesus's disciples exit, preach, and cast out demons (6:12–13)

In the received text, these verses (6:12–13) occur just before the Herod banquet scene. After the banquet and entombment, Jesus's disciples return and report to him (6:30). The Herod banquet scene provides the time lapse necessary for the disciples' missionary activity offstage. But if the original Herod material was instead, as I have proposed, the report of a messenger to the Chorus, then in the performed play there was no time for the disciples to exit and return *in the world of the play*. In addition, the disciples' missionary trip is irrelevant to the plot and the subplot, and is never mentioned again. For these reasons, I believe 6:12–13 were added by an editor.

Jesus privately explains what defiles a person (7:17–23)

Jesus is Stage Center. He has just spoken to the disciples and Chorus, "there is nothing outside a person that by going in can defile, but the things that come out are what defile" (7:15). Then in 7:17, Jesus "left the crowd and entered the house," where he explains his teaching to the disciples.

I have eliminated the next two scenes in the received text, the healing of the Syrophoenician woman's daughter (7:24–30) and the healing of the deaf-mute man (7:31–37) (p. 100). The following scene is the Second Feeding Miracle. Verses 7:17–23 do make sense as a prelude to the Second Feeding Miracle, so I will retain them for the moment.

Let us look at the verses immediately *before* 7:17–23.[*] In verses 7:1–15, Jesus attacks the Pharisees' rules about eating. He states that what goes in cannot defile, but what comes out can defile. Verses 7:17–23 amplify his statement. But the staging is problematic. Jesus speaks 7:17–23 *in a house*. Taken literally, this staging means that Jesus and disciples climb to the second level to enter the house (that is, stand in front of the small door Stage Left or on the stairs below it). But in the next scene, they enter the boat and travel to Bethsaida. They would have to immediately descend the stairs to reach the boat! If Mark had written 7:17–23, he would not have placed the

---

[*] Mk 7:16 is often omitted from modern versions as an editorial interpolation.

conversation *in the house*. Mark would have written something like, "Jesus took his disciples aside and told them privately..." The actors would move only a few feet, and remain near the boat. Verses 7:17–23 display poor dramaturgy. They fail the DC.

But, you may say, perhaps Mark wrote most of 7:17–23 and an editor added the "house" location. I respond that the contents of the speech argue against Markan authorship. It is didactic: it explains a wise saying, whereas elsewhere Mark trusts the audience/reader to interpret wise sayings. Also, this passage does not have any consequences in the world of the play. It slows down the action. Overall, my judgment is that Mark did not write 7:17–23 in his polished text.

Boat trips to and from Dalmanutha (8:10, 8:13)

In the received text, after the Second Feeding Miracle, Jesus and his disciples enter the boat and cross the orchestra to Dalmanutha (8:10). There, some Pharisees demand a sign. Jesus tells them not to seek a sign (8:11–12). Jesus and the disciples then depart from Dalmanutha in the boat (8:13) and go to the other side. During this return trip, Jesus tries to make the disciples recognize the significance of the bread they had distributed at the feeding miracles (8:14–21).

This sequence, if staged, has a number of problems. First, the outbound trip does not have interesting theatricality. Second, the boat trip to see Pharisees is not necessary: Jesus has already encountered Pharisees in Galilee. Third, the trip begins Stage Left and goes to Stage Right. Stage Right has been used twice for Gentile territories (Gerasa and Bethsaida), yet now there are Pharisees Stage Right! Fourth, on the return trip, Jesus refers to two feeding miracles (8:19–21), but Mark wrote only one feeding miracle. (This is enough to imply that an editor has intervened.) Taking all these problems together, I conclude that the boat trips to and from Dalmanutha are not by Mark. (However, the location name "Dalmanutha," and the conversation with Pharisees about the sign [8:11–12] may be by Mark.)

The boat conversation "we have no bread" (8:14–21)

On the supposed return boat trip from Dalmanutha, this is the conversation in the received text (8:14–21):

> [14] Now the disciples had forgotten to bring any bread; and they had only one loaf with them in the boat. [15] And he cautioned them, saying, "Watch out—beware of the yeast of the Pharisees and the yeast of Herod." [16] They said to one another, "It is because we have no bread." [17] And becoming aware of it, Jesus said to them, "Why are you talking about having no

bread? Do you still not perceive or understand? Are your hearts hardened? [18] Do you have eyes, and fail to see? Do you have ears, and fail to hear? And do you not remember? [19] When I broke the five loaves for the five thousand, how many baskets full of broken pieces did you collect?" They said to him, "Twelve." [20] "And the seven for the four thousand, how many baskets full of broken pieces did you collect?" And they said to him, "Seven." [21] Then he said to them, "Do you not yet understand?"

In verse 8:14, the disciples have only one loaf of bread. In verse 8:15, Jesus warns against the yeast of the Pharisees. Verse 8:16 is continuous with 8:14: the disciples reason with each other because they have no bread.* Jesus then speaks on the topic of "no bread." Obviously an editor has been involved. I propose that the editor replaced Jesus's original line at 8:15 with the current verse 8:15.

Another problem with this scene is that Jesus refers to *two* feeding miracles. But Mark's play included only the Second Feeding Miracle. That makes the entire passage suspect. Turton agrees, "A chiasm can be constructed, but it makes no sense at all, merely an artistic arrangement of the sentences.... The writer of Mark never had a hand in this one."[64] I believe that 8:14 and 8:16–21 were written by an editor.

Jesus's warning against the yeast of the Pharisees in 8:15 may be by Mark but moved from elsewhere. "Yeast of the Pharisees" is a vivid expression that meant "interpretation of Scripture according to the Pharisees." In the same way that wild yeast/leaven enlarged dough and made bread more digestible, interpretation enlarged the meaning of Scripture and made it more understandable/digestible.

The term "yeast of Herod" requires explanation. Perhaps the term was a topical reference, now lost. Or it was added by an editor to conform to the mention of "Herodians" (allies of the Pharisees) in 3:6.

Jesus prays on a mountain (6:45–46)
In the received text, Jesus goes and prays on a mountain (6:45–46) just before the first boat trip to Bethsaida: "[45] Immediately he made his disciples get into the boat and go on ahead to the other side, to Bethsaida, while he dismissed the crowd. [46] After saying farewell to them, he went up on the mountain to pray." If the scene is staged as written, the disciples are in the boat, traveling *to* Bethsaida, while Jesus stays behind and prays on

---

* In Greek, 8:16 is narrative, not dialogue. The disciples seem to try to understand whatever Jesus originally said in 8:15.

the mountain. But both the mountain and Bethsaida are Stage Right! The scene is not performable and fails the PC. I believe that verses 6:45–46 were added by an editor after the original Bethsaida section had been disrupted.

■■■

Now I discuss more scenes in and adjacent to the Bethsaida section.

Boat trip to Bethsaida (now missing)
In the received text, Jesus walks on water during the boat trip *to* Bethsaida. I will propose, below, that this water walk occurs during the boat trip *from* Bethsaida. I cannot guess at what interesting theatricality occurred in performance on the boat trip *to* Bethsaida because the entire scene is missing. I can only say that the topic of bread—a theme in the play—is appropriate just before a feeding miracle.

The Second Feeding Miracle (8:1–9)
I believe that this scene (8:1–9) is original to the polished text, but the performance was somewhat difference than the narrative. In the received text, one of the disciples asks, "How can one feed these people with bread here in the desert?" (8:4). This is a classic set-up line. The Jesus actor should respond, "Like this!" (miracle occurs). But in the received text, Jesus does not seize the moment and perform the miracle. Instead, he prays, then anticlimactically orders the distribution of the food from bottomless baskets:

> [5] He asked them, "How many loaves do you have?" They said, "Seven." [6] Then he ordered the crowd to sit down on the ground; and he took the seven loaves, and after giving thanks he broke them and gave them to his disciples to distribute; and they distributed them to the crowd. [7] They had also a few small fish; and after blessing them, he ordered that these too should be distributed. [8] They ate and were filled; and they took up the broken pieces left over, seven baskets full. [9] Now there were about four thousand people. And he sent them away.

The above scene is poor theater. The Chorus members and the audience only gradually realize that a miracle is occurring, as they observe that the food will not run out. The scene is tedious to enact: The Chorus must recline (not "sit down"). The audience must see loaves and fishes distributed to every Chorus member and they must eat onstage. Then the disciples must pick up the leftovers. These problems tell me that 8:1–9 in the received text cannot be a condensed version of the performance.

Was there, instead, an intermission for refreshments at this scene? After all, Jesus has rejected the Pharisees' concerns about unclean food. He has stated, "there is nothing outside a person that by going in can defile" (7:15). And the miracle involves the distribution of food. The problem here is that the performance was too short for a full intermission away from the theater. (I estimate that the entire performance was about 1 hour 40 minutes.) But perhaps there was a short break for stretching, etc.

I suggest that the line "How can one feed these people with bread here in the desert?" referred to the audience and was a cue for the distribution of a gift of food *to the audience.*[*] The audience members, who accept (and eat?) food not approved by the Pharisees affirm their commitment to the congregation's doctrine that all food is clean.

The stilling-of-the-storm (4:35–41) and water-walk scenes (6:45–52)

These two scenes seem to make the same doctrinal point: Jesus can control the forces of nature. Did Mark write both scenes? Let's examine their staging.

In the stilling-of-the-storm scene (4:35–41), Jesus and disciples are in the boat in the orchestra. "A great windstorm arose, and the waves beat into the boat, so that the boat was already being swamped" (4:37). The disciples "bail water" energetically. Meanwhile, Jesus is "in the stern, asleep on the cushion" (4:38). The disciples rouse him. He calms the sea, and the boat crosses to Gerasa Stage Right.

The scene is theatrically interesting, with sound and wind effects, and the disciples' physical actions and emotions. The scene has a practical purpose in the play: I propose that the Jesus actor, once roused, bails water and throws the cushion overboard. In the next scene, the acrobatic Roman soldiers somersault off the mountain into the orchestra—and land on the cushion. The stilling-of-the-storm scene provides them with their landing mat.

I note that the narration of the scene begins, "On that day, when evening had come..." (4:35). However, in performance the boat trip cannot take place in the evening because there is no indication that the scene in Gerasa, where they arrive, takes place at night in the world of the play. So I suggest that the term "evening" is an artifact of the polished text. Mark placed "evening" in the narrative in order to justify the (necessary) presence of the cushion: Jesus sleeps on it.

Now to the water-walk scene (6:45–52). The water-walk scene is also theatrically interesting, with wind effects and the Jesus actor "walking on

---

[*] This gift could be a snack, a souvenir of the performance—or both. It was common for audiences at public entertainments to be given gifts (or tokens for gifts). Guests at dinner parties could take food home and were usually, if not always, given gifts.

water." In the next scene in my proposed original sequence, the Pharisees demand a sign that Jesus is extraordinary. As mentioned, the audience has just seen that sign (Jesus walks on water!) and feels superior to the Pharisees.

So both scenes are theatrically interesting, and they have different purposes in the play. I believe that Mark wrote both scenes.

Healings of the deaf-mute, the blind man of Bethsaida, and blind Bartimaeus

I discuss the three scenes in Table 2 together because (in their current form in the received text) they are duplicative and lack interesting theatricality. Are they by Mark?

TABLE 2. HEALINGS OF DEAF-MUTE AND BLIND MEN

	Deaf-mute (7:31–37)	Blind man of Bethsaida (8:22–26)	Blind Bartimaeus (10:46–52)
Performed?	No	Yes	No
Written by?	Editor, no obvious reason	Mark	Editor, to replace Mark's Jericho scene
In GMatthew?	No	No	Yes

The healing of the deaf-mute (7:31–37)

In the received text, Jesus heals the daughter of a Syrophoenician woman (7:24–30). That scene is by an editor. Then—still without his inner disciples—Jesus travels through Sidon towards the Sea of Galilee in the Gentile Decapolis. There, Jesus heals a deaf-mute man (7:31–37).

The healing of the deaf-mute man is stageable. But it has no interesting theatricality: Jesus has already used words of power to heal the daughter of Jairus. The healing of the deaf-mute does not connect to the action of the previous scene or the following scene. There is no stage direction to place the Jesus actor into position for his next scene. These observations, taken together, make the scene fail the DC. Also, the scene-level chiasm has an unMarkan center.[65] I believe this scene was written by an editor.

The healing of the blind man of Bethsaida (8:22–26)

In the received text, Jesus and the disciples travel by boat to Bethsaida (6:45). Again by boat, they travel to and return from Dalmanutha (8:10–13). Then, suddenly "they came to Bethsaida" (8:22) without information about their travel. Obviously Mark's polished text has been edited and its original sequence disturbed.

Above, I discarded the boat trips to and from Dalmanutha. What remains? There is still a boat trip to Bethsaida (6:45). The verse "they came to Bethsaida" (8:22) may be present in the received text because an editor, faced with the disruptions to this section and the presence of the Dalmanutha material, wanted to ensure the reader knew that the healing of the blind man occurred in Bethsaida. The editor wanted to preserve Mark's link between Bethsaida and the blind man. So let us assume that in performance, the healing of the blind man did occur in Bethsaida, after the (one and only) boat trip there.

Here is the scene in the received text (Mk 8:22–26):

> [22] They came to Bethsaida. Some people brought a blind man to him and begged him to touch him. [23] He took the blind man by the hand and led him out of the village; and when he had put saliva on his eyes and laid his hands on him, he asked him, "Can you see anything?" [24] And the man looked up and said, "I can see people, but they look like trees, walking." [25] Then Jesus laid his hands on his eyes again; and he looked intently and his sight was restored, and he saw everything clearly. [26] Then he sent him away to his home, saying, "Do not even go into the village."

The scene is performable. Although the scene does not seem to have interesting theatricality, the fact that the healing takes place "out of the village" suggests an unusual staging. The scene-level chiasm is Markan.[66] On the other hand, the scene is a simple healing just after the audience has been distracted by the receipt of gifts: the healing does not seem dramatic enough to re-engage them in world of the play. And why is this scene at the center of a plausible multi-scene chiasm (p. 92)? It must be important. I suggest that Mark did write this scene, and its importance existed in the world of the audience. I discuss this scene further in Chapter 6.

The healing of blind Bartimaeus (10:46–52)

In this scene (10:46–52), the only interesting element is the name "Bartimaeus." The Greek-speaking audience (or reader/listener) would have immediately recognized "Bartimaeus" as a neologism that combined the Aramaic "*bar*" (son of) and "*Timaeus*," a dialogue by Plato. "By the end of the first or the beginning of the second century Plato's works, especially the *Timaeus*, were established as authoritative texts conveying philosophical truth."[67] Like Genesis, the *Timaeus* concerns the nature of the Creator.[68] To Mark's audience, in the context of the performance, the word "Bartimaeus" therefore probably meant something like, "[Judean or Para-Judean] Son of Greek Civilization."

This healing is another theatrically dull scene. The man's restored "sight" seems to be only physical. If Mark had written this scene, the man's recovery of his "sight" would have had additional meanings. Turton assesses the chiastic structure of the scene as "clear and quite beautiful, almost suspiciously so. The center of the chiasm seems somewhat unMarkan. Also unMarkan is the lack of saying that can be unplugged from its context."[69] Together, these features suggest that the scene has been edited away from Mark's original, or was added by an editor.

The healing of Bartimaeus follows a scene set in Jericho, now missing from the received text. I propose that both the healing of Bartimaeus and the (original) Jericho scene had the same function in the play: they added Gentiles to Jesus's followers. I suggest that the editor who cut Mark's Jericho scene from the polished text wrote the healing of Bartimaeus as a replacement. This editor knew how to imitate Mark's style, and knew that the polished text condensed a performed play.

The original scene in Jericho

In the received text, Jesus and the twelve disciples come to Jericho, then immediately leave it (10:46). In GMatthew, there is no scene set in Jericho, but there is a healing of two blind men (Mt 20:30–34). Therefore, the Jericho material in GMark had been edited before Matthew got a copy.

The audience at Mark's play would have known that Jericho was the first city in Canaan conquered by the Israelites under Joshua. Therefore, when the Jesus actor approaches "Jericho," the audience maps him onto their mental knowledge of the biblical Joshua. Then, Jesus leaves Jericho with his disciples "and a large crowd" (10:46). This stage direction suggests that some (Gentile) multitudes are now followers of Jesus. (Some or all of these followers will participate in the parade that enters Jerusalem [11:7–11].) Something occurred in Jericho that caused multitudes of Jericho to follow Jesus.

Other scenes

Now I turn to scenes outside the Bethsaida section. First I discuss the calling of Levi. Then I discuss the major scenes of the plot (Temptation, Recognition, ascension) and their current forms in the received text. I discuss the Olivet Discourse and the staging of Jesus's death. Then, having discussed Jesus's exit from the stage during the ascension scene, I circle around and discuss his *entry* to the stage. That segues into a reconstruction of the original sequence of scenes in Act I in which he recruits disciples, appoints them, and informs the audience of his mission on earth.

The calling of Levi (2:13–14)

Here is the action of the scene in the received text (2:13–14): Jesus and the four disciples walk along the sea side (the stage edge). An actor, obviously a tax collector, is seated at a table. Jesus says, "Follow me." The man stands up, picks up his table and stool, and follows Jesus and the Four to the "house" on the upper level.

This scene is stageable, but it is dramatically dull. The only purpose of the scene is to show the audience that Jesus has (successfully) called a tax collector. Furthermore, the man's identity is improbable: He sits beside the Sea of Galilee. But taxes were collected in the towns, not at the sea side. And the man cannot collect customs because the Sea of Galilee was entirely inside the empire.

Who wrote 2:13–14, Mark or an editor? If Mark had written the scene and the tax collector was named to the audience, he would have had some significance later in the play. But he does not.* Therefore, I conclude that an editor wrote 2:13–14 (as backstory to 2:15–17). The name "Levi" was created by the editor.

The Temptation

The Temptation scene introduces Satan, the antagonist in the plot. The scene should have some dramatic extensivity. Yet in the received text, the entire scene is this: "[Jesus] was in the wilderness forty days, tempted by Satan; and he was with the wild beasts; and the angels waited on him" (1:13).

The reader/listener cannot imagine the scene in performance, because there are no details on how Jesus was tempted/tested by Satan. There is no information on how the angels entered or when and how they exited. Wild beasts cannot be brought on stage, and imitation wild beasts (costumed actors?) belong in a children's play and set the wrong tone for Mark's play. The time interval of "forty days" cannot be shown, and if mentioned in dialogue, creates a time lapse in the world of the play that the audience is expected (unreasonably) to overlook. The scene fails the PC—it is not performable. The scene fails the DC—it is poor playwriting. In addition, a scene-level chiasm cannot be constructed.

I propose that the scene in GMatthew, Mt 4:1–11a, is essentially copied from Mark's polished text. Here is Mt 4:1–11a:

---

* However, it is possible that one of the outcasts who dines with Jesus and is identified by the scribes to the audience as a tax collector (2:16) *does* become one of the "follower" disciples later in the play.

¹ Then Jesus was led up by the Spirit into the wilderness to be tempted by the devil. ² He fasted forty days and forty nights, and afterwards he was famished. ³ The tempter came and said to him, "If you are the Son of God, command these stones to become loaves of bread." ⁴ But he answered, "It is written, 'One does not live by bread alone, but by every word that comes from the mouth of God.'" ⁵ Then the devil took him to the holy city and placed him on the pinnacle of the temple, ⁶ saying to him, "If you are the Son of God, throw yourself down; for it is written, 'He will command his angels concerning you,' and 'On their hands they will bear you up, so that you will not dash your foot against a stone.'" ⁷ Jesus said to him, "Again it is written, 'Do not put the Lord your God to the test.'" ⁸ Again, the devil took him to a very high mountain and showed him all the kingdoms of the world and their splendor; ⁹ and he said to him, "All these I will give you, if you will fall down and worship me." ¹⁰ Jesus said to him, "Away with you, Satan! for it is written, 'Worship the Lord your God, and serve only him.'" ¹¹ Then the devil left him.

I imagine the action of Mark's play as follows: The Jesus actor is Stage Center. The stage crane carries in a second actor who wears a robe. He tells Jesus to enter the "bucket."* They rise. The second actor tells Jesus to command the stones to become loaves of bread. Jesus answers with a quotation from Scripture. The stage crane swings them to the top of the scene building. The other actor says, "If you are the Son of God, throw yourself down" (Mt 4:6). Jesus answers, "Do not put the Lord your God to the test" (Mt 4:7). (By now the audience suspects that the angel is Satan, the heavenly adversary.) The stage crane swings them to the top of the mountain. The other actor offers Jesus all the kingdoms of the world. Jesus refuses and in the process introduces the actor to the audience, "Away with you, Satan! for it is written, 'Worship the Lord your God, and serve only him.'" Jesus exits the bucket onto the mountain. Probably the Satan actor is deposited onto a "perch" near the top of the scene building: he remains on earth, and will appear in this spot later in the play to oversee *his* "mission on earth."

The next verse in GMatthew "and suddenly angels came and waited on him" (Mt 4:11b) is logistically problematic. Angels should enter the stage via the stage crane. Unless there is a second (or third) stage crane, the bucket of the stage crane used by Jesus would have to be withdrawn, then loaded with the angels, then lowered to the stage. All of this takes time, while the audience

---

* The Satan actor shows Jesus the kingdoms of the world. The simplest staging seems to me a stage crane with a bucket that held two actors. (This two-person stage crane will be used at the end of the play, when Jesus ascends with an angel.) But possibly there were two stage cranes that moved independently.

waits. The action of the angels has no dramatic value: they briefly interact with the Jesus actor, then disappear. And their help cannot be *reported* by the Jesus actor because there is no other actor onstage for him to speak to! So I conclude that the angels in Mt 4:11b are not from Mark's polished text: an editor of GMatthew wrote Mt 4:11b to harmonize with Mk 1:13.

My proposed original Temptation scene is appropriate for the beginning of the play. It is theatrical: Satan and Jesus move around in the heavens, then descend to the earth. The play's motif of bread is introduced. The Satan actor is introduced by name, and his conflict with Jesus is established. The Satan actor is physically placed on the set, and the audience now knows where to look for him later in the play.

But an editor of GMark deleted the verses that are now Mt 4:3–10, and condensed the verses that are now Mt 4:1–2 and Mt 4:11a into Mk 1:13. The editor added details in Mk 1:13—"wild beasts" and "angels"—probably to point to related stories in Scripture.

The Recognition (8:27–38)

The staging of the Recognition scene in the received text is not quite clear. A small change will clarify the dramatic action.

First, Peter recognizes Jesus as the Christ (8:29):

> [29] He asked them, "But who do you say that I am?" Peter answered him, "You are the Messiah." [30] And he sternly ordered them not to tell anyone about him.

Jesus now trusts the disciples to support him in his mission. He tells them about his mission:

> [31] Then he began to teach them that the Son of Man must undergo great suffering, and be rejected by the elders, the chief priests, and the scribes, and be killed, and after three days rise again. [32] He said all this quite openly.

But Peter can't accept these predictions and rebukes Jesus:

> And Peter took him aside and began to rebuke him.

Jesus responds:

> [33] But turning and looking at his disciples, he rebuked Peter and said, "Get behind me, Satan! For you are setting your mind not on divine things but on human things."

What was the content of Peter's rebuke? Probably something like, "You must stay alive, you are our teacher, we can't live without you!" Jesus then rebukes Peter. That exchange makes sense. But the stage directions don't make sense. Why does Mark mention that Jesus has turned and looked *at his disciples*? Whom does Jesus address with "Get behind me, Satan!"?

The Recognition is a pivotal scene. It is located in the middle of the play, which makes it a candidate for the climax of the plot—especially because it mentions Satan. So I will assume that in this scene, Satan has acted against Jesus, and Peter is the third character of the climax.

I propose the following staging of the scene: The Jesus actor foretells his fate to the disciples. Peter takes Jesus aside and rebukes him for planning to abandon them (as Peter understands it). The two actors have moved a few steps away from the group, and turned slightly away from the audience. Facing away from the audience, the Jesus actor sees the Satan actor high up on the scene building in the background behind Peter. Jesus realizes that Peter's rebuke was caused by Satan's influence (or entrancement). That is, Satan has "taken over" Peter, presumably recently. Jesus then addresses *the Satan actor*, "Get behind me, Satan!"* Jesus returns his attention to Peter and adds: "For you are [because of Satan's influence] setting your mind not on divine things but on human things."

In this proposed reconstruction, Satan is present onstage at the climax of the plot. Jesus remains committed to his mission, but now he knows that his chief disciple—who a minute earlier had seemed to understand it—is entranced and therefore, like the Satanic spirits in the possessed multitudes, an agent of Satan.† I note that the audience members see the Satan actor and know that Peter is entranced. It is not clear if the other disciples—who do not see the Satan actor—know that Peter is entranced. They may be entranced themselves. Any verses that concerned when and how Peter was taken over by Satan are missing.

This scene takes place "on the way" to "the villages of Caesarea Philippi" (8:27). "The way" is the orchestra. A centered staging in the orchestra is appropriate for the climax of the plot. As in the Temptation, the Jesus actor looks upward across the stage, past his disciples, towards the top of the scene building and Satan's "perch." Jesus's gaze traverses a larger volume of space than the action of scenes that concern only earthly matters.

The Olivet Discourse (13:5–37)
The Olivet Discourse (13:5–37) (sometimes inaccurately called the "Little

---

* Note that "Get behind me, Satan!" here in the Recognition is very similar to "Away with you Satan" (Mt 4:10) that I have proposed was in Mark's original Temptation.

† Peter remains possessed until the cock crow at 14:72.

Apocalypse"[70]) is, in the received text, a long, continuous speech. I ask you to read aloud the first few verses, 13:5–12.

Do it now.

Without looking at the text again, can you relate, in order, the gist of each verse you have just read?

Do it now.

The gists are: beware being led astray—do not be alarmed that wars will come—there will be disasters—when you are tried, the Holy Spirit will speak through you—families will betray each other. Or, in brief: be careful—don't worry—bad things will happen—don't worry—bad things will happen.

Is the speaker building up to a point? What is that point? Based only on these verses, can you predict the topics of the next few verses?

If you can't answer yes to these questions, the audience at the performance couldn't. A rule of playwriting, says Grebanier, is that "*any given speech must convey only one important dramatic idea and/or only one ruling emotion*" (italics in original).[71] Mark could write a speech with a single idea, as demonstrated by Jesus's praise of the anointing woman at Bethany (Mk 14:6–9). But the Olivet Discourse is a hodgepodge. Therefore, we can reasonably infer that it has been edited.

To reconstruct Mark's original version of the Olivet Discourse, I will assume that it builds to a point. I will assume that its theme was suitable for Jesus's "Last Words."[72] I will assume that the speech commented on, foreshadowed, or echoed other scenes, speeches, or themes in the play. I will assume that Mark constructed it in a chiasm.

When I started work on the reconstruction, I did not have any assumptions about the speech's theme. I only assumed that it would be suitable as Last Words. I retained vivid language from the received text as likely to be original. Once I had posited several lines as originally by Mark, the possibilities for the remaining lines narrowed.

I suggest the following chiasm as an approximation of Jesus's original Olivet Discourse. The numbered verses are extracted from the received version of Mark 13:

> A [5] Beware that no one leads you astray, [22] False messiahs and false prophets will appear and produce signs and omens.
>> B [7] When you hear of wars and rumors of wars, do not be alarmed; this must take place, but the end is still to come. [8] For nation will rise against nation, and kingdom against kingdom; there will be earthquakes in various places.
>>> C [24] But in those days, after that suffering, the sun will be darkened, and the moon will not give its light, [25] and the stars will be falling from heaven, and the powers in the heavens will be shaken.
>>> D [26] Then they will see 'the Son of Man coming in clouds' with great power and glory.
>>> D' [missing—about the Son of Man in heaven]
>>> C' [27] Then he will send out the angels, and gather his elect from the four winds, from the ends of the earth to the ends of heaven.
>> B' [missing—about the earth]
> A' [23] But be alert; I have already told you everything. [31] Heaven and earth will pass away, but my words will not pass away.

Jesus pauses, then in a second speech, addresses a different topic, the importance of watching for these events:

> A [32] But about that day or hour no one knows, neither the angels in heaven, nor the Son, but only the Father. [33] Beware, keep alert; for you do not know when the time will come.
>> B1 [34] It is like a man going on a journey, when he leaves home and puts his slaves in charge, each with his work,
>> B1' and commands the doorkeeper to be on the watch.
>> B2 [35] Therefore, keep awake—for you do not know when the master of the house will come, in the evening, or at midnight, or at cockcrow, or at dawn,
>> B2' [36] or else he may find you asleep when he comes suddenly.
> A' [37] And what I say to you I say to all: Keep awake.

The reconstructed Olivet Discourse contains two sections. In the first section, the A brackets warn the hearers about being led astray; the B brackets concern activities on earth; the C brackets concern activities in the heavens; and the D brackets concern the Son of Man in the heavens. The focus moves from the congregation to the earth to the heavens to the Son of Man, then reverses. The gist of this proposed speech is: "Remain committed. The heavens will convulse and the elect will see the Son of Man. There will be consequences in the heavens and on the earth, and this is what they will be. I have spoken."

In the world of the play, this proposed speech is appropriate for the disciples. The play is set before the Jewish War. The war *will* be a disaster. Galileans and Judeans will be killed, enslaved, and displaced. All Judeans will suffer when they lose the earthly Temple, the focus of their ethno-religious identity. An apocalyptic speech is consistent with life in the world of the play.

Functionally, the speech prefigures scenes in the Passion and tells the audience what to expect. The B bracket predicts earthquakes; there may be an earthquake effect at Jesus's death. The C bracket (13:24–25) prefigures the darkness at noon and the convulsed forces in the heavens (the tearing of the Temple veil). I suggest that the D bracket prefigures a staged ascension scene where Jesus ascends to the clouds. (Appropriately, this culmination of Jesus's mission on earth is placed in the center of the chiasm.) The final, A′ bracket mentions "heaven and earth" (back-referencing my proposed C and D brackets). Mk 13:31 "rounds off" the Last Words.

The second chiasm, 13:32–37, is good advice. In the world of the play, it prefigures the disciples' failure to watch in Gethsemane. And in the world of the audience, the command to watch tells *them*, "stay tuned, more entertainment is ahead."

Jesus's cry from the cross (15:34)

If the crucifixion scene in the received text is entirely original, Mark preserved only one line of dialogue spoken by Jesus on the cross. That line must be important. Jesus calls out loudly from offstage, "*Eloi, Eloi lema sabachthani?*" (15:34) ("My God, My God, why have you forsaken me?"). This is the first line of Psalm 22, in Aramaic.

Mark uses several elements of Psalm 22 in the Passion. I think he expected the audience to recognize that Jesus is quoting Psalm 22. If his expectation was valid, the Jesus actor could have pronounced "*Eloi*" like the Greek sun god "*Hēlios*," i.e., "*Hēlios, Hēlios, lema sabachthani?*" ("Thou sun, Thou sun, why hast thou forsaken me?")[73] and the audience would have still recognized the emulation of Psalm 22.* The line as *actually spoken*, then, informs the audience that the sun has disappeared, that is, the stage is in darkness. This line was logistically critical to the performance, because the ambient light was still daylight.

Mark knew that the reader/listener of the polished text would not experience the sonic mash-up of "*Eloi*" and "*Hēlios*." They would be Greek-speakers, and some would not know Aramaic or Psalm 22. They might interpret "*Eloi*" as only "*Hēlios*." That is why Mark provided the reference in the polished text, "My God, my God, why have you forsaken me?" (15:34).

In performance, the spoken line received another interpretation. "When some of the bystanders heard it, they said, 'Listen, he is calling for Elijah'" (15:35). The Chorus does not hear "*Eloi*" or "*Hēlios*." They hear "*Elias*" (Greek for "Elijah"). The Chorus sees Jesus as a man (albeit a healer with special powers) who calls on the more powerful Elijah to help him. (Many Judeans saw Elijah as the precursor to the Messiah.) The audience, however, knows that the Chorus is wrong and the real situation is the reverse: Jesus doesn't call on anyone: *he* is the Messiah (and John the Baptist was his Elijah). One line: three meanings, and placed at a moment of maximum drama. This is a master playwright at work.

The empty tomb scene (16:1–8)
This is the action of the last scene of the Gospel in the received text: Three women approach the open tomb. A young man in a white robe is inside. He tells the women that Jesus has ascended. They run away without speaking.

This scene (16:1–8) cannot be the original ending of the play. The other actors and the Chorus cannot see inside the tomb. Therefore, they do not know why the women are running away. They have no reason to leave the stage. The play ends with the young man, Pilate, the soldiers, Peter, most of the Chorus, and possibly the Council still onstage! Mk 16:1–8 fails the DC.

In the received text, the young man in a robe reports to the women that an ascension has occurred. I suggest that his report condenses the performance; a staged ascension was the original last scene of the play.

Earlier in the play, the audience was given several hints that they will see an ascension scene. Jesus says that he will be killed, then rise (Mk 8:31, 9:31, 10:34). Jesus says that dead people rise and are "like angels in heaven" (12:25). In the Olivet Discourse, Jesus says, "Then they will see 'the Son of

---

* The technical term for this wordplay is "paronomasia," from *paronomazein*, *para-* + *onoma* (name).

Man coming in clouds' with great power and glory" (13:26). During the trial, Jesus says, "'you will see the Son of Man seated at the right hand of the Power,' and 'coming with the clouds of heaven'" (14:62).

My proposal for the performed ascension scene

What occurred in Mark's performed ascension scene? I make the following assumptions: The Jesus actor is carried by the stage crane to the heavens. There is at least one angel present. The scene answers the question of the plot and therefore it is very likely that the Satan actor is present. At the end of the scene, all the actors exit the stage.

In the received text of the Passion, there are two loose ends: Peter's presence in the courtyard, and the cut ear of the slave of the high priest. I asked if those two elements set up some action in the ascension scene. As I did so, I came up with the following proposal. I did not innovate—I used only materials from the received text (and my reconstructions in this book).

Here is my proposal for the action and (approximate) key dialogue of the ascension scene in Mark's performed play:

> PILATE *and* SOLDIERS *are on the upper level of the stage. The* HIGH PRIEST *and* COUNCIL *(and* PHARISEES?*) are on the lower level, Stage Center. The* CHORUS *is Stage Left.* PETER *and the* SLAVES OF THE HIGH PRIEST *are in the orchestra.* SATAN *is present on a "perch" near the top of the scene building. On the stage crane, an* ANGEL *descends to the stage near the tomb Stage Right. He steps off. He rolls away the disc door of the tomb. The* JESUS *actor is alive inside, dressed in a white robe. The wrapped, headless corpse of* JOHN THE BAPTIST *is still inside and visible to the audience. The* ANGEL *leads (assists?)* JESUS *onto the stage crane (or a second stage crane). They ascend, then pause above the scene building. Only* SATAN *sees them.*

> PETER *notices that the* SLAVE OF THE HIGH PRIEST *has a damaged ear, points to it, and says:* His ear! It is bleeding! Look!

> *The* SLAVE OF THE HIGH PRIEST *feels his ear, looks stricken. The other* SLAVES *look stricken. The* HIGH PRIEST *and* COUNCIL *see the blood. Horrified by having participated in a trial conducted by an impure high priest, and by his pollution of the Temple, they flee.* * *So do the* SLAVES OF THE HIGH PRIEST *and some of the* MULTITUDES *(pro-Council Judeans).*

---

* It is reasonable to infer that "*the* slave of the high priest," who had accompanied the guards sent by the Council to arrest Jesus, served as the personal representative of the high priest. (Otherwise, the actor would be called "*a* slave of the high priest.") The high priest had to be a perfect physical specimen (Philo of Alexandria, *Special Laws* 1.16.80). Therefore, it seems probable that the personal representative of the high priest also had to be a perfect physical specimen. However, I have not found any texts that say this.

PETER (pointing at the tomb): Look, Jesus's body is not in the tomb! (pause) He has risen! Just as he said he would! (pause) Glory to Jesus the Son of God, who has risen and sits at his Father's right hand! Glory to God who is served by the true high priest in the Temple made without hands!"

Some of the MULTITUDES run towards the tomb to see for themselves. Some flee through the parodoi. Others are jubilant. For PILATE and (all?) SOLDIERS, this is just another day in the provinces: they exit quietly through the royal door of the scene building and close it behind them. PETER leads the jubilant MULTITUDES, possibly singing, on a march out of the theater.* *JESUS and the ANGEL continue their ascent and disappear into the heavens (behind a cloud?). SATAN withdraws. The stage and orchestra are now empty.*

This proposed ascension scene has these virtues:

- It is theatrical.
- It *shows* doctrine.
- It gives dramatic value to the cutting of the ear of the slave of the high priest during the arrest scene, and explains Peter's presence with the slaves of the high priest in the courtyard of the house of the high priest.†
- It gives dramatic value to Peter's weeping in 14:72: the actor will quickly transit from despair to exultation.
- It creates a tableau in which actors with speaking roles are posed simultaneously on *five* levels: the orchestra (Peter), the lower stage (the high priest and Council), the upper stage with the scene building (Pilate), (near) the top of the scene building (Satan), and the heavens (Jesus). Mark's tableau emulates and *surpasses* the four-level tableau at the end of Euripides's *Orestes*, "the most spectacular climax in all of Greek tragedy."[74]
- It is structurally parallel to the Temptation within the entire play.

---

* Peter leads Jesus's followers. Peter, who had been "dumb as a rock," is now "the rock of the church." I suspect that Mark always intended Peter's name to have these two meanings—*sequentially*—within the context of the play. But without Mark's original ascension scene, the received text supported only the first meaning.

† I suggest that in Mark's original arrest scene, *Peter* (not an anonymous bystander) grabbed a sword from a guard, lashed out, and cut the ear of the slave of the high priest. Either Peter did not realize he had drawn blood, or he knew but did not recognize its significance because he was still entranced by Satan. The guards arrested Peter and placed him in the custody of the slaves of the high priest in the courtyard. Later, a pro-Peter editor erased Peter's participation in the arrest scene.

- It answers the question of the play: Jesus does complete his mission to die and rise.
- It shows the audience Satan's reaction to the outcome of *his* mission.
- It provides reasons for all the remaining actors onstage to exit.
- A raucous mêlée is created by some of the exiting actors.
- It is compatible with the young man's report of ascension in the received text (16:6).

The empty-tomb scene as a replacement for the ascension scene

At some point, an editor excised Mark's ascension scene from the polished text and replaced it with 16:1–8. Now the last words of the text were awkward: "*ephobounto gar*" ("they were afraid for"). Here is my proposal for the editor's thoughts: "With the odd phrase '*ephobounto gar*' I left the reader a clue that the original scene has been changed. I created the young man in the tomb as a messenger who reports that Jesus has ascended. I specified that the messenger is a young man (*nēaniskon*), not an angel—if he is an angel, the reader would wonder how he had entered the stage. But the young man's white robe—the costume of an angel—tells the reader not to take him at face value. It is necessary that this messenger speak to at least one actor. There was an earthquake when Jesus died on the cross; some Chorus members fled in fear. I moved their "flight in fear" to later, when they see the empty tomb. I gave them a reason to go to the tomb—to anoint Jesus—that duplicates the anointing at Bethany (they don't actually anoint him, as that would be superfluous). At the tomb, they hear the messenger's speech. So, in my new, replacement scene, I used materials already in the play. I didn't distort the polished text's account of the performance: I just condensed the performance into a report. I made only a minimal change to the sequence of events (I moved the fleeing, frightened women from the earthquake scene to the empty tomb scene). I respected and conserved Mark's work. The reader who had seen the play or heard about it would not say that I have *innovated*."

Why did the editor replace the ascension scene with the empty tomb scene? Possibly the editor was concerned about the political implications of Jesus as Son of God. Possibly the Roman congregation wanted to erase the implicit doctrine about Jesus's "body" and/or "nature," to allow for diverse views among the congregants. Another possible reason is evident only when the ascension scene is reconstructed: the disciples (except for Peter and possibly Judas) have already left the stage. When Peter leads the multitudes (Chorus) out of the theater, the other disciples are not present. At some point, the Roman congregation was invested in promoting the historicity of the other eleven disciples. Their absence from the original ascension scene diminished their credibility and utility as founders of other congregations, since Peter knew more about Jesus's ascension than they did. The empty tomb scene made *all* the disciples equal.

Jesus's entry to the stage
Given that Jesus exits the stage on the stage crane, it would be logical for him to *enter* the stage on the stage crane. That would show the audience that he is a heavenly being. He is onstage briefly—baptized and named the Son of God. Then the Temptation scene brings Satan to the stage and introduces the plot. But the problem with this scenario is that the stage crane is used twice in three scenes (entrance and Temptation).

Alternatively, we can take the received text at face value: the Jesus actor just appears onstage (1:9). Let us imagine the staging. In tragedy, "the protagonists always entered the stage through the middle or royal door."[75] Although GMark as a whole is not a tragedy, it has a tragic section. I propose that at 1:9, the Jesus actor opens the royal door of the scene building, enters the upper stage, then walks down to the lower level. He meets John the Baptist, is baptized, and is named the Son of God. Seeing this sequence, the audience knows only that the Jesus actor is the protagonist. They do not think of him as a heavenly being. But then the Satan actor appears on the stage crane. Satan promises Jesus all the kingdoms of the world. This scene informs the audience that the Jesus character is not an ordinary human being. Only now, when it is relevant in the scene, is Jesus' heavenly identity provided to the audience.

I think the second alternative is a dramatically more effective opening for the play. And it does not require two uses of the stage crane (Jesus, then Satan) in rapid succession. In addition, if the royal door is not opened by Jesus when he enters the stage, who opens it? When?

The entry of the Chorus, and reconstruction of Mk 1
My proposed ascension scene includes the exit of the Chorus. That raises a question I have not addressed: How does Mark stage the *entry* of the Chorus?

The Temptation initiates Jesus's mission on earth. In the received text, the next five scenes are Mk 1:16–45. (I assume that they are all original, and no scenes are missing.) The Chorus must be introduced during this sequence.

There is only one line that can serve as the entry of the Chorus. It is 1:45, the last line of the healing of the leper. He exits proclaiming, "so that Jesus could no longer go into a town openly, but stayed out in the country; *and people came to him from every quarter*" (emphasis added). That is, the Chorus enters. Their entry is informal, as appropriate for a play in the genre of mime.

However, several earlier scenes in the received text involve Chorus members. In 1:16–20, Jesus calls disciples from the boat and the seaside. The position of this scene *before* the entry of the Chorus makes sense only if the fishermen are heavenly beings. As they are not, I propose that originally, the calling of the fishermen *followed* the healing of the leper and the entry of the Chorus.

The healing of the possessed man in the synagogue at Capernaum (1:21–28) and the healing of Simon's mother-in-law (1:29–34) are also prior to the entry of the Chorus. Are they original (but out of sequence), or were they written by an editor? Here are my observations about these scenes:

Jesus heals the possessed man on the Sabbath, and the synagogue attendees do not object. But later, in the same synagogue, Jesus heals on the Sabbath (the man with a withered hand, 3:1–6)—and meets hostility because he heals on the Sabbath: "They watched him to see whether he would cure him on the sabbath, so that they might accuse him" (3:2). Why is there no hostility in the earlier scene? And it is poor dramaturgy for Mark to begin the play with a healing that has no theatricality and no obvious emulation. The healing of the possessed man fails the DC. I believe it is by an editor.

Now to the healing of Simon's mother-in-law (1:29–34). The scene has no interesting theatricality. Even if the healing is enacted, and not reported, the woman merely stands up. Then, "she began to serve them" (1:31). Her service—washing feet or serving food—is dramatically dull, slows down the play and has no consequences later in the play. Even if the actors referred in dialogue to the woman's status as a mother-in-law, and that status was interesting to the audience, the *action* of the scene remains unacceptably dull. The scene fails the DC and therefore is very likely by an editor.

Also before the entry of the Chorus, Jesus prays alone, in a deserted place (1:35). Only the audience hears his lines. A religious prayer that the audience already knows has no theatrical value and does not advance the plot. Instead, I propose that in this prayer, *Jesus reviews his plans to fulfill his mission on earth and prays for God's help*. This speech gives the audience the "master plan" by which they understand Jesus's behavior throughout the play. (This is also the time for Jesus to explain the rationale for his itinerary in Galilee.)

Logically, this prayer should immediately follow the Temptation scene. Jesus should inform the audience of his plans *before* the entry of the Chorus and before he calls the fishermen as disciples. (The fishermen, who are not yet onstage, will perforce know less than the audience about Jesus's identity and plan. The fishermen will not understand Jesus's actions or his disclosures about his fate. It is not fair to see them as dim. They are underinformed.)

With these observations in mind, I propose the following original sequence of events at the beginning of Mark's performed play:

1. (1:1–11, 1:14a). Voice of God speaks. John and his disciples enter. Jesus enters. John baptizes. Guards enter and seize John. The guards exit, followed by John's disciples/baptizees.* Jesus remains onstage. The dove descends and the Voice of God proclaims that Jesus is his son.

2. The original Temptation scene. Satan enters via the stage crane; Jesus also enters the stage crane (or a second one) and dialogues with Satan. Jesus descends onto the mountain and Satan exits the stage crane onto the scene building.

3. (1:35) Jesus is alone onstage. He "prays"; the audience overhears his plans to fulfill his mission on earth, and possibly his itinerary.

4. (1:40–45) A leper approaches Jesus. Jesus heals him (stage magic). The Chorus enters from all directions, then goes to its holding area(s) on the stage. (During this distraction, the boat is brought in and the fishermen enter.)

5. (1:14b–20) Jesus walks towards the boat, then calls the Three. They follow him. (The boat remains.)

At this point, Jesus and his antagonist have been introduced, the Chorus is onstage, the audience has been informed of Jesus's plans, the inner disciples have joined Jesus, and he is ready to begin his earthly mission in Capernaum.

I suggest a possible additional detail for this proposal: Perhaps the leper had been a follower of John the Baptist. The leper had asked John for healing but John could not (or did not have time to) heal him. The leper exited with John's followers. In this case, when *prior to the entry of the Chorus* the leper approaches Jesus at 1:40, the audience has seen the leper before and knows that he is an earthly being with an earthly problem. They are not confused by the possibility that he is a heavenly being.

Conclusions about reconstruction
Limits of reconstruction
In Appendix E, I apply my insights—mainly from Chapters 3 and 4—and

---

* John's disciples/baptizees must exit so that the Jesus actor is alone onstage for the descent of the dove and the Temptation.

take a first step toward proposing the stage action of Mark's performed play. But Appendix E is only a first step, for the following reasons:

It is very likely that I have retained scenes and dialogue that have been edited (or are entirely by an editor). For example, at 2:23–28, Pharisees suddenly appear and comment that the disciples are harvesting grain on the Sabbath. Jesus responds with a clever speech that conveys his doctrine. This "scene" is an exchange of dialogue and had no dramatic value. It has no consequences in the play. Because I do not know who wrote the scene, and if it was actually staged, I retain it. As another example, in Act IV, Jesus's parable teachings are too lengthy to be effective in performance. But because I cannot determine which parables came from the hand of Mark, and which parables were added by an editor, I have retained them all.

I cannot reconstruct scenes that were excised by editors and are absent from GMatthew. The excised scenes include the original scene in Jericho and the boat trip to Bethsaida.

I cannot reconstruct the dialogue of the performed play and I do not even try. Mark omitted dialogue when he wrote the polished text. He folded some dialogue into narration. Editors have added, deleted, and changed dialogue. Some—it is impossible to tell how much—of the play's dialogue is lost. At the trial, multiple witnesses spoke, but only the gist of some of their speeches is preserved. Possibly at times the actors spoke "logistical" lines like "Let's go to X now" that Mark omitted from the polished text. I don't know if the Chorus spoke only indistinct words, or recognizable lines. I do not know *which* Chorus members spoke those lines.

I also do not have Mark's notes about the characterization of the roles. How does Satan play his role? Does the Chorus have divided loyalties, or do they sway, as a whole, from pro-Jesus to pro-Council and back again? Does the Barabbas actor emulate a known person or dramatic role? How is Pilate played?

Much of a performed play is nonverbal. The scenes in performance were necessarily longer and more visually complex than they appear in the received text. As Grebanier points out, "An episode that comes and goes on the stage too briefly will not have had time to penetrate the audience's consciousness."[76]

I do not know the conventions for audience participation in or reaction to theatrical performances. Was it expected for audiences to interrupt scenes with applause? To dialogue directly with the actors during the performance?

If the actors directly addressed the audience, how did the audience react? How long were such interruptions, if any?

Therefore, Appendix E has a number of limitations. It is not accurate in length, because I include scenes and lines that I suspect are not original. It is missing scenes that I cannot reconstruct. Appendix E is not accurate in width, because even in original (or proposed original) scenes I cannot provide all the original dialogue or stage directions for the contributions of the actors. And some material in the received text—particularly dialogue concerning doctrine—may have been seamlessly changed by editors and I have not identified it.

So what use is Appendix E? It is a repository of my observations and insights from this book. It is a step toward reconstructing Mark's performed play. It shows that my observations and insights make for a performable and entertaining play. Though not entirely correct—for reasons mentioned above—it provides a foundation for further work on reconstructing Mark's performed play.

The performed play had fewer healings than the received text

Now that I have given you a tool to imagine the (original) Gospel as a performed play, I can address an important aesthetic question about the received text of the Gospel: the action prior to the Passion is often theatrically dull. In particular, there are many healings that are repetitive and lack theatricality. I will first address the healings, then the dullness.

I think it is useful to list the healings in the received text (Table 3). I add my conclusions about which ones are original and which ones are not.

TABLE 3. HEALINGS IN THE RECEIVED TEXT

Healing scene	By Mark?	Theatrical element
Possessed man (1:21–28)	Probably not	Removal of possession
Simon's mother-in-law (1:29–31)	Probably not	None
Multitudes around the door (1:32–34)	Probably not	Removal of lameness, etc.
Leper (1:40–45)	Yes	Stage magic
Paralytic (2:1–12)	Probably	Removal of paralysis
Man with a withered hand (3:1–6)	Yes	Stage magic

4 - Some Reconstruction of the Performance, and Editors in Rome

Healing scene	By Mark?	Theatrical element
Demoniac of Gerasa (5:1–20)	Yes	Behavior of demoniac before *and* after healing (possession/loud proclaiming)
Woman with hemorrhage and Jairus's daughter (5:21–43)	Probably	Jesus touches taboo females? Woman with hemorrhage and story to tell is guest star? Magic words?
Multitudes healed at Gennesaret (6:53–56)	No	None
Syrophoenician woman's daughter (7:24–30)	No	None
Deaf-mute (7:31–37)	No	Magic word
Blind man of Bethsaida (8:22–26)	Yes	The (Gentile) congregant who plays the role
Epileptic boy (9:14–29)	Yes	The (comedic) failure of the disciples to heal the boy
Blind Bartimaeus (10:46–52)	No	Man's line: people look like trees

In the received text, the healing of the woman with hemorrhage and Jairus's daughter (5:21–43) are theatrically dull. The scenes do not add new information: Jesus has already demonstrated that he heals people with these kinds of conditions. On the other hand, the two healings are intercalated and the action is stageable. I am not sure if these healings are original, so I retain them.

I note that in my proposed *original* sequence of Mk 1 (p. 114), at the onset of his mission on earth Jesus heals three actors in succession (leper, paralytic, withered hand). This focus on healings establishes Jesus's identity as a healer, and impresses the multitudes, who consequently begin to pay attention to him. Their attention alarms the Council, initiating the subplot conflict.* The five subsequent healings that I propose were written by Mark are diverse. One has a possibly dead girl, one has a possible female guest star, one has a male guest star (the demoniac of Gerasa), one is a teenager (the epileptic boy), and one is probably played by a congregant (the blind man of Bethsaida). The result is that all of the eight probably original healings in the performed play had some unique element and some inherent theatricality. When you think about the performance of the Gospel, you should try to mentally exclude the other healings.

---

* In performance, the multitudes' "following" of Jesus implies only that some actors flock to the Jesus actor when he is nearby. They are not necessarily all committed followers, or favorable to Jesus all the time. If they were, there would be no suspense!

Duration of the play

I estimate a duration of 1 hour 40 minutes for the entire performance, based on my run-through of my reconstructed play in the miniature theater. Most scenes go by rapidly. Only the trial seems a few minutes longer in performance than in the received text. Even though the Temple Incident and the arrest scene are theatrically interesting, they can be fairly brief. And there is no reason to think that there were dimensions to the performance (e.g., choral songs) that are missing from the received text.

The genre of the performed play, redux

Now I return to a question that I addressed in Chapter 1: What kind of play is the Gospel? By this time the reader has thought of the Gospel as a performed play, and imagined the staging of some of the scenes. The reader may have referred to Appendix E. I now take Appendix E as the basis for discussion.

I have said that the genre of the performed play was literary mime. The mime genre allowed the playwright a great deal of freedom. Mime was the only genre in which Mark could write a play that was a journey story into which was woven a mini-tragedy. The play inferable from the received text has a number of characteristics of mime. I believe that if the audience were asked about the genre of the play, they would have said it was a mime that included a tragedy. But there is another dimension to the answer.

Think of a performance of the received harmonized nativity story. The characters do not develop. Each scene is self-contained. Each scene illustrates a story already known. "Oh, look, there's Baby Jesus in the manger." "Oh, here come the Magi." The pre-Passion scenes in the Gospel of Mark have the same self-contained, static feeling; no internal development in the scenes; and characters who do not change as the play continues.

I suggest that Mark borrowed this illustration or "tableau" style from the dramatizations of known stories presented by the mystery cults of heroes, gods, and goddesses, such as Osiris, Dionysus, and Persephone. The style of the scenes told Mark's audience that Jesus was like these figures. But Mark was not referring to known stories. Mark took the bold step of writing what was very likely the *first* dramatization of the nascent scenarios around the Jesus figure that were known in his congregation and other congregations of the Jesus movement. Mark's audience entered the theater prepared to accept the Jesus figure placed in dramatic scenarios, e.g., "we have a great high priest who has passed through the heavens" (Heb 4:14) and "he himself was tested by what he suffered" (Heb 2:18). The audience could appreciate the enactment of scenarios from Scripture, e.g., "All who see me mock at me; they make mouths at me, they shake their heads" (Ps 22:7). The audience could accept teachings and sayings they had already associated with their Jesus figure in these scenarios as long as the presentations were not contradictory. Mark enacted scenarios, qualities of the Jesus figure, and teachings, within a story unified by a plot and a subplot. He wrote a play—and the first draft of a myth.

In his play, Mark did not use all the scenarios, qualities, and teachings that his congregation had concerning the Jesus figure. Mark selected those elements that he found useful. We cannot treat the Gospel as a summary of the congregation's entire doctrine concerning their Jesus figure. To do so is to unconsciously accept the traditional Christian view that Mark wrote down everything that Peter told him, and Mark had no doctrine about Jesus outside the edges of the received text of the Gospel.

I suggest that the attendees—who had never seen a dramatized story about their Jesus figure—experienced *all* the scenes in the play as containing emulations to be recognized. That mental activity kept them interested in dramatically inert scenes like the calling of the fishermen in the boat: "Oh, I see: this scene emulates the calling of Elisha. How clever." By the time they had appreciated the emulation(s), the scene was over.

Mark used a variety of theatrical techniques to keep the audience engaged in the play. The healings vary. The stilling of the storm, the water walk, the entry to Jerusalem, the Temple Incident, the arrest, and the crucifixion are theatrical. The Passion is filled with interesting sights and sounds: the torches that illuminate the arrest and trial, the staging of the trial, the mocking, and so on. The Temptation and ascension scenes use the stage crane. Jesus teaches wisdom, delivers pithy sayings that always win arguments, spars with his Judean competitors, speaks his Last Words, and serves as the protagonist of a mini-tragedy. Peter is a foolish foil to Jesus. The actors playing the Council, Pharisees, and Satan can exaggerate their villainy. The play uses the entire performance space: stage, orchestra, parodoi, and audience area. And undoubtedly Mark used other theatrical arts—costumes, music, props, decoration of the scene building, etc.—to enrich his story. Each scene had something new.

I see the performed play as a hybrid, perhaps unique in history. It had the structure of a mime play and some theatrical elements particular to mime. Its static scenes and its focus on an unchanging son of God imitated the enactments of pagan mystery cults.

This hybrid had a very short life. Mark's play was consistently entertaining only if the audience recognized at least some of his emulations and did not have a version of the gospel story. Once the gospel story had been disseminated, an audience at another performance of the play would perceive the play as an *illustration* of the gospel story, just as a modern Christian perceives a nativity play as an illustration of the harmonized nativity story. This second audience would not experience Mark's innovation in hybridizing mime and mystery enactment. I do not know if Mark thought about this problem, but it was moot, because he wrote the play with the intent of staging it only once.

Pre-Matthean editors of the Gospel

I date the performance of the Gospel to 90–95 CE (Chapter 6). Before 150 CE, Matthew obtained a copy of the (edited) polished text, and revised it for his own use.[*]

I see two rounds of editing in Rome prior to GMatthew. The simplest scenario, which I will assume in my discussion, is two individual editors, but other individuals might have made smaller changes. Both main editors knew that Mark had referenced the Elijah-Elisha cycle in Kings. Both editors were conservative about Mark's work. When they added or changed scenes, they often duplicated material already in the polished text.

The earlier editor knew that the polished text preserved a performance. I think that this editor changed the polished text under duress. I call this individual "S-Mark" for "Secretary of Mark" or "Stage Manager of Mark." S-Mark knew Mark's style and wrote scenes that were stageable, but were nonMarkan in other ways. S-Mark, I think, replaced the original scene set in Jericho with the healing of Bartimaeus, and replaced the original Herod material with a flashback and an obviously unstageable banquet scene. S-Mark is probably the editor who replaced the ascension scene with the empty tomb scene and its report of ascension.

The later editor also knew that the polished text had preserved a performance, but made edits that were not performable within the entire play. This editor added three unstageable scenes: the First Feeding Miracle, the anti-Gentile Syrophoenician woman scene, and the healings at Gennesaret (or edited the original scene behind it). This editor enlarged the Olivet Discourse. There is internal evidence that an editor wanted to emphasize

---

[*] I cannot date GMatthew more precisely because "Matthew" might have begun his revision of Mark's polished text *before* GMarcion—or *in response to* GMarcion.

that Jesus came *first* for Judeans: In the First Feeding Miracle, Jesus feeds Judeans with five loaves of bread (Scripture).[77] And he feeds Judeans *before* he feeds Gentiles. The Syrophoenician woman compares herself to a dog. I suggest that this editor expanded the dinner with outcasts to make the calling of Levi a separate scene, a duplicate of the calling of Simon Peter. "Levi" was the eponymous founder of the Judean Temple musician caste, the Levites. The editor not only gave Levi his own scene, the editor made his calling *prior to* the calling of the Three.

Part II: Context and Aftermath

CHAPTER 5

Mark and the Roman Congregation

IN THIS CHAPTER, I present what little I have been able to infer about Mark and his congregation from the play itself and from a scenario in which a play about the Jesus figure was presented as entertainment in a theater.

Mark's biography
To have presented his play before the congregation, Mark must have had their respect and trust. He was very likely middle-aged (or older) at the time of the performance. (As was the Jesus character in the play.)

Honored playwright
I have given numerous reasons to infer that Mark was a highly skilled playwright. He creates scenes with multiple resonances. There are three simultaneous meanings of Jesus's cry on the cross. The possessed centurion speaks the truth—but is not credible because he is possessed. The march to the cross enacts the precession of the equinoxes. Mark skillfully manages the logistics of the play: He provides characters' names in the midst of a relevant action. The stilling-of-the-storm scene places the landing mat for the drowning pigs. Peter's sword strike during the arrest scene lays the groundwork for the exit of all the actors onstage at the end of the play. There are many more scenes that show Mark's skill.

If, as I have proposed, Mark played the role of Jesus, then when the Jesus character referred to his own biography, the audience might assume that those references also applied to Mark.* Therefore, those lines must be at least *compatible* with his real-life biography. There are two such lines that Mark preserved in the polished text. I suggest that these lines also applied to Mark's biography in the world of the audience.

---

* One would like to know how often such double entendres of identity were used in theatrical presentations and if audiences were on the lookout for them. Mark was not innovating: Nero had scandalized (and delighted) the public when he sang tragedies while wearing a mask of his own features (Suetonius, *Nero* 21.3).

First, when Jesus teaches in the synagogue, the Chorus asks, "Where did this man get all this? What is this wisdom that has been given to him? What deeds of power are being done by his hands! Is not this the carpenter (*tektōn*), the son of Mary?" (6:2b–3a). Jesus has not handled wood, or crafted anything physical, so the word *tektōn* must be metaphorical. A contemporary use of *tektōn* was "skilled interpreter of Scripture."[78] Jesus is a skilled interpreter of Scripture. The audience could not be faulted if they also applied *tektōn* to the actor, Mark, as praise for *him* as a skilled crafter of plays/play*wright*.

Second, now that the concept "Jesus = Mark = playwright" is activated in the audience's minds, Mark adds a layer. The audience hears the Jesus character say, "Prophets are not without honor (*atimos*), except in their hometown, and among their own kin, and in their own house" (6:4). The audience knows that Jesus has not been honored in the world of the play. And it is strange that Jesus notices that he has not been honored: He has not sought honor. He has Cynic values. He has dined with outcasts and touched taboo females. Even if we see 6:4 as a commonplace, it does not resonate at that moment in the world of the play. The Greek word translated as "honor" is *atimos*. Its root, *timé*, means "perceived worth." Later, the woman at Bethany will accurately perceive Jesus's worth: she will anoint him with expensive oil. Mark is using 6:4 to foreshadow the recognition in Bethany of Jesus's true worth. But the line has to be meaningful to the audience at the time they hear it. I suggest that the Mark expected the audience to accept "prophets are not without honor" when it was spoken because it was meaningful *in the world of the audience*: they knew that the actor playing Jesus—Mark—had been honored.

Possibly estranged from some of his family
The line "Who are my mother and my brothers?" (3:33) is spoken by Jesus in the world of the play. These lines *might* apply to Mark in the world of the audience. Perhaps Mark's mother and brothers had not shared his beliefs, or were estranged from him. On the other hand, the line may have simply existed to set up the saying "Whoever does the will of God is my brother and sister and mother" (3:35).

However, the line, "And are not his sisters here with us?"(6:3) is probably just an observation. It suggests that Mark's biological sisters were present at the performance. "Here with *us*" implies that they were guests.

Of Judean heritage
The Jesus character of the play had to map onto the Biblical Joshua, a hero of both Judeans and Samaritans. If the actor who played the role of Jesus

were a Gentile, the audience would have been constantly reminded that the story was fiction.

In the play, Jesus is an interpreter of Scripture who is taken seriously by people who had Scripture as their heritage. At this early stage in the development of the Jesus movement, I think that a convert would not have felt he had the authority to assert *on behalf of the sect*, "The sabbath was made for humankind, and not humankind for the sabbath" (2:27). Or to disagree *on behalf of the sect* with the way Pharisees interpreted the Law (7:13).

Mark was not a Samaritan. Mark's Jesus is involved with the *Jerusalem* Temple, not the Samaritan temple on Mount Gerizim. I conclude that Mark was of Judean heritage.

The name "Mark"

The text we know as the Gospel of Mark does not include the name of the author—at least, not overtly. The author is traditionally known as "Marcus" (or Greek "Markos"). The Latin name is not expected in an ethnic Judean who had a good education in Scripture and wrote in Greek. (Latin names were rare among men interred in the catacombs of the first-to-fourth-century Roman synagogues.[79]) "Marcus" is not the Latin version of a Judean name (as "Josephus" is of "Yosef"). So what is the source of the attribution to Marcus/Markos?

Not long after the performance, the Roman congregation had good reason to hide the real name of the Gospel's author. I suggest that they placed the new name on the label of the scroll(s) of the polished text. ("Marcus," a very common first name in Rome, may have served as the Roman "John Doe.") Once the congregation was invested in the story that the Gospel was the biography of Jesus of Nazareth as told by Petros to Marcus/Markos, the attribution could not be changed. Eventually, the orally transmitted memory of the author's real name died out and the name on the scroll was the only name left.

Dates

Many scholars date the Gospel to the 70s.[80] This date is consistent with a scenario where Peter was a historical person who gave Mark information about Jesus of Nazareth, a historical Judean who had lived during the time of Pontius Pilate (died c. 36 CE). But if Mark's Jesus is a heavenly figure, we can infer only that Mark wrote after 36 CE.

As discussed above, I think that the Olivet Discourse is heavily edited, and it functions in the play as Jesus's Last Words. It may refer to the Jewish War, but literature as well as ancient and recent history could have given Mark imagery of apocalypse. The Olivet Discourse cannot help us date the Gospel.

I have suggested that the Joseph of Arimathea character maps onto Flavius Josephus. An insult to a living person is more potent than an insult to a dead person. Therefore, if I am correct that Joseph of Arimathea parodied Josephus, we can infer that he was still alive at the time of the performance. Josephus had settled in Rome in the early 70s; he died c. 100.

Later, I discovered a plausible occasion for the performance of the play, in 90–95 CE. I discuss it in Chapter 6.

Characteristics of the congregation

Internal material in the Gospel offers little information about the congregation. Jesus teaches with parables and sayings. He lives simply and has disciples. I infer that the congregation admired simple-living philosophers.

From the *fact* of the performance of a complex, entertaining, and well-constructed *new* play in a theater, I infer that the host or benefactor of the congregation was well-to-do. A wealthy host would have worshiped with social equals. Therefore, the congregation as a whole was prosperous. Their admiration of the simple life must be understood in that context.

The play explicitly welcomes Gentiles to the congregation. In the play, Jesus teaches and heals Galileans and Judeans, but he also travels to Gentile areas and acquires Gentile followers. Jesus performs the feeding miracle in Gentile Bethsaida. Jesus asks, "Who are my mother and my brothers?" (3:33). The answer is: the audience. The last loyal follower of Jesus is a Gentile: the healed demoniac/naked young man.

It is important to remember that Mark wrote an *entertainment*. For the performance to take place, the welcome to the Gentiles (as well as all doctrine expressed in the play) only had to be *acceptable* to the congregation's leaders *in the context of an entertainment on a single occasion*. We cannot infer that the play was an x-ray or average of the congregation's doctrine in its entirety, or on any issue.

I also note that the Jesus character is the protagonist of a play. He is onstage in almost every scene. We should not infer that the Jesus figure was the focus of the congregation's devotion or their intellectual speculation. *Jesus was the protagonist of a play.* Of course the play was all about him.

CHAPTER 6

The Occasion of Performance

IN THIS CHAPTER, I focus on the performance as a phenomenon in the world of the audience. I propose that the Roman aristocrat, Flavia Domitilla, engaged Mark to write and direct the play. She produced the play and presented it to the congregation in a private theater on her property. I argue that these circumstances of performance explain the pro-Gentile attitude of the Gospel. Not long after the performance, Flavia was exiled and her family killed. I discuss the possibility that these events were related to the performance.

The benefactor of the congregation

The dinner in Bethany

I discovered the benefactor of the congregation when I imagined the staging of the dinner in Bethany (14:3–9):

> ³ While he was at Bethany in the house of Simon the leper, as he sat at the table, a woman came with an alabaster jar of very costly ointment of nard, and she broke open the jar and poured the ointment on his head. ⁴ But some were there who said to one another in anger, "Why was the ointment wasted in this way? ⁵ For this ointment could have been sold for more than three hundred denarii, and the money given to the poor." And they scolded her. ⁶ But Jesus said, "Let her alone; why do you trouble her? She has performed a good service for me. ⁷ For you always have the poor with you, and you can show kindness to them whenever you wish; but you will not always have me. ⁸ She has done what she could; she has anointed my body beforehand for its burial. ⁹ Truly I tell you, wherever the good news is proclaimed in the whole world, what she has done will be told in remembrance of her."

"Wherever the good news is proclaimed in the whole world, what she has done will be told in remembrance of her." This is a promise, overheard by the characters onstage and the audience, that the woman will have eternal fame. Yet in the world of the play, she has only spent money! Does that deed deserve eternal fame?

Imagine that the anointing woman was played by an ordinary actor, usually a slave or freedwoman. The promise of eternal fame would affect her persona in the Chorus for the rest of the play. The audience would wonder when the other Chorus members will notice her—after all, such an extravagant promise must have consequences in the world of the play! But she is never referred to again.

Therefore, an ordinary actor from the Chorus could not have played that role. Who else was available? Perhaps the anointing woman was played by a *congregant*. The scene honors her for her contributions to the congregation *in the world of the audience*. The woman came up to the stage, anointed the Jesus actor, then returned to her seat. The audience *saw* her: her name did not have to be spoken. That is why her name is not given in the polished text.

I thought that this scenario was possible, so I imagined it further. To receive this honor during the performance, this congregant was likely the congregation's benefactor. She sat in the front row. The audience members applauded when she resumed her seat.

If the role of the anointing woman was played by the benefactor, the play had only one performance. If at a subsequent performance another woman—actor or congregant—was promised eternal fame, the first promise would be revealed as only playacting, as existing only in the world of the play.

The Bethany dinner scene does contain hints that the anointing woman is the congregation's benefactor. The dinner guests (probably disciples) assert that the money the woman has spent on the anointing oil should have been given to the poor. In the world of the play, their position is valid: Jesus has praised Cynic simplicity and told the disciples not to put on two tunics. Jesus has told a rich man to give away his riches. But Jesus *defends* the woman. He shifts the issue from the high price of the oil to the woman's intention. *She has done what she could*: she has acted within the constraints of her life situation. (It just so happens that her wealth has enabled her to give Jesus the anointing he deserves.) Jesus's defense of her action makes sense if it refers to the benefactor in the world of the audience.

Flavia Domitilla, the benefactor

I suggest that the congregation's benefactor was Flavia Domitilla, a niece of the current emperor, Domitian. Elite women were benefactors of public and private organizations.[81] Flavia would have had access to a theater, or the resources to build one for the occasion. The historical Flavia Domitilla was involved with Judean religion: The Talmud mentions that Flavia's husband, Titus Flavius Clemens, was a convert to Judaism.[82] The Roman historian

Cassius Dio (d. 235 CE) wrote, "Domitian slew, along with many others, Flavius Clemens the consul, although he was a cousin and married to Flavia Domitilla, who was also a relative of the emperor's. The charge brought against them both was that of atheism, a charge on which many others who drifted into Jewish (*Ioudaion*) ways were condemned" (*Epitome of Cassius Dio* 67.14.1–2).*

Flavia was born before 69 CE. She was a granddaughter of the emperor Vespasian (ruled 69–79 CE) and a niece of the emperors Titus (ruled 79–81 CE) and Domitian (ruled 81–96 CE). Flavia was married to her second cousin, Titus Flavius Clemens ("Clemens"). He was a senator and served as consul in the spring of 95. At some time earlier, Domitian openly designated their two young sons to succeed him as emperor (Suetonius, *Domitian* 15.1).

The official orthodox history is consistent with Flavia as benefactor of Mark's congregation. During the second century, Jesus-movement leaders attempted to systematize and standardize belief and practice. In the institutional history of the orthodox church, the Pope/Bishop of Rome in 88–99 CE was Clement I. The name "Clement" tells us that later orthodox leaders linked their church to the congregation of Flavia and her husband Clemens.†

The performance in the context of benefaction
Dinner-party and evening-event entertainment
In Mark's Rome, dinner was the major meal of the day and the main occasion for private social life. Dinner parties generally began in the late afternoon (3:00–4:00 pm), but some people dined around sunset.[83] A drinking party—short or long—followed. The guests contributed to the entertainment during the meal and the drinking party with jokes, stories, readings, and so on; the host or hosting organization presented professional entertainers. The entertainment ranged from the simple—musicians, dancers, storytellers—to the complex and lavish, e.g., themed dinners.[84]

---

* The terms "Judaism" and "Jewish" here reflect the social reality in the world of the historian. The historical Flavia and Clemens belonged to a sect within the *Judean* cultural universe.

† Possibly one of Flavia's freedmen or clients had taken her husband's name "Clemens" and served as an official of the congregation. Alternatively, later orthodox churchmen, for their official history, retroactively assigned the chronologically appropriate papal name "Clement" to the congregation's leader in the 90s.

It is reasonable to assume that dinner parties, or, more broadly, evening events, were a major topic of gossip. It is also reasonable to assume that the elite competed to provide unique, high-quality, spectacular events that would be talked about and add to their prestige. Elite evening events, therefore, cannot be expected to follow a pattern. Only food, wine, and the provision of entertainment were the constants. There must have been professional dinner party managers/consultants in this social space—the Roman equivalent of today's elite wedding planners.*

Here, the question is, were plays performed at evening events? New Comedy was very popular at dinner parties,[85] but it is impossible to distinguish in the records the performance of whole plays from the performance of selected scenes, or dramatic readings. (New Comedy needed very little infrastructure.) There are almost no contemporary references to the performances of whole plays at evening events. Eric Csapo observes, "Even on a restricted scale the cost of private theater (which always, it seems, included dinner) was prohibitive to all but the wealthiest."[86] The *Historia Augusta* (Hadrian 1.26.4) seems to give a data point, when it states that the emperor Hadrian, "at his banquets…always furnished, according to the occasion, tragedies, comedies, Atellan farces, players on the sambuca, readers, or poets." However, the *Historia Augusta* was written more than 250 years later. The author could have simply *inferred* from the presence of a Greek theater on the grounds of Hadrian's Villa at Tivoli that Hadrian had used it for entertainment at banquets. (However, the location and large size of the Greek theater suggests that those occasions, if any, were rare.[87])

Still, the Greek theater at Hadrian's Villa is one of the very few private theaters from the early Empire partially extant.† It is the best stand-in for the features and proportions of Flavia's theater. At the Greek theater, the seating rows are of ordinary width. That means that the audiences for those plays *always* ate dinner at another location. I assume that Mark's audience also ate dinner offsite.

---

* My proposed professional "dinner party manager" obtained services and entertainments that were beyond the capabilities of the host's household slaves. Examples are new plays, luxury goods, and exotic entertainers. These managers also had valuable inside information on dinner parties hosted by other members of the elite. Could Mark have worked in this profession?

† The other theaters are: Domitian's theater at his summer residence in Castel Gandolfo, the theater on the grounds of the Villa at Pausilypon (Posillipo), and the Odeon (South Theater) at Hadrian's Villa.

Flavia's role in the entertainment

When I first hypothesized that Flavia had played the role of the anointing woman, I still assumed that the Gospel was in some sense a "religious" play and Flavia's involvement was secondary to the overall religious purpose of the event: On behalf of the congregation, Mark conceived and created the event; Flavia was surprised and pleased by the honor given to her during the play. But then I worked backward from the fact of performance. If the play was performed in a theater, it had been rehearsed in a theater. If Flavia provided the theater for the performance, she had provided the theater for rehearsals. She must have helped plan the performance. At minimum, Flavia had engaged Mark's services as writer and director. Mark must have discussed with her the content of the play, and gotten her approval for his proposal. Flavia, in other words, *produced* the play.

As producer of the play, as host of the evening, and as benefactor of the congregation, Flavia would have expected recognition during the performance. Mark cleverly placed that recognition *inside the play's storyline*. So when the audience honored the woman at Bethany for buying expensive oil to anoint Jesus in the world of the play, they honored Flavia for her benefaction in the world of the audience.

Originally I wondered if the play's action was interrupted for rituals that involved the audience: baptisms of congregants after John's baptizing, installation of congregational officials who "take up the cross and follow," celebration of the Eucharist. I have concluded that these activities almost certainly did not take place. The scenes of the play were much shorter than any of these interactive ceremonies. Strict time limits on them could not be enforced, and therefore they could spoil the rhythm of the play. And they would spotlight congregants other than Flavia and her family.*

The play in the sequence of evening events

Now the question arises: Did the audience eat before the play, after the play, or at both times?

In the section on lighting (p. 61), I concluded that the entire play was performed during the day. At Passover, sunset in Rome occurs at approximately 6:30 p.m. So let us assume that the audience met at Flavia's estate at 2:00 p.m., after the daily bath. Let us assume that the performance took 1 hour 40 minutes.

If the play is over by 6:30 p.m., it began before 4:50 p.m. Because the Roman breakfast and lunch were light meals, the audience must have *also* eaten before

---

* However, possibly a few (pre-selected) congregants donated/"put in large sums" (12:41).

the performance. This repast, between 2:15 p.m. and 4:30 p.m., could be only a light and informal meal. If there was a religious service as well (to put the audience in the right frame of mind, and possibly to prime them to recognize Mark's Scriptural references/emulations), the meal was only a snack.

Therefore, the play must have been followed by a full dinner, with wine—and more entertainment. The audience may have recognized they were watching a masterpiece of theater, and they may have wanted the play to be remembered. They may have discussed the play at length that night, and for weeks or months afterward. But it was not the last event of the evening. The audience also wanted to have dinner and dink. The play was embedded in their world; only later was it extracted from their world, and its author and its theatrical origins erased.

Implications of benefaction for Mark's compositional process

I suspect that Mark's play was the result of a felicitous meeting of preparation and opportunity. Flavia knew Mark through his previous work as a playwright, possibly for other evening events. (That is how she knew he could produce a high-quality play.) Flavia approached Mark and asked him if he could write a new play for her to present to her guests. Or Mark told Flavia that he had an idea for a new play, and she scheduled the performance. In either case, I suggest that Mark had already written some of the material he would use: an arrest-trial-conviction tragedy, and possibly dramatic material based on the Elijah-Elisha cycle. Mark had to guarantee that he would stage the play on a specific date.

Implications of benefaction for the performance

- The play was new and written for the occasion.
- The only actor who might have improvised was Mark, playing Jesus.
- With an essentially unlimited budget, Mark could use (and write for) a very large Chorus with no doubling.
- With an essentially unlimited budget, Mark could use real nard, a real donkey for the entry to Jerusalem, and two stage cranes.
- With an essentially unlimited budget, Mark could have had the theater designed (or modified) to fit his script: for example, a place for the Satan actor on the scene building.
- The play was performed only once.*

---

* The breaking of the alabaster jar of expensive oil symbolized the unique performance of the play. I am indebted to reviewer Kim Trimiew for this insight.

I suggest that Mark presented a copy of the polished text to Flavia after the performance, in front of the audience (or at the dinner afterwards). When Mark made the official record of the play a *condensed* version, he guaranteed the singularity of the event—a further honor to Flavia. However, he could expect that the audience would remember the occasion, and Flavia's partisans/clients in the congregation would ensure that the polished text in the library of the Roman congregation would survive, as evidence of the occasion and Flavia's benefaction.

Elements of the play compatible with Flavia Domitilla as benefactor

1. Jesus never disputes with Gentiles or makes Gentiles look bad

If Mark had written for an exclusively Judean audience, he might have shown Jesus's superiority to Gentile philosophers.

2. Jesus is presented as a Cynic philosopher, i.e., he is culturally Greek as well as Judean.

Jesus lives a simple life ("do not put on two tunics"), has a house but spends most of his time outdoors, teaches with clever sayings (*chreiai*), and dines with outcasts.

3. Despite his Cynic values, Jesus deals gently with rich people

In the play, Jesus criticizes wealth, then pivots. He says, "How hard it will be for those who have wealth to enter the kingdom of God!" (10:23). The disciples are amazed. (They believe that wealth is a sign of divine favor.[88]) Jesus repeats his statement, with a subtle revision, "Children, how hard it is to enter the kingdom of God!" (10:24). Now, *everyone* will have difficulty entering the kingdom of God. Mark does this again. Jesus compares a rich man's ability to enter the kingdom of God to a camel's (in)ability to pass through the eye of a needle. The disciples ask, "Then who can be saved?" (10:26). Jesus answers, "For mortals it is impossible, but not for God; for God all things are possible" (10:27). So perhaps God will allow Flavia and Clemens to pass through the eye of a needle and enter the kingdom of God. They *have* given away some of their riches!

While the Temple operated, female Judeans were not required to pay the Temple tax,[89] but in the Gospel, the poor widow puts coins in the contribution box. Mark values her contribution above that of the rich: "For all of them have contributed out of their abundance; but she out of her poverty has put in everything she had, all she had to live on" (12:44). Jesus praises the poor widow because *proportionately*, she gave more than others. Now the congregation could gracefully accept Flavia's (enormous) donation, because she was obviously not doing it in order to receive praise. It merely came from her abundance, what she had to spare.

4. The audience sees the woman at Bethany purchase expensive oil
In the received text, the owner of the house at Bethany is Simon the Leper (*Simōnos tou leprou*). The placeholder name "Simon" is followed by "*tou leprou*," which looks like a coded term. ("Leper" adds no theatrical value to the play: the audience already knows that Jesus associates with lepers. And Jesus doesn't heal the owner.) Why does Mark tell the reader to imagine a scene that involves "*tou leprou*"?

Greek *leprou* = Aramaic *gar'ba*. Aramaic did not use vowel points, so when written, *gar'ba* was spelled the same as *garaba* (jar maker or jar merchant). Mark is playing a game with the reader/listener: Can they figure out that *leprou/gar'ba* is not an accurate description of the house owner? The reader who knows Aramaic recognizes that *gar'ba* is a near-word to *garaba*/jar merchant. The Simon character is a jar merchant and "sells" the oil to the woman. (The stage action is obscured in the received text [14:3]: the woman only "came" with the oil.)

Now imagine the performance: Jesus and disciples sit in front of the house door on the upper level Stage Right. (The Jesus actor must sit upright so that the audience below can see him.) Flavia enters the stage. She purchases the jar from the house owner.* She breaks the jar and anoints Jesus. The disciples, who have observed her purchase, complain about the expense. Jesus tells the audience that she will have eternal fame. Flavia returns to her seat.

5. The woman at Bethany recognizes Jesus's true nature
The woman at Bethany knows and accepts that Jesus will die soon, and she anoints him in advance of his death. She is the only character not inhabited by Satanic spirits who recognizes Jesus's true identity as the Son of God. In addition, the woman at Bethany *prepares* Jesus for death by anointing him (for burial in the world of the play, for his high priestly role in the world of the audience).

6. The blind man of Bethsaida may have been played by Flavia's husband
In my reconstruction of the Bethsaida section, the healing of the blind man of Gentile Bethsaida (8:22–26) is the first scene after the distribution of gifts to the audience. The blind man is not a Chorus member. When he is partially healed, the blind man says that other people look like trees, walking. Even though that line is obscure, we can be sure that a Chorus

---
* Perhaps Flavia used real money (a very public donation to the congregation).

member would not say that about other Chorus members. Did he step out of the Gentile multitudes at the Second Feeding Miracle? Where did this actor come from?

I suggest he was played by Flavia's husband, Titus Flavius Clemens. Here are my reasons. First, the placement of the scene immediately after the semi-intermission, while the audience is not yet re-immersed in the play, is compatible with a staging that is partly in the world of the audience and partly in the world of the play—that is, a congregant plays a bit part in the play. Second, the scene is set in Gentile Bethsaida, and Clemens was a Gentile. Third, the scene ends when Jesus sends the man to his home. This creates an exquisite staging that is valid simultaneously in the world of the play and the world of the audience: I propose that after the healing, Jesus takes the blind man by the hand and leads him "out of the village" (8:23). That means the actors go to the edge of the audience area. After the healing, Jesus tells Clemens to go home but "do not even go into the village" (8:26). That command means that Clemens exits the theater through a parodos. He has not gone *through* the village (the audience area). But he does go to his home in the world of the audience—the property around the theater! Clemens then re-enters the theater from the back and walks through the audience to his front-row seat. The audience applauds.[*]

7. Jesus speaks praise to only one character in the play: the woman at Bethany
In the Gospel, the inner disciples (Peter, James, and John) are underinformed, and for the last half of the play, Peter is under the influence of Satan. Jesus never praises the inner or outer disciples. The poor widow is commended, but not to her face. A scribe "answered wisely," but Jesus praises him with a negative: "You are not far from the kingdom of God" (12:34). That is the highest praise Jesus gives to any character—except the woman who anoints him at Bethany. Jesus promises *her* eternal fame.

The bias of the play
If Mark wrote his play on commission from Flavia, the play's tone and content were shaped by her benefaction. We must see the play's welcome to Gentiles in the context of benefaction, where flattering the benefactor was of paramount importance. We cannot infer that Mark's congregation was

---

[*] The reader may ask if a high-ranking Roman, the father of future emperors, would let himself be "healed" by the spit of an actor during a play. I answer that the dramatic logic of the staging points to Clemens. The polished text may have been edited to change the interaction between Jesus and the man before he leaves for his home. The other canonical gospels omit this healing, which is consistent with it being specific to Mark's audience.

focused on welcoming Gentiles, or that Gentiles were a majority (or even a substantial minority) of the congregants.

Sequelae of the performance

The historical record retains only a few bits of data on Flavia and her family. Clemens served as consul in early 95; the family was still in Domitian's good graces. But later that year, Flavia was exiled to a .6-square-mile island, Pandateria (now Ventotene). She probably died there. Clemens was killed. Their sons—future emperors—disappear from the historical record. It looks like Domitian decided in 95 to eliminate the family.*

One might suppose that Domitian acted against Flavia and Clemens for religious reasons: Domitian was threatened by Mark's theology and Jesus was a competing "son of God." Or Domitian felt Flavia's Judaizing was inappropriate or disloyal. But I think those inferences are wrong. Domitian must have known that Flavia had been participating in a Judean sect: her sons were being educated in his palace! The boys attended the performance of Mark's play, or knew about it. Flavia and Clemens would have consistently worshiped the emperor, if only for self-preservation. And Mark would have been careful to avoid sensitive political issues; caution was always required when working for the elite. So although Domitian may have officially charged Flavia and Clemens with atheism, his *reason* for eliminating them was likely something else.

Pat Southern, the author of a biography of Domitian, speculates on his motives: "The fact that Domitian had adopted Clemens' two young sons, renaming them T. Flavius Vespasianus and T. Flavius Domitianus and clearly marking them out as his successors, may have given Clemens and his wife Domitilla delusions of grandeur, affecting their behavior in a way intolerable to Domitian."[90] That is possible but I have a related suggestion.

Flavia lived in a social context where her presentation of a new play to her guests—whatever her motives—was perceived as political. For centuries, rich and socially ambitious Greeks and Romans had sponsored theatrical performances in order to display their status and acquire/strengthen their political ties. In Flavia's time, private theatrical performances were as political as public performances.[91] Because Flavia was a member of the imperial

---

* The Letter of Clement (1 Clement) may refer to these events from a congregational leader's point of view. The first line reads, "Owing, dear brethren, to the sudden and successive calamitous events which have happened to ourselves..." The writer of 1 Clement associates Clement's papacy with events that are "calamitous" to the congregation. This is an accurate description of a purge of Flavia and her family and associates.

family, her production of the Gospel would be discussed by the guests, and the official and unofficial "gossip columnists" of the day. Domitian was a cautious and defensive person. Southern writes, "Mistrust and its attendant alienation seem to have been built into his character from the earliest times."[92] It is possible that Domitian interpreted the *production* of the Gospel play to a private and well-to-do audience as evidence that Flavia and Clemens were establishing their own power base. But it seems to me that the audience for the play was likely mainly ethnic Judeans of the congregation (along with slaves and Flavia's household) and therefore socially relatively innocuous (Roman Judeans weren't politicians or Senators). It would be helpful to know if Flavia and Clemens had a *program* of benefaction, i.e., they produced other events and *were* raising their public profile. If so, perhaps Domitian's paranoia was justified. That is all I can say about Domitian's motives for eliminating his designated heirs.

In September of 96, Domitian was assassinated by conspirators, among them Flavia's steward Stephanus. Domitian had no heir. The same day, the Senate appointed as emperor an elderly senator, Marcus Cocceius Nerva.

The Praetorian Guard (palace guard) demanded that the (partly pro-Flavia) conspirators be punished, but Nerva did not act. A year later, in October 97, some members of the Praetorian Guard besieged the palace and held Nerva hostage. He agreed to hand over the conspirators to the Praetorian Guard for punishment.

The Roman congregants might have wondered if, like the pro-Flavia conspirators, they would be seen as anti-Domitian (or anti-emperors in general). They were no longer protected by their association with Flavia. This context may explain the action of the editor I call S-Mark. S-Mark knew the play thoroughly. S-Mark revised the original ascension scene, and replaced the Jericho scene with the healing of Bartimaeus. I note that these scenes concerned the ascent of the son of God and a mission to the Gentiles, issues that could be deliberately misinterpreted by the authorities.

Was S-Mark in fact Mark, revising his own polished text under duress? Mark was a top artist of his day, "not without honor," and with—it is reasonable to assume—an ego to match. I don't think that Mark would have altered his polished text, the record of a play he had written and staged for the family of future emperors. I think that if congregational leaders had asked him to change his text to, for example, put less emphasis on the concept 'Jesus is the son of God,' Mark would have said, "that's your problem, not mine." Mark would have dared the congregational leaders to alter the record of Flavia's recent benefaction *on their own authority*.

But obviously they did. I think that S-Mark would not have altered the polished text if Mark were still alive. So my best guess about Mark's future is that he was killed in the purge, or died shortly after the performance of the play.

CHAPTER 7

The Second Century

OVER THE NEXT 100 years, the Jesus movement ramified, and orthodox Christianity and Judaism separated out of the Judean ethnic identity. The orthodox church, headquartered in Mark's Roman congregation, created its own canon, and promoted the concept of the human Jesus of Nazareth, with the subplot of Mark's play as his biography. To do this, they blurred the plot of the play, forgot the *fact* of performance, suppressed Mark's real biography, and redefined "Mark" as the selfless *amanuensis* of the historical Peter.

The Roman congregation
A third place for ethnic Judeans

The editor who followed S-Mark added the anti-Gentile Syrophoenician woman scene and the pro-Judean First Feeding Miracle. The material that had flattered Flavia and her family remained in the polished text, but there was also material now that denigrated Gentiles and showed that Jesus had fed ethnic Judeans with bread (interpretation of Scripture) before he fed Gentiles.

Why did this editor make these changes? As discussed earlier, Mark's Jesus extended a welcome to Gentiles, through elements such as the statement that all foods are clean, and the fact that the last loyal follower of Jesus is a Gentile. I suggest that the Roman congregation's pro-Gentile reputation is why Marcion visited Rome and thought that he had a chance for a leadership role there. Possibly, after the Romans excommunicated Marcion and returned his donation, they decided to revise the polished text (and perhaps also their official position) to make it clear that while Jesus did come for Gentiles, he came for Judeans first.

What was the congregation's identity during the second century? The imagery of the Catacombs of Domitilla testifies to an ethnic Judean identity. I suggest that the congregation experienced a steady stream (and majority) of ethnic-Judean members. The congregation occupied a unique social niche. Throughout the second century and beyond, there must have been many well-to-do Hellenized ethnic Judeans in Rome who wanted to maintain their ethnic identity—Scripture as their history and YHWH as their god—yet dine with Gentiles and participate in public life. They were in the same social and cultural position as the eighteenth- and nineteenth-century European Jews who created Reform Judaism.[93] Mark's congregation was perfectly positioned to be their gathering place.

Insights from decorations in the Catacombs of Domitilla

Flavia donated to her congregation the Catacombs of Domitilla. They are the oldest Christian catacombs in Rome. The entrance, the Crypt of the Flavians, is still extant, about three miles southeast of the Forum. A nineteenth-century archaeologist describes it:

> The crypt is approached through a vestibule, which was richly decorated with terra-cotta carvings, and, on the frieze, a monumental inscription enclosed by an elaborate frame. No pagan mausolea of the Via Appia or the Via Latina show a greater sense of security or are placed more conspicuously than this early Christian tomb. The frescoes on the ceiling of the vestibule, representing biblical scenes, such as Daniel in the lions' den, the history of Jonah, etc., were exposed to daylight, and through the open door could be seen by the passer. No precaution was taken to conceal these symbolic scenes from profane or hostile eyes. We regret the loss of the inscription above the entrance, which, besides the name of the owner of the crypt, probably contained the *lex monumenti*, and a formula specifying the religion of those buried within.[94]

The frescoes of the crypt depict scenes from Scripture. There are no Jesus-movement images, or scenes from the four-gospel story (the writer would have mentioned them). Inside the catacombs, the earliest decorations come from Scripture or Hellenistic culture.[95] Among the second-century images, 20 are from Scripture, 96 are general/decorative and Jesus-movement themes that do not refer to the four-gospel story, and only 16 are from the four-gospel story.[96] We can infer that at the end of the second century, the four-gospel story had only recently entered the mythos of the Roman congregation.

The future headquarters of orthodoxy and the Pope

The question arises whether it was Flavia's congregation, or a second Jesus-movement congregation in Rome, that became the headquarters congregation of orthodoxy and the home of the Bishop of Rome (the Pope). I respond that later orthodox leaders emphasized their continuity from Pope Clement I (and his "predecessors") and therefore from the congregation of the historical Flavia Domitilla and Titus Flavius Clemens. Second-century orthodox leaders *wanted* to trace their heritage to the congregation of Flavia and Clemens. As there is no evidence extant of a *second* elite Jesus-movement congregation in Rome at the end of the first century CE, I conclude that Flavia's congregation was the direct ancestor of the orthodox churches and the papacy.

The development of Jesus of Nazareth

I think that it is now useful to provide a timeline for the conversion of Mark's heavenly Jesus figure into a being that had lived on earth, Jesus of Nazareth.

In the mid-late first century CE, there are congregations of Judeans (and possibly Samaritans) that have a spiritual Jesus figure. Some Judeans have the concept of a Messiah/Christ/anointed one, a being (earthly, heavenly, or some combination thereof) who will in some sense "save" or liberate the Judean *ethnos* and/or certain individuals, or serve as the heavenly high priest. "Jesus" and "Christ" are two different concepts, both varied.*

- By 80 CE. A congregation of the Jesus movement is established in Rome. The congregation has a Judean identity. It has a heavenly Jesus figure and relaxed interpretation of the Law.

- 90–95. Mark, a member of the Roman congregation, writes and stages a play produced by the benefactor of the congregation, Flavia Domitilla. The play's protagonist is a heavenly Jesus who comes to earth, dies on earth, then ascends. The play expresses doctrine that the Jesus figure is also Christ, who for the congregation is probably the anointed high priest in the heavenly Temple.* Mark writes a condensed text to preserve the performance, the "polished text."

- 96–140s. At least two editors in Rome, with distinct agendas, edit the polished text. (They work prior to GMatthew.)

- ?110s–130s. Marcion of Sinope (died c. 160) is active in Asia. He teaches that Jesus's Father is a different god than YHWH. Marcion values (early versions of some of the texts we know as) the Letters of Paul, and may have written some of them himself.

- Late 130s. Marcion goes to Rome, where he participates in Mark's congregation and makes a large donation. In 144 the leaders excommunicate him and return his donation.

- c. 144–160. Marcion builds his sect in the East, using a gospel described by church historians as an early version of the Gospel of Luke. (A plausible scenario is this: Marcion revised GMark and

---

* It is not known when and where the (local versions of the) concepts of "Jesus" and "Christ" were first combined.

expanded it with sayings; Luke later expanded GMarcion into canonical GLuke.[97] I propose that Marcion copied and revised GMark and added material from the sayings collection in the Roman congregation's library *while he was in Rome.*)

- 100s–140s. Matthew obtains a copy of Mark's edited polished text, and revises it for use in his Law-observant congregation. (It is not clear if Matthew began this work before Marcion published GMarcion; or if the presence of GMarcion in circulation in the East, Matthew's territory, motivated Matthew to "go back to the source" and obtain a copy of GMark to revise for his own use.)

- 130s–150s. Justin Martyr in Rome knows some elements of the Gospel story but does not appeal to a canon of authorized texts. Justin rejects a human Jesus of Nazareth.[98]

- 140s–150s. In response to the popularity of Marcionite doctrine and GMarcion, an orthodox editor expands that text into the Gospel of Luke, and writes the Acts of the Apostles. Acts redefines the disciples as apostles, thereby allowing contemporary orthodox church leaders to trace their received authority through these apostles to the human Jesus of Nazareth.

- 140s–160s. An orthodox writer creates/assembles the text now known as the Gospel of John. The story is ultimately based on the story in GMark.

- 150s–170s. The Roman congregation backs a canon that includes four gospels, the Acts of the Apostles, and (the orthodox version of) the Letters of Paul. Bishop Polycarp of Smyrna may be the publisher[99] of this orthodox canon and the author of Luke/Acts.[100] Other sects of the Jesus movement have other sets of sacred books.

- c. 180. Irenaeus, the orthodox Bishop of Lugdunum (now Lyon) writes *Against Heresies*. In several places in his works, he refers to a fleshly or human Jesus who had lived in Judea. Irenaeus symbolizes the crystallization of orthodoxy.

Jesus the Nazarene becomes Jesus of Nazareth

A constituency already existed for Irenaeus's advocacy of Jesus of Nazareth. Several factors had already encouraged ordinary Christians to accept the idea that the Jesus of the four-gospel story had been, in some sense, a human being who had lived on earth.

The Gospel story enters the mythos

Marcion and Matthew seem to have been the first writers to adapt Mark's story for use outside the Roman congregation. Because their gospels were both based on GMark, Mark's story began to create a mythos around "Jesus." Other writers wrote gospels based on GMark, or using characters from Mark's story. Matthew, I think, played an important role because he made Mark's story usable in his congregation for sermons, pulpit teachings, and children's lessons. Children of the congregation would assume that the Jesus of the story was as historical as Moses, David, and Elijah. Even if these children were later told that the gospel story was not objectively true, it remained true in the sense that it was part of the culture's narrative that their community took seriously. In this way, a "historical, human Jesus on earth" could develop a constituency at the same time that educated adults continued to think of Jesus as a heavenly figure. I add that this dissemination of Mark's story to anti-Law (Marcion) and pro-Law (Matthew) communities started the process of giving Christians of different sects a common culture focused on a historical human Jesus. Eventually the orthodox's definition of "Jesus of Nazareth" became politically preeminent.

The usefulness of Jesus of Nazareth to the orthodox

Irenaeus wrote that Jesus had "lived" in Judea, "Learn then, ye foolish men, that Jesus who suffered for us, *and who dwelt among us*, is Himself the Word of God....He, namely, the Only-begotten Son of the only God, who, according to the good pleasure of the Father, *became flesh* for the sake of men..." (*Against Heresies* 1.9.3, emphases added).

I do not know how Irenaeus understood the nature of his Jesus figure. Contemporary thought allowed for more categories than the mutually exclusive "human" and "heavenly." In Irenaeus's extant works, there are a few references to the four-gospel story, far too few (in my opinion) if he saw the four-gospel story as the biography of Jesus of Nazareth.

But the orthodox had a practical reason to advocate for a human Jesus of Nazareth. With their uninterrupted custody of Mark's text, they could claim that they had the earliest and therefore the most accurate story of Jesus's "life" (or "life on earth"). The teachings of this historical human being—and his personally appointed followers—were more authoritative than the teachings of Marcion and the leaders of gnostic sects, who knew their Jesus only through revelation. As Walter Bauer says, "If Jesus *in person* already has ordered the gospel to be preached in Edessa by his *apostle*, then the teaching of Marcion, Bardesanes, or even Mani immediately is unmasked and condemned as a human work by way of imitation" (emphases added).¹⁰¹ The orthodox needed to make only a few small changes to the canonical gospels: they made Jesus the Nazarene into Jesus of Nazareth, and redefined disciples as "apostles." (The official orthodox history is the Acts of the *Apostles*.) Church leaders could now say that these apostles had appointed bishops, who in turn had authorized their successors, among whom were the current bishops of orthodox congregations.

I think it is likely that the Roman congregation throughout the second century and beyond included members who continued to understand the Jesus of the gospel story as a heavenly figure, and understood his "time on earth" as ahistorical and mythical. They knew that the Gospel of Mark was a preserved play about a heavenly Jesus. They knew that Mark had worked for Flavia. They knew that the Gospel was not the history of Jesus of Nazareth, who had appointed apostles, who had delegated authority to the founders of the orthodox churches of the day. But because a human Jesus of Nazareth was potent ammunition against Marcionites and other gnostics, the congregants kept quiet (or were ignored by their leaders). One must wonder how long the memory of Mark and his life-situation survived.

"Mark" in the second century

The orthodox creation of a link between "Mark" and a human Peter

The earliest extant reference to "Mark" as a writer is in a text by the church historian Eusebius c. 300 CE. Eusebius says that

> Papias (c. 125) wrote that
> the presbyter/elder John (c. 125) said that
> Peter (c. 60?) told Mark the sayings and doings of the Lord.*

Obviously, Eusebius's statements are not historically reliable. We can say only that Eusebius states what *he* understood (or wanted) to be history: Peter

---

* "[says Papias]: And the presbyter said this. Mark having become the interpreter of Peter, wrote down accurately whatsoever he remembered. It was not, however, in exact order that he related the sayings or deeds of Christ. For he neither heard the Lord nor accompanied Him. But afterwards, as I [Papias] said, he accompanied Peter, who accommodated his instructions to the necessities [of his hearers], but with no intention of giving a regular narrative of the Lord's sayings. Wherefore Mark made no mistake in thus writing some things as he remembered them. For of one thing he took especial care, not to omit anything he had heard, and not to put anything fictitious into the statements" (Eusebius, *Church History* 3.39.15).

and "Mark" were connected to an early text about Jesus. Peter had provided the information about Jesus to Mark, who wrote it down accurately.

A second early data point is 1 Peter, a letter that connects Peter and Mark, in Rome ("Babylon"): "Your sister church in Babylon, chosen together with you, sends you greetings; and so does my son Mark" (1 Pt 5:13).

Both Papias and 1 Peter are known to Irenaeus.[*] He links Mark and Peter when he writes, "Mark, the disciple and interpreter of Peter, did also hand down to us in writing what had been preached by Peter" (*Against Heresies* 3.1.1). This is the pivot, the moment of the sleight of hand that officially erased Mark's real history. Read the sentence again, "Mark, the disciple and interpreter of Peter, did also hand down to us in writing what had been preached by Peter." Irenaeus does not state that the polished text of the Gospel of Mark was "what had been preached by Peter." But as far as we know, Irenaeus and his readers/hearers knew only one text by "Mark." Irenaeus's readers/hearers would have inferred that the Gospel of Mark was Mark's record/transcript of "what had been preached by Peter." Mark's version of the gospel story was factually accurate but not necessarily complete: "information" about Jesus of Nazareth from other texts could also be valid.

Irenaeus's statement of a link between Mark and a human Peter that erased Mark's history anticipated the orthodox policy going forward. Church leaders could now treat the story "preserved" in Mark's text as having originated with Peter. Other apostles of Jesus of Nazareth could be assigned as the authors of ideologically compatible texts and founders of other congregations. Mark's gospel story was objectively true history of Jesus of Nazareth. The story could be expanded, with spinoffs, sequels, and prequels, and texts purportedly written by the participants. The founding narrative of a religious civilization was under construction.

"Mark" outside Rome

The Coptic Orthodox Church of Alexandria traces its founding to "Mark." But the orthodox sect did not have a significant presence in Egypt through the second century. The *Catholic Encyclopedia* notes, "During the first two centuries of our era, though Egypt enjoyed unusual quiet, little is known of the ecclesiastical history of its chief see, beyond a barren list of the names of its patriarchs."[102] The orthodox church fathers of Alexandria, Clement of Alexandria (c. 150–c. 215) and Origen (c. 184–c. 253), do not mention Mark.[103] How did Mark come to be associated with Egypt?

---

[*] Irenaeus quotes 1 Peter in *Against Heresies* 5.7.2, and mentions Papias in 5.33.4.

Walter Bauer suggests, "There is some reason to suppose that Rome placed at the disposal of orthodox Alexandria the figure of Mark as founder of the church and apostolic initiator of the traditional succession of bishops. At all events, it is not easy to imagine from what other source he could have come."[104] If my presentation in this book of Mark's life-situation is correct, Mark was firmly identified with Rome. But at some point, the Roman congregants' loyalties to Mark's memory had faded, and they could recast him as needed. (This new version of "Mark" needed to be credible only to the orthodox congregants of Alexandria, not to all Christians in Egypt—or in Rome.)

Elsewhere in Christendom, only one major pre-modern building is named for Mark: Saint Mark's Basilica in Venice. This church was so-named because in 828 CE, merchants from Venice stole purported relics of Mark from Alexandria. A church was built to house the relics, then rebuilt and enlarged in the Middle Ages.

Summary

I hope I have convinced you that the orthodox story of Jesus of Nazareth did not originate in Peter's preaching. The orthodox story is ultimately based on a story that first entered the world in a play performed once in Rome in the early 90s CE.

The play was written by the author known to history as "Mark." He was a brilliant playwright who had worked for the elite of Rome. Mark wrote and directed a play in the genre of mime, into which he incorporated a previously written or outlined tragedy. He wrote the play for Flavia Domitilla, a niece of the emperor Domitian and the benefactor of her Jesus-movement congregation. Flavia produced and presented the play in a private theater. During the performance, Flavia played the anointing woman at Bethany. Mark—in the role of Jesus—assured her that she would have eternal fame.

Mark preserved and condensed the experience of performance into a narrative with a narrator. Mark polished this text with literary features: pointers to his sources in Scripture and other literature, chiasms, coded meanings, etc. This polished text was edited at least twice in Rome before Matthew obtained a copy. Mark's edited polished text is ultimately the basis of the other three canonical gospels.

Editors in Rome would erase the play's plot, in which Satan tempts Jesus to abandon his mission on earth to die and rise. Eventually, the Roman congregation would promote as literally true Mark's *subplot* about an earthly Jesus who only wants to teach and heal, but is opposed by Pharisees and a narrow-minded Judean Council.

Mark was essential to the creation of Christianity. But so was Flavia. She gave Mark an opportunity to write and present a play about the Jesus figure. And because Mark knew that Flavia's partisans would guard the polished text as a record of Flavia's benefaction, Mark could justify investing the time to produce a *literary* work of the highest quality, one commensurate with Flavia's social status. We think of Flavia only as the donor of catacombs later used by Christians. I submit we should also recognize her catalyzing role in the creation of the Gospel of Mark.

APPENDIX A

~The Gospel According to Seneca~

Many people have noticed the similarities in the Passion story and tragedy. The Passion has a single line of action and takes place during a short span of time (36 hours in the received text of GMark), in a few adjacent locations. The plot of the Passion is suitable for a tragedy: the accusation, trial, conviction, and punishment of a nonconformist by the Establishment.

Livio C. Stecchini and Jan Sammer are the only scholars, to my knowledge, who propose that a Passion play was staged before Mark wrote his text, and who *also* imagine the staging of that play, scene by scene.[105] I found their book, *The Gospel According to Seneca*, valuable because they apply their knowledge of classical plays and contemporary stage conventions to the Passion story, and propose staging details that enhanced my reconstruction of the stage action of Mark's play. For example, "The three synoptic gospels state that Simon of Cyrene carried the cross for Jesus, whereas according to John Jesus went out carrying the cross. Christian iconography usually presents Jesus as carrying the horizontal cross-bar, whereas Simon carries the pole. This solution is substantially correct. The normal Roman practice was to march the condemned one to the place of execution with his hands tied securely to the two extremities of the horizontal piece of the cross, which passed behind his neck; the vertical pole was often already standing at the place of execution."[106] A crossbar weighs less than a full cross, yet conveys the theatrical point equally well. Another example is their discussion of the arrest scene, where they review the use of torches in contemporary theater and propose that the arrest party carried torches to indicate to the audience that the arrest took place at night.[107]

But I want to draw the reader's attention to four limitations of their work. First, the book is based on research done in the 1970s and earlier. After Stecchini's death in 1979, Sammer used Stecchini's notes to assemble/create/write the book, which is not complete.[108] Stecchini cannot finish the book or update it in the light of recent scholarship.

Second, Stecchini and Sammer propose that the Passion story was a *fabula praetexta*, a Roman historical drama written by the Roman philosopher

Seneca the Younger (c. 4 BCE–65 CE). I see multiple problems with this proposal. Many elements of the Passion come directly from Scripture (for example, Jesus's cry on the cross and the gambling for his clothing emulate Psalm 22). But Seneca would not have known Scripture well enough to reference it so extensively. Also, Seneca wrote in Latin in an elaborate literary style, but the canonical gospels are written in simple Greek. Seneca's plays are full of long speeches, but the canonical gospels are narratives that include short speeches (teaching passages excluded). Would the gospel authors "translate" Seneca's work into such a different form? Also, Seneca was the tutor of the Emperor Nero. Why would Seneca write a play about a Judean Cynic who claimed to be the/a son of God? The authors answer: Seneca wrote because "Paul's protracted court proceedings brought about the need for some sort of an apology of Jesus, in the manner of Plato's *Apology of Socrates*, to account for the scandal of the cross."[109] This is not plausible. The story that "Paul" (whoever he was) went to Rome, and was tried there originates in the Acts of the Apostles, and Acts is not trustworthy as history. And even if "Paul" was tried in Rome, he would have been an unimportant representative of a tiny sect: Seneca would not have known that Paul existed. So if this earlier play existed, we cannot postulate Seneca as its author. (Sammer does not endorse Seneca's authorship.[110]) This leaves us without a real-life situation in which a Passion play about "Jesus" had an audience.

Third, Stecchini and Sammer propose that the Gethsemane scene was the prologue to the original Passion play.[111] I think that Mark's original play that he used as the Passion began earlier, at the Last Supper or a prologue to it. In Chapter 2 I discuss the original Passion.

Fourth, the play that Stecchini and Sammer reconstruct is *a harmonization of the stageable material in the four canonical gospels*. They propose that John had a copy of Seneca's script; Mark and Luke saw the play and wrote about it afterwards; Matthew knew it through GMark.[112] If you read their book, you must de-harmonize their reconstructed play. A scene found only in GJohn cannot be used to reconstruct the Passion in GMark. A scene found in GMatthew may or may not have originated in GMark.*

---

* I note that the fact that GMatthew and GLuke contain nonMarkan material that is *stageable* does not require that the authors saw a staged Passion play. Like their contemporaries, the authors attended the theater, the mass medium of their time. They thought theatrically and presented stories theatrically. GJohn is widely acknowledged to be a later, composite document, and it has also been edited. Its Passion story could have been based on the Passion in a synoptic gospel.

APPENDIX B

"Paul" and Acts

Here I make explicit why I do not consider the Letters of Paul or the life of Paul (as portrayed in the Acts of the Apostles) in my discussion of Mark's life-situation. The reader may ask:

If Paul was in Rome in the 50s–60s CE, did he influence Mark, Mark's congregation, or other members of the Jesus movement?
Answer: The Acts of the Apostles and Paul's Letter to the Romans are the two texts that place "Paul" in Rome. The Acts Seminar says, "Acts can no longer be considered an independent source for the life and mission of Paul."[113] In Romans, Paul merely states his plan to visit Rome; there is no evidence in the letter that he ever arrived. So we cannot infer that Paul was ever in Rome. Mark's pro-Gentile stance, which is sometimes seen as Pauline,[114] can be explained as a welcome to Flavia and her family.

Did Mark know any of the Letters of Paul?
Answer: The *current* versions of the Letters of Paul were created by orthodox editors some 50–60 years after Mark wrote the Gospel. The longer letters are composites of first- and second-century material of various origins.[115] Some of that material may have come from the library of the Roman congregation. Marcion as well as the later orthodox editors of the letters had access to the Roman congregation's library. So did Mark. All of them could have known the same pre-Markan documents. We do not have to assume that Mark knew any works by "Paul."

APPENDIX C

Times of Day in the Received Text

Table 4 shows the times of day that are specified in the scenes of the received text of the Gospel.

Parentheses indicate where the time of day is *implied* in the scene. "NS" indicates that the time of day is not specified.

In the Comments column, I note scenes that I think are not original, or are out of order. I do not mention edits that affect only dialogue.

TABLE 4. TIMES OF DAY IN THE RECEIVED TEXT

Scene	Time of day	Comments
I:1 Baptisms (1:4–11)	(Day)	
I:2 Jesus in wilderness 40 days, tested by Satan (1:12–13)	(Day)	Scene is not original. Original scene was staged in daylight.
I:3 Jesus calls fishermen (1:14–20)	(Day)	
I:4 Capernaum synagogue. Jesus heals possessed man (1:21–28)	Day	Scene is probably not original.
I:5 Jesus heals Simon's mother-in-law, multitudes (1:29–34)	Day to evening	Scene is probably not original.
I:6 Jesus prays "in the morning, while it was still very dark," disciples seek him out, Jesus proclaims (1:35–39)	Dawn to day	The Jesus actor can rub eyes to indicate "early morning."
I:7 Jesus heals a leper (1:40–45)	(Day)	
II:1 Jesus heals the paralytic (2:1–12)	(Day)	
II:2 Jesus calls Levi (2:13–14)	(Day)	Scene is probably not original.
II:3 Jesus has dinner with tax collectors and outcasts (2:15–17)	NS; day is possible	Dinner parties usually began during daylight.
II:4 Discussion of fasting (2:18–22)	(Day)	

Appendix C - Times of Day in the Received Text

Scene	Time of day	Comments
II:5 Disciples gather grain, Sabbath was made for humankind (2:23–28)	Day	
III:1 Jesus heals man with a withered hand (3:1–6)	(Day)	
III:2 Jesus departs for the seaside (3:7–12)	(Day)	
III:3 On the mountain, Jesus calls the Twelve (3:13–19a)	(Day)	Jesus calls only Three.
III:4 At home, Jesus teaches Satan cannot drive out Satan, bind the strong man (3:19b–30)	NS; day is possible	Dinner parties usually began during daylight.
III:5 Jesus's true family (3:31–35)	(Day)	Continues previous scene.
IV:1 Jesus teaches Parable of the Sower from a boat (4:1–9)	Day	
IV:2 Jesus explains the parable, teaches more parables (4:10–34)	(Day)	
IV:3 In the boat, Jesus sleeps, then stills storm (4:35–41)	Evening	In performance, "evening" is implied by Jesus's sleeping. Scene can be staged in daylight.
V:1 In Gerasa, healing of demoniac and drowning of "pigs" (5:1–20)	(Day)	
V:2 Jesus heals daughter of Jairus, woman with hemorrhage (5:21–43)	(Day)	
VI:1 On Sabbath, Jesus teaches in the synagogue, "Is not this the carpenter?", prophet without honor (6:1–6a)	Day	
VI:2 Jesus teaches in the villages (audience) (6:6b)	(Day)	
VI:3 Jesus instructs the disciples, then they exit and heal the multitudes (6:7–13)	(Day)	Beginning of heavily edited and reordered Bethsaida section. (6:12–13 is probably not original).
VI:4 Herod's banquet and the account of killing of John the Baptist (6:14–29)	NS	Banquet scene is not by Mark. My proposed original scene (a report of John's death) can take place in ambient daylight.
VI:5 The disciples tell Jesus what they have done; travel to deserted place (6:30–32)	NS	Scene is not original.

Appendix C - Times of Day in the Received Text

Scene	Time of day	Comments
VI:6 Feeding of 5,000 (First Feeding Miracle) (6:33–44)	NS	Scene is not original.
VI:7 Boat trip, Jesus walks on water (6:45–52)	Near-dawn	The specified time is between 3:00 a.m. and dawn, compatible with ambient daylight.
VI:8 Healings at Gennesaret (6:53–56)	(Day)	Not stageable, not original.
VII:1 Teachings on purity and defilement (7:1–23)	(Day)	
VII:2 Jesus heals Syrophoenician woman's daughter (7:24–30)	(Day)	Scene is not original.
VII:3 Jesus heals deaf-mute (7:31–37)	(Day)	Scene is not original.
VIII:1 Feeding of 4,000 (Second Feeding Miracle) (8:1–9)	(Day)	
VIII:2 Boat trip to Dalmanutha (8:10)	(Day)	Scene is not original.
VIII:3 Pharisees demand a sign (8:11–12)	(Day)	
VIII:4 Boat trip from Dalmanutha and discussion of bread (8:13–21)	(Day)	Scene is not original (some dialogue may be original).
VIII:5 Jesus heals blind man of Bethsaida (8:22–26)	(Day)	
VIII:6 Peter recognizes Jesus as the Christ, Jesus rebukes Peter (8:27–8:33)	(Day)	
VIII:7 Jesus tells crowd to take up the cross and follow (8:34–9:1)	(Day)	
IX:1 Transfiguration (9:2–13)	(Day)	
IX:2 Jesus heals epileptic boy (9:14–29)	(Day)	
IX:3 On the way, Jesus predicts his death (9:30–32)	(Day)	
IX:4 Display of little child, Jesus teaches in Capernaum (9:33–50)	(Day)	
X:1 Jesus teaches on divorce and adultery (10:1–12)	(Day)	
X:2 Jesus blesses little children (10:13–16)	(Day)	

Scene	Time of day	Comments
X:3 Jesus teaches about riches, promises reward (10:17–31)	(Day)	
X:4 Jesus predicts his death, James and John request honor (10:32–45)	(Day)	
X:5 Jesus heals blind Bartimaeus (10:46–52)	(Day)	Not original, replaces original scene set in Jericho.
XI:1 Entry to Jerusalem (11:1–11)	(Day)	
XI:2 Jesus curses the fig tree (11:12–14)	Day	"On the following day"
XI:3 Temple Incident (11:15–19)	Day to evening	"And when evening came, Jesus and his disciples went out of the city."
XI:4 Withered fig tree (11:20–25)	Day	"In the morning"
XI:5 Jesus asserts his authority to interpret Scripture (11:27–33)	(Day)	
XII:1 Jesus teaches in the Temple, the widow contributes (12:1–44)	(Day)	
XIII:1 Olivet Discourse (13:1–37)	(Day)	
XIV:1 Chief priests and scribes plot, woman anoints Jesus at dinner (14:1–11)	NS	Dinner parties usually began during daylight.
XIV:2 Disciples get room for Last Supper (14:12–16)	Day	"On the first day"
XIV:3 Last Supper (14:17–25)	Evening	"When it was evening." Starting here, all scenes of the play are in continuous time.
XIV:4 Jesus speaks to disciples on Mount of Olives, Peter promises loyalty (14:26–31)	(Evening or night)	
XIV:5 Jesus prays in Gethsemane (14:32–42)	(Night)	Disciples drowse, sleep to indicate "night."
XIV:6 Arrest of Jesus (14:43–52)	(Night)	Torches indicate night.
XIV:7 Trial before the High Priest (14:53–65)	(Night)	Peter warms himself at the fire. Fire and torches indicate "night."
XIV:8 Peter is in courtyard of High Priest (14:66–72)	Night to dawn	Peter warms himself at the fire. Cock crows indicate dawn. Fire can be extinguished.

Appendix C - Times of Day in the Received Text

Scene	Time of day	Comments
XV:1 Jesus is brought before Pilate and condemned (15:1–15)	Morning	"As soon as it was morning," Implies previous scenes were at night.
XV:2 Soldiers mock Jesus (15:16–20a)	(Morning)	
XV:3 March to cross (15:20b–21)	(Morning)	
XV:4 Crucifixion (15:22–32)	Day	"It was nine o'clock in the morning"
XV:5 Darkness at noon (15:33)	Complete darkness	"When it was noon, darkness came over the whole land until three in the afternoon." Indicated by Jesus's cry, actors stumbling, etc.
XV:6 Jesus dies during darkness (15:34–41)	Darkness	"At three o'clock Jesus cried out." Lighting special effects may have been developed for daylight shows.
XV:7 Joseph of Arimathea obtains Jesus's body and entombs it (15:42–47)	Evening	"When evening had come." "Evening" can be conveyed by dialogue or acting.
XVI:1 Young man at tomb, women flee (16:1–8)	Sunrise	"Very early on the first day of the week, when the sun had risen." Scene is not original.

APPENDIX D

Model of the Two-Level Miniature Theater

Once I learned about the two-level stage in the Theater of Dionysus in Athens, I constructed a two-level miniature theater (Figure 2) for the purpose of blocking my reconstructions of the play.

Initially, I thought that the best model for Flavia's theater would be the Greek Theater at Hadrian's Villa (HV). But from the tiny drawing of the ground plan I was able to obtain,[116] I could not determine the width of the upper stage, or the height of either the lower or upper stages. Therefore, I also used a printout of the drawing of the Theater of Dionysus (TD) (Figure 1). All "TD" numbers come from that printout. Table 5 shows that the proportions of the stage and wings of HV and TD are similar, providing a range I could use for the miniature theater.

TABLE 5. PROPORTIONS OF THE STAGE AND WINGS OF HV AND TD

	HV (drawing)	TD (drawing)
Length of lower stage including wings	46 mm	7.8 cm
Length of lower stage between wings	30 mm	4.8 cm
Length of wings	8 mm each side	1.5 cm each side*
Ratio of length of one wing to length of entire stage	8 mm / 46 mm = .17	1.5 cm / 7.8 cm = .19
Width of lower stage	7 mm	1.5 cm (estimate)
Ratio of width of stage to length of entire stage	7 mm / 46 mm = .15	1.5 cm / 7.8 cm = .19

*The stage in the drawing of TD does not have wings. I use the space allotted to the seated Chorus.

Appendix D - Model of the Two-Level Miniature Theater

For the two-level model, I used the proportions of TD but made the wings narrower (as in HV) and the main stage a little longer and wider (deeper) (Table 6).

TABLE 6. MEASUREMENTS OF THE TWO-LEVEL MINIATURE THEATER

	TD	Proposed TD dimensions at 20 mm/1 foot*	At 1:12 scale	At 1:24 scale	Actual
Length of lower stage including wings	7.8 cm	39 feet	39"	19.5"	18.25"
Length of each wing	1.5 cm	7.5 feet	7.5"	3.75"	2.75"
Length of lower stage between the wings	4.8 cm	24 feet	24"	12"	12.75"
Width of lower stage	1.5 cm	7.5 feet	7.5"	3.75"	4.5"
Height of lower stage above orchestra	60 mm	3 feet	3"	1.5"	2"
Height of back wall of lower stage	1.2 cm	6 feet	6"	3"	3.25"
Height of upper stage	3 cm	15 feet	15"	7.5"	7"
Width of upper stage	1 cm	5 feet	5"	2.5"	2.75"
Height of back of stage, from orchestra to above royal door	4.8 cm	24 feet	24"	12"	12"
Length of each set of large stairs between levels	2 cm	10 feet	10"	5"	6.5"†
Height of royal door	1.7 cm	8.5 feet	8.5"	4.25"	4"
Height of smaller doors	1.4 cm	7 feet	7"	3.5"	3.5"

---

* In the real TD, the wall behind the lower level had to be no lower than the tallest actor wearing headgear. If the wall is 6 feet high, then the scale of the drawing of TD is 1.2 cm = 6 feet, or 20 mm = 1 foot (sixth line of table).

† I made one of the staircases longer and shallower because in Mark's performed play, there is a lot of climbing between stage levels, and the stairs should not be steep. In addition, some scenes with a number of actors may have been staged on these stairs.

Appendix D - Model of the Two-Level Miniature Theater

	TD	Proposed TD dimensions at 20 mm/1 foot*	At 1:12 scale	At 1:24 scale	Actual
Diameter of disc door		4.5 feet (estimate – audience can see seated actor inside)*	4.5"	2.25"	2.25"
Height of rock wall		5 feet (estimate)	5"	2.5"	2.5"
Width of couch		2.5 feet	2.5"	1.25"	1.25"
Width of large stairs		2.5 feet	2.5"	1.25"	1.5"
Width of royal door	70 mm	3.5 feet	3.5"	1.75"	2"
Length of boat		7 feet (5 actors/ 3 double seats)	7"	3.5"	3"
Width of smaller doors	50 mm	2.5 feet	2.5"	1.25"	1.5"
Height of mountain		5.5 feet (estimate based on height of actor hidden behind it)	5.5"	2.75"	2.75"

I reiterate that my only purpose in building the miniature theater was to block the play, that is, test out the flow of the actors' movements in a model that was within the mainstream of contemporary theater design. The dimensions I used were good enough for this purpose. The miniature theater cannot tell us the absolute size or proportions of Mark's theater. We *can* assume that it was smaller than HV. And we can assume that its proportions and features were modified to provide the best viewing experience for the relatively small audience.

■ ■ ■ ■ ■

---

* After I made the model, I discovered that 4.5 feet was the right size: see endnote 47.

APPENDIX E

A Partial Reconstruction of the Action of the Performed Play

Introduction

Behind the received text is Mark's polished text. Behind Mark's polished text is a performance. Here, I provide a script for the performance, incorporating my insights and reconstructions, mainly from Chapters 3 and 4. I focus on the physical action and omit most of the received dialogue. I provide key lines mainly to orient the reader.

The playscript below is not the same as the one Mark wrote, which can never be reconstructed. See the section "Limits of reconstruction," p. 116.

The reader may wonder if the script below is what I want to have happened in the play. I have no interest in promoting any doctrine. I strongly believe that Mark, as a playwright, always kept the performability and entertainment value of his play foremost in his mind, and I must do the same. I offer what I think are plausible proposals, based on several years of involvement with the Gospel. Information about my choices here can be found by looking up the scene or role in the table of contents or index.

TIME: c. 30 CE
PLACE: Province of the Galilee and Province of Judea

Major speaking roles
JESUS (middle-aged or older, bearded like a philosopher)
SATAN
PETER
HIGH PRIEST
PONTIUS PILATE

Disciples*
JAMES
JOHN
JUDAS

Chorus
MULTITUDES
JOHN'S DISCIPLES
OUTCASTS (a female poisoner, a tax collector, prostitutes?)
SLAVES
BUYERS/SELLERS
PHARISEES
SCRIBES
ELDERS
SADDUCEES†
HERODIANS
CHIEF PRIESTS
BYSTANDERS
GUARDS
ATTENDANTS
ROMAN SOLDIERS (acrobats)

Bit parts (some have lines)
JOHN THE BAPTIST
ZEBEDEE
MAN WITH AN UNCLEAN SPIRIT
LEPER
PARALYTIC
MAN WITH A WITHERED HAND
DEMONIAC (a comic guest star, not circumcised)
WOMAN WITH HEMORRHAGE (possibly a guest star)
JAIRUS
WIFE
JAIRUS'S DAUGHTER
BLIND MAN OF BETHSAIDA
SMALL CHILD
FATHER OF EPILEPTIC

---

* The other members of the TWELVE might be bit-part characters like the LEPER and LEVI.

† "SADDUCEES" in the received text (12:18) might in performance be "CHIEF PRIESTS."

EPILEPTIC
RICH MAN
SCRIBE
POOR WIDOW
MAN WITH A PITCHER (SIMON OF CYRENE)
SIMON THE JAR-MERCHANT (SIMON THE LEPER)
WOMAN WITH PERFUME
SLAVE OF THE HIGH PRIEST
MAIDSERVANT OF THE HIGH PRIEST
BARABBAS
CENTURION (one of the ROMAN SOLDIERS)
JOSEPH
ANGEL

Costumes
- garment and leather belt for JOHN THE BAPTIST
- robes for SATAN, ANGEL, and JESUS (in ascension scene)
- ordinary tunics and cloaks (the default costume) for JESUS, DISCIPLES, MULTITUDES, etc.
- props/costumes that distinguish each faction/sect: PHARISEES, HERODIANS, SCRIBES, CHIEF PRIESTS, ELDERS
- white tunic and cloak for JESUS (donned at Transfiguration)
- soldier costumes for ROMAN SOLDIERS
- costume for PILATE
- pre-torn garment (for HIGH PRIEST)
- loincloth (for fleeing YOUNG MAN)

Set and properties (in approximate chronological order of initial use)
- a stage crane with a "bucket" that holds two actors
- trees and plants
- a curtain, probably decorated with the constellations of the night sky, to hang above the scene building
- pole with a dove on a string
- wheeled boat that holds five actors (JAMES, JOHN, ZEBEDEE, SERVANTS)
- fishing nets
- false skin or makeup for LEPER
- stretcher/mat
- couch
- benches and stools
- standard (flagpole of a Roman legion) with boar on the flag

- cushion (landing mat)
- headless "body," wrapped in a linen shroud stained with blood
- cloud (for Transfiguration)
- bread for the disciples to eat
- soft foliage
- donkey
- leafy fig tree
- dead fig tree
- collection chests
- tables for Temple Court
- real coins
- live doves (probably on leashes)[117] in cages
- breakable white flask containing scented liquid
- pitcher of water and washing bowl
- table for Last Supper
- wine, bread, plate and cups (for Eucharist)
- swords and clubs
- torches
- a brazier with "fire" inside
- artificial blood (for ear of SLAVE OF THE HIGH PRIEST)
- whips
- purple (dark red) cloak
- material for crown of thorns
- reed
- bones for gambling
- one cross beam (with rope to tie it)
- cup and "poison"
- two sponges with reeds
- a "corpse" wrapped in plain linen (placed by JOSEPH)

Gifts for audience (distributed at feeding miracle)

Set

The play is staged in a Greek theater with a two-level stage.

- The lower level is deeper than the upper level. The lower level has a back wall 5–6 feet high.
- On the lower level, against the back wall, two sets of wide stairs lead to the upper level. The larger and more visible stairs are Stage Left.
- The scene building on the upper level has a large "royal" door in the center, flanked by two smaller doors.

- The door Stage Left and the stairs below it are used for all the house/indoor scenes before the Last Supper, except the healing of Jairus's daughter and the dinner at Bethany. The dinner is held in front of the door Stage Right.
- Wings project a few feet into the orchestra on both sides of the lower stage.
- The orchestra extends a bit beyond the outer edges of the wings.
- Small staircases are on the outside of each wing and center stage.
- The theater has a parodos (side exit) outside each wing, and an exit at the back of the audience area.
- A garden set on the wing Stage Right contains trees and plants, and a rock wall partly covered by a large stone disc. The disc rolls away to reveal the inside of the tomb. The tomb has two shelves.
- In front of the garden, a mountain at least 5½ feet in height overlooks the orchestra. There is a staircase on the back side of the mountain. There are several steps and a "seat" visible to the audience on the side of the mountain.

Lighting
- The entire play is staged in ambient daylight.
- There may be lightning or other visual effects during "darkness at noon."
- The arrest party carries torches; these torches remain onstage and illuminate the trial in the house of the high priest.
- PETER in the courtyard is near a fire in a brazier. The fire is extinguished to indicate "dawn."
- There may be extra lighting in the heavens when Jesus ascends at the end of the play.

Opportunities in the script for music
- Comedy music accompanies the Temple Incident.
- Music accompanies the parade that enters Jerusalem.
- A hymn is sung by JESUS and DISCIPLES while seated at the Last Supper.

Stage Right	Stage Left
← Country	City, Marketplace, Harbor →

Audience

Comments

In the script below, I use the word "Act" instead of "Chapter" to prevent confusion with the chapters of this book.

Direct quotations (with verse numbers) are from the New Revised Standard Version (NRSV).

I have used *[italic text in brackets]* for substantive additions or edits that I have made to the received text (positive changes). I do not use them for stage directions implied in my reconstructions of the action, or in my proposed sequence of scenes.

I have *silently* deleted verses and the corresponding verse numbers that I believe are not by Mark (negative changes).

The staging in the performance was more complex and varied than the narrative in the polished text, or than provided in my stage directions here. In particular, at any given time Chorus members may be visible in several areas of the stage. The visual component of the staging cannot be recovered.

The received text gives little information on other issues relating to the Chorus. It is not clear *how many* actors are in the Chorus and *which* members of the Chorus are onstage at any given time. Nor is it clear how many members of the Chorus are pro-Jesus or skeptical, and when they change their allegiance. And the *acting* and any dialogue spoken by the Chorus are missing.

Unless I specify that an actor or group of actors exits the stage, I assume that they remain in the location of their previous scene.

■ ■····················■····················■····················■····················■····················■ ■

THE PLAY

PROLOGUE
(1:1–3)
Empty stage. VOICE OF GOD speaks.

(1:4–11, 1:14a)
The Wilderness. JOHN THE BAPTIST and Chorus members enter and go to Stage Center. JOHN stands on the center stairs or in the orchestra (the Jordan River), and baptizes other actors. They go to the side.

JESUS enters the stage through the royal door of the scene building (the door remains open throughout the play). He goes downstairs. JOHN baptizes him. Above the stage, the curtain opens and a dove descends.

The VOICE OF GOD speaks.* GUARDS enter from Stage Left. They take JOHN and exit. The Chorus members *[including the LEPER]* follow them.† JESUS alone remains, Stage Center.

ACT I, SCENE 1
[The original Temptation scene.
The Wilderness. SATAN enters on the stage crane. JESUS enters the "bucket." The actors converse throughout the scene. The crane swings them to the top of the scene building. Then it swings them to the top of the mountain Stage Right. There, JESUS exits the crane and descends the mountain. The crane deposits SATAN on the scene building.‡ He withdraws. The crane withdraws.]

ACT I, SCENE 2
(1:35)
"A deserted place," Stage Center. JESUS prays. *[He explains his plans and prays to his Father for strength.§ Possibly he also explains his itinerary.]*

ACT I, SCENE 3
(1:40–45)
(location not specified) A LEPER enters and kneels facing JESUS. JESUS heals him and tells him to be silent. However, the cured LEPER goes out proclaiming, "so that Jesus could no longer go into a town openly, but stayed out in the country; and people came to him from every quarter" (1:45). *[This scene is the entry of the Chorus. Some actors go to the synagogue (in front of the royal door) on the upper level, others to the holding area Stage Left.]* Meanwhile, JAMES, JOHN, ZEBEDEE, and SERVANTS bring the boat through the parodos Stage Left and tie it up adjacent to that wing. They enter the boat. PETER enters Stage Left and goes to the wing.

---

* The received text does not state if JOHN sees the heavens open and hears the VOICE OF GOD.

† Some of these actors will return to the stage as JOHN'S DISCIPLES. Possibly some later become followers of JESUS.

‡ The SATAN actor will appear here later in the play.

§ JESUS, I suggest, intends to teach and heal the multitudes in order to provoke the COUNCIL to kill him. This is the only scene in the received text that gives him the opportunity to state this goal, *prior to the entry of the Chorus and the calling of the fishermen*. Note that the audience now knows JESUS's master plan but the inner disciples do not.

ACT I, SCENE 4
(1:14b–20)
The Sea Side. PETER is fishing with a net into the "sea" below. "Proclaiming the kingdom of God," JESUS walks along the stage edge (the sea side) towards Stage Left and calls PETER, JAMES, and JOHN (not by name). They follow him. ZEBEDEE and SERVANTS quietly step out of the boat, and exit through the parodos. The boat remains.

ACT II, SCENE 1
(2:1–12)
Capernaum, the house. JESUS, the THREE, MULTITUDES, and SCRIBES are present in front of the door. Jesus teaches. Four MULTITUDES try to carry the PARALYTIC on a stretcher up the stairs to JESUS. Eventually they succeed. JESUS heals the PARALYTIC and addresses the SCRIBES. The PARALYTIC, stands, takes his mat/stretcher, and goes downstairs.

ACT II, SCENE 2
(2:15–22)
Capernaum, the house. JESUS and members of the MULTITUDES (LEVI and OUTCASTS, a poisoner, possibly prostitutes)* enter the house door. The THREE are about to follow, but the SCRIBES ask, "Why does he eat with tax collectors and sinners?" (2:16). JESUS emerges and answers. Someone asks JESUS why his disciples do not fast. JESUS answers.

ACT II, SCENE 3
(2:23–28)
The Countryside. JESUS and the THREE descend to the lower level and cross the stage to Stage Right. The THREE "harvest" grain from a plant. PHARISEES observe and comment. JESUS defends the disciples. PHARISEES, JESUS, and the THREE go up to the synagogue.

ACT III, SCENE 1
(3:1–6)
Capernaum, the synagogue. JESUS heals the MAN WITH A WITHERED HAND. MULTITUDES observe. Jesus says, "Is it lawful to do good or to do harm on the sabbath, to save life or to kill?" (3:4). PHARISEES and HERODIANS observe, then conspire.

---

* The SCRIBES inform the audience that these actors are sinners/outcasts, but some of the actors might wear distinctive costumes.

ACT III, SCENE 2
(3:7–12)
The Sea Side. JESUS and the THREE descend the steps Stage Left to the lower level and walk along the edge of the stage. The THREE get the boat ready for JESUS to teach from in 4:1.* Meanwhile, MULTITUDES enter the stage from several directions and try to touch JESUS. Some—possessed by demonic spirits—fall down and cry out, "You are the Son of God!" (3:11).

ACT III, SCENE 3
(3:13–19)
JESUS walks along the stage edge to the mountain Stage Right, then sits on the mountain. He calls the THREE over and formally appoints them as disciples. *[He does not give them the power to preach or exorcise.]* He speaks their names ("Peter" and "Boanerges"). They climb to the upper-level "house."

ACT III, SCENE 4
(3:20–35)
Capernaum, the house. JESUS and the THREE are crowded by the MULTITUDES. SCRIBES from the synagogue area say that JESUS has Beelzebul in him. JESUS teaches "Binding of the Strong Man."

MULTITUDES tell JESUS that his mother and brothers are among the crowd.† Looking at the audience, JESUS replies, "Here are my mother and my brothers!" (3:34). JESUS and the THREE descend the stairs Stage Left and move toward the front edge of the stage.

ACT IV, SCENE 1
(4:1–35)
The Sea Side. The MULTITUDES gather at the edge of the stage. JESUS enters the boat and sits.‡ JESUS teaches the audience and the

---

* Mk 3:9 reads "He told his disciples to have a boat ready for him because of the crowd, so that they would not crush him." The THREE move the boat from its initial position and "ready" it for JESUS's use.

† The audience need not identify actors with these roles. (They will never be seen again.) Their presence can be reported. This scene sets up 6:3, "Is not this the carpenter, the son of Mary...?"

‡ There are problems here. 4:10–12 (and possibly also 4:13–20) are by an editor: we know this because JESUS is in the boat, then suddenly "when he was alone" he teaches privately. It may be that only 4:1–9 is original. Also, the parable material in the received text is too long and varied for a single speech; the performance speech was shorter.

MULTITUDES.* JESUS says to the THREE, "Let us go across to the other side" (4:35). The MULTITUDES withdraw.

ACT IV, SCENE 2
(4:36a, 4:37–41)
The Sea of Galilee. The THREE enter the boat and cross the orchestra to the wing Stage Right. A storm rocks the boat. The THREE "bail water" while JESUS "sleeps" on a cushion. The THREE rouse him. *[In front of the mountain, JESUS throws the cushion overboard.]* He rebukes the wind and waves. They stop. The THREE are amazed.

ACT V, SCENE 1
(5:1–20)
(Gentile) Gerasa, Stage Right. The boat ties up on the outer side of the wing. JESUS and the THREE exit the boat to the stage. The DEMONIAC, who is naked or nearly so, enters from behind the tomb. *[ROMAN SOLDIERS are standing in the parodos. One carries a standard with the image of a boar.]* Several MULTITUDES (swineherds) enter *[with the SOLDIERS]*.

JESUS exorcises the DEMONIAC. *[The demonic spirits enter the ROMAN SOLDIERS. The "possessed" acrobatic SOLDIERS ascend the stairs to the wing, then climb the mountain. They jump off and somersault onto the cushion in the orchestra and "drown."]* The MULTITUDES exit excitedly through the parodos Stage Right. More MULTITUDES enter from Stage Right.† The healed DEMONIAC, now "clothed," sits on the mountain.‡ JESUS tells him to go to his home. The DEMONIAC walks, comically "proclaiming," through the audience and exits out the back. Meanwhile, the Gerasene MULTITUDES exit. *[The (dead) SOLDIERS stand up, take the cushion*

---

* JESUS is teaching from a boat, *below* the stage. If this stage direction is original, to address both the audience and the actors onstage, he faces Stage Center—a mirror image of his position on the Mount of Olives Stage Right when he gives the Olivet Discourse (13:3). The two scenes are chiastically parallel within the play as a whole.

† The swineherds cannot tell it "in the city" (5:14) because they cannot exit to Stage Left. They cannot go through the garden set because it is the home of the DEMONIAC and does not "connect to" any other location. The swineherds must exit through the parodos Stage Right (to the country). Possibly "the city" is revealed by dialogue, or by the costumes/demeanor of some of the new entrants.

‡ The term "clothed" may simply mean that the DEMONIAC is no longer naked. I suggest he wears a loincloth, which he will wear (and lose) as the YOUNG MAN at the arrest scene, and is wrapped in a himation. (This new costume was stashed behind the tomb.)

and also exit through the parodos Stage Right.] During the distraction of the DEMONIAC's speech and exit, JESUS and the THREE enter the boat and recross the orchestra to Stage Left.

ACT V, SCENE 2
(5:21–43)
Town in Galilee. JESUS and the THREE tie up the boat and ascend to the stage. MULTITUDES are present, including WOMAN WITH HEMORRHAGE. JAIRUS descends the stairs from the upper level.

JAIRUS asks JESUS to heal his daughter. JESUS and the THREE follow JAIRUS to the stairs. The WOMAN touches JESUS. He addresses her. The WOMAN falls down and tells her story. JESUS takes the THREE upstairs. The MULTITUDES above are weeping.

JESUS, JAIRUS, his WIFE and the THREE go to the GIRL, who is lying on a bed. JESUS says, "*Talitha, koum!*" and the GIRL stands up.* JESUS tells JAIRUS and WIFE to give the GIRL something to eat.

ACT VI, SCENE 1
(6:1–6a)
Capernaum, the synagogue. JESUS and the THREE walk to the synagogue Stage Center. There, JESUS teaches. The MULTITUDES say, "Is not this the carpenter, the son of Mary?" JESUS responds, "Prophets are not without honor…" (6:4). He lays hands on a few sick people and cures them.

ACT VI, SCENE 2
(6:6b)
The villages. JESUS descends from the stage on the outer steps Stage Left and visits the audience, possibly directing his "teachings" at several attendees. Meanwhile, the THREE wait on or near the stairs between the upper and lower levels, Stage Left.

ACT VI, SCENE 3
(6:7–11)
The Wilderness. JESUS returns to the stage and calls over the THREE.

---

* JAIRUS's entry to the stage through the royal door would inform the audience that he is connected with the synagogue. Perhaps Mark described him as an "*archisynagōgos*" in the polished text to inform the reader that the scene with the girl occurred inside the *royal* door, and not one of the two house doors. The term need never have been spoken.

He tells them how to behave as disciples and gives them power over Satanic spirits. *[JESUS and the THREE retire to the stairs.]*

ACT VI, SCENE 4
[The original Herod scene plus 6:29.
Galilee. The MULTITUDES are Stage Left, possibly also Stage Center. A MESSENGER from Herod enters Stage Left and announces that JOHN THE BAPTIST has been executed by order of Herod. The MESSENGER explains the backstory. He exits with JOHN'S DISCIPLES.] The MULTITUDES exclaim that JESUS's powers must have been due to JOHN. JOHN'S DISCIPLES, carrying an obviously headless body, re-enter from the parodos Stage Left. They cross the stage to the tomb. They roll the door open, place the body in the tomb, roll the door closed, and exit Stage Right.

ACT VII, SCENE 1
(7:1–15, 8:15)
The Wilderness. JESUS and the THREE descend the stairs. DISCIPLE(S) eat. SCRIBES and PHARISEES observe, then descend the stairs. They criticize the THREE for eating with unwashed hands. JESUS responds with criticism of the PHARISEES. JESUS calls the MULTITUDES over to listen. He teaches them and the audience about defilement. *[He also warns of the leaven of the Pharisees (8:15).]* JESUS and the THREE go to the boat Stage Left.

ACT VII, SCENE 2
[Boat trip to Bethsaida.
JESUS and the THREE enter the boat and cross the orchestra to the wing Stage Right. Possibly, JESUS teaches about food and purity, and mentions bread.]

ACT VIII, SCENE 1
(8:1–9)
Bethsaida. JESUS and the THREE tie up and exit the boat. JESUS addresses the THREE but refers to the *audience*, "I have compassion for the crowd" (8:2). The THREE ask, "How can one feed these people with bread here in the desert?" (8:4) *[JESUS gives an answer that prompts the THREE to distribute gifts to the audience.*]*

---

* The gifts may have been hidden behind the rock wall.

ACT VIII, SCENE 2
(8:22–26, 6:45)
Bethsaida. Some people *[congregants or actors]* escort the BLIND MAN *[an audience member]* to JESUS *[who is in the audience area]*. JESUS leads the BLIND MAN to a visible spot in the audience area, and heals him. JESUS sends him home and says, "Do not even go into the village" (8:26). The BLIND MAN exits through the parodos Stage Right (to the country). *[He re-enters from the back of the audience and retakes his seat.]* JESUS goes to the edge of the orchestra Stage Right. Meanwhile, the THREE have entered the boat and are crossing the orchestra from Stage Right to Stage Left.

ACT VIII, SCENE 3
(6:47–51)
The Sea of Galilee. The THREE strain to row. JESUS walks behind them. The THREE see him and are terrified. JESUS speaks to them. He enters the boat and the wind drops. The boat reaches Stage Left.

ACT VIII, SCENE 4
(8:11–12)
"Dalmanutha."* JESUS and the THREE tie up the boat and climb to the stage. PHARISEES demand a sign that JESUS is extraordinary. JESUS tells the PHARISEES that there will be no sign.†

ACT VIII, SCENE 5
(8:27–9:1)
The way to the villages of Caesarea Philippi. JESUS and the THREE walk to Stage Center. (Stagehands remove the boat.) JESUS stands on the steps to the orchestra (now "the way"). *[The SATAN actor is visible to the audience near the top of the scene building.]* JESUS asks the THREE, "Who do people say that I am?" (8:27). PETER responds that JESUS is the anointed one. JESUS says he will be killed. PETER rebukes him. JESUS turns around *[and sees SATAN*

---

* The word "Dalmanutha" is probably not spoken and, if original, is probably an artifact of the polished text. The audience needs to know only that JESUS is now back in Judean territory (Galilee); that information is conveyed by the presence of PHARISEES.

† From the PHARISEES' point of view, their demand for a sign makes sense: the last time they saw JESUS (Act VII, Scene 1), he had taught a different doctrine about their signature issue: ritual purity. They are escalating their challenge to him.

behind PETER. *No other actor sees SATAN.*] JESUS rebukes SATAN *[for entrancing PETER]*, "Get behind me, Satan" (8:33). *[SATAN withdraws.]**

JESUS tells the THREE, the MULTITUDES, and the audience to take up their cross and follow him. *[Nine FOLLOWERS (JUDAS, and possibly actors whom JESUS has healed/impressed, such as LEVI) separate themselves from the MULTITUDES.]* JESUS and the THREE go to the mountain.

ACT IX, SCENE 1
(9:2–13)
The mountain. JESUS climbs the mountain and disappears behind the back. PETER ascends a step or two; JAMES and JOHN remain at the base. PETER offers to build structures for Jesus, Moses, and Elijah. A cloud descends and the VOICE OF GOD speaks. The cloud lifts. JESUS, now dressed in a white tunic and cloak, and PETER descend the mountain. The THREE ask JESUS about "rising from the dead" and if Elijah must come first.

ACT IX, SCENE 2
(9:14–27)
(location not specified) JESUS and the THREE walk to Stage Center. SCRIBES have descended from the upper level and are arguing with the FOLLOWERS. Some MULTITUDES run toward JESUS. The FATHER OF THE EPILEPTIC says that his son is possessed, and "your disciples" (the FOLLOWERS) could not cure him. *[The THREE try and fail to cure him.]*

The MULTITUDES bring the EPILEPTIC to JESUS. The EPILEPTIC falls, rolls, and foams at the mouth. JESUS heals him and helps him to stand up. EPILEPTIC and FATHER exit. SCRIBES and MULTITUDES withdraw.

ACT IX, SCENE 3
(9:30–32)
[unknown location]† JESUS and the *[new group of]* TWELVE walk through the orchestra. JESUS predicts that he will be betrayed but the TWELVE do not understand him. They contest who is the greatest.‡

---

* At some point before PETER's rebuke, SATAN has possessed/entranced PETER. Perhaps this possession occurred earlier in the scene: possibly PETER *looked behind him,* like Lot's wife and Orpheus, and saw SATAN on the scene building.

† The boat has been removed, therefore the orchestra is no longer the Sea of Galilee. The action is no longer in Galilee.

‡ It is understandable that the THREE "pull rank" on the FOLLOWERS. The THREE, after all, have been with JESUS for longer, and were given power over Satanic

Appendix E - A Partial Reconstruction of the Play   175

ACT IX, SCENE 4
(9:33–50)
[unknown location] Stage Center.* JESUS asks the TWELVE what they were discussing. They do not answer. JESUS teaches "Whoever wants to be first must be last of all and servant of all" (9:35). A CHILD is introduced (and probably displayed in a tableau). JESUS teaches the TWELVE and the audience to welcome him and to resist temptation. The CHILD is returned to its caretaker.

ACT X, SCENE 1
(10:1–9)
Judea on the other side of the Jordan. JESUS and the TWELVE walk. MULTITUDES and PHARISEES are present. PHARISEES ask about divorce and JESUS answers.†

ACT X, SCENE 2
(10:13–16)
[unknown location] Stage Center. Young children are brought up to the stage. DISCIPLES interfere. JESUS says, "Let the little children come to me" (10:14). He blesses them. The children are returned to their caretakers.

ACT X, SCENE 3
(10:17–31)
[unknown location] Stage Center. The RICH MAN enters running, and kneels. He asks about eternal life. JESUS tells him to follow the commandments and to sell all his goods and give the money to the poor. The RICH MAN exits. JESUS discourses on how to enter the kingdom of God. PETER says, "Look, we have left everything and followed you" (10:28). JESUS says that his followers will be rewarded.

ACT X, SCENE 4
(10:32–45)
The Way to Jerusalem. JESUS, followed by the TWELVE, descends the

---

spirits (although they failed to exorcise the EPILEPTIC). This scene also provides an opportunity for the THREE to comically (mis-)explain JESUS's teachings/identity.
  * This scene, and the three subsequent scenes, which involve many actors, must be performed on the lower stage Stage Center, or centered in the orchestra.
  † I omit 10:10–12 because "then in the house" is not stageable. There is no reason why JESUS would keep this teaching "secret" from the PHARISEES and MULTITUDES.

steps Stage Center into the orchestra. JESUS predicts his Passion. The THREE are amazed and the FOLLOWERS are afraid. JAMES and JOHN ask to sit next to JESUS in heaven, and promise to drink his cup. JESUS teaches, "whoever wishes to be first among you must be slave of all" (10:43).

ACT X, SCENE 5
[(10:46) The original Jericho scene.]

ACT XI, SCENE 1
(11:1–11)
The Way to Jerusalem. A donkey waits in the parodos Stage Left. JESUS sends two DISCIPLES "into the village ahead of you" (11:2). BYSTANDERS comment but allow the DISCIPLES to take the donkey to JESUS. He sits on it.

The Judean (and Gentile?) MULTITUDES (and the TWELVE?) spread their cloaks and foliage in the orchestra. The parade commences and continues through the audience area. (Meanwhile, stagehands set up the tables and other props Stage Center, which is now the Temple Court. The leafy fig tree is placed in the orchestra near the wing Stage Left.)

Having returned to the orchestra, JESUS gives the donkey to DISCIPLES, who return it. The MULTITUDES go to the holding area Stage Left. JESUS ascends the central stairs and looks around.* He returns to the orchestra. He and the TWELVE walk to Bethany Stage Right.

ACT XI, SCENE 2
(11:12–14)
The Way to Jerusalem. The next day.† JESUS and DISCIPLES‡ descend to the orchestra, and see the fig tree. JESUS curses it.

---

* When JESUS "looks around" the Temple Court set, he *assesses* it and plans the Temple Incident for the next day.

† "The next day" may have been indicated by a visual display of the now ongoing "Temple Court activities."

‡ The text does not specify how many DISCIPLES accompany JESUS in the Temple and in Bethany. I think that the stage would be cluttered if all twelve are *always* present. (In the Temple Incident, MONEYLENDERS, DOVE SELLERS, and ATTENDANTS are present, and MULTITUDES, CHIEF PRIESTS and SCRIBES observe.) The possibility that fewer than twelve are present is why I use the imprecise "DISCIPLES" from here until the Last Supper, when twelve *are* needed.

ACT XI, SCENE 3
(11:15–19)
Jerusalem, the Temple Court. JESUS and DISCIPLES climb the steps to Stage Center. In a choreographed scene, probably accompanied by music, the DISCIPLES disperse and block the Temple ATTENDANTS from carrying objects across the stage. Meanwhile, JESUS overturns the tables and stools; coins spill, and fallen cages open. Birds (on leashes) escape. Children from the audience run into the orchestra to pick up the scattered coins.

JESUS addresses the actors *and* the children, "Is it not written, 'My house shall be called a house of prayer for all the nations'? But *you* have made it a den of robbers" (emphasis added) (11:17). The children return to their seats. The DISCIPLES release the ATTENDANTS. The CHIEF PRIESTS and SCRIBES, who have observed this scene, conspire.

JESUS and DISCIPLES descend on the center steps into the orchestra and walk to Bethany Stage Right.

Pause in the action*
Stagehands clean and reset the Temple Court with benches. The collection boxes for the Temple are brought out (or revealed). A dead fig tree replaces the leafy fig tree.

ACT XI, SCENE 4
(11:20–25)
The Way to Jerusalem. JESUS and DISCIPLES enter the orchestra and walk towards the dead fig tree. JESUS tells the DISCIPLES to have faith.

ACT XI, SCENE 5
(11:27–33)
The Temple Court. JESUS and DISCIPLES ascend to the stage. CHIEF PRIESTS, SCRIBES, and ELDERS ask JESUS the source of his authority. He refuses to tell them.

ACT XII, SCENE 1
(12:1–44)
The Temple Court. JESUS teaches. He tells the parable of the vineyard,

---

* This pause in the action gives the audience—particularly children—a few moments to enjoy their "loot," then settle down before the play resumes.

directing it at the CHIEF PRIESTS, SCRIBES, and ELDERS. They are ready to arrest JESUS, but are deterred by the enthusiasm of the MULTITUDES. The Council members return to the upper level. One SCRIBE remains.

The conspirators send PHARISEES and HERODIANS down from the upper level. They ask about paying taxes. JESUS asks them to show a coin, and they do. JESUS tells them, "Give to the emperor the things that are the emperor's" (12:17).

PHARISEES and HERODIANS step aside. Enter SADDUCEES.* The SADDUCEES ask about seven brothers and one wife. JESUS answers.

SADDUCEES step aside. The SCRIBE who has remained steps forward. He asks about the most important commandment. JESUS says, "You are not far from the kingdom of God" (12:34). The SCRIBE steps aside.

JESUS teaches the MULTITUDES about David's son. He tells the MULTITUDES to beware of the SCRIBES. Meanwhile, the MULTITUDES contribute coins to the collection chests.

JESUS sits opposite the collection chests. The MULTITUDES continue to contribute coins.† The POOR WIDOW contributes. JESUS praises her to the DISCIPLES. JESUS and the THREE walk to Stage Right. The actors in the Temple Court withdraw.

ACT XIII, SCENE 1
(13:1–37)
A DISCIPLE exclaims, "what large stones and what large buildings!" (13:2). JESUS predicts all the buildings will be thrown down. The THREE ask when this will occur. JESUS sits on the mountain and gives the Olivet Discourse, addressing the THREE and the audience. JESUS commands the listeners to "watch."‡

ACT XIV, SCENE 1
(14:1–11)
Bethany, the house. JESUS and the THREE climb the stairs to the house

---

* There have been no stage direction to introduce these actors as "Sadducees," and the audience does not recognize them. That is not how Mark introduces new characters. I suggest that the actors who asked this question were the CHIEF PRIESTS. Later, for unknown reasons, an editor of the polished text changed their identification to "Sadducees."

† "Many rich people put in large sums" (12:41). Possibly (pre-selected) congregants came forward to contribute publicly to collection chests on the edge of the stage.

‡ I suggest pp. 70–71 that possibly the Olivet Discourse *followed* the Last Supper.

Stage Right (Bethany). JUDAS joins them. Nearby, the CHIEF PRIESTS and SCRIBES conspire.

JESUS sits at dinner. A WOMAN from the audience enters the stage. She buys a small white jar from the house owner. She goes to JESUS, breaks the jar, and pours its aromatic contents over his head. She returns to her seat.

DISCIPLES condemn the WOMAN for wasting money on expensive oil. JESUS responds that she has anointed his body for its burial. She will have eternal fame. *[The audience applauds.]*

JUDAS leaves and conspires with the CHIEF PRIESTS. The CHIEF PRIESTS, SCRIBES, ELDERS, and PHARISEES exit through the royal door but leave it open.* JESUS and DISCIPLES descend the stairs.

Stagehands set up benches and a long table (or a few small tables) in front of the royal door.

ACT XIV, SCENE 2
(14:12–16)
Jerusalem. The TWELVE ask where they will celebrate the Passover. JESUS sends two DISCIPLES "into the city" (14:13) (towards Stage Left). They find the MAN WITH A PITCHER. He shows them the (new) dining set on the upper level, then they return to JESUS.

ACT XIV, SCENE 3
(14:17–26)
Jerusalem. An upper room. JESUS and the TWELVE go upstairs. They sit in a row in the center of the upper stage. JESUS sits in the center; JUDAS sits next to him. *[The MAN WITH PITCHER accompanies them. He pours water into a bowl. They wash their hands. He exits.]*

JESUS predicts that he will be betrayed by "one of the twelve, one who is dipping bread into the bowl with me" (14:20).

JESUS blesses bread and wine, and distributes them to the TWELVE.

JESUS and the TWELVE sing a hymn. They descend to the lower level and go to the mountain.†

---

* When the Council members and PHARISEES exit, the area in front of the royal door of the scene building is no longer "holy precincts of the Temple" and is available as the "upper room" for the Last Supper.

† For the first time in the play, actors have crossed the entire upper stage in consecutive scenes: First, JESUS and entourage ascend the stairs Stage Left to the upper stage,

ACT XIV, SCENE 4
(14:27–31)

The Mount of Olives. JESUS sits on the mountain and tells the TWELVE they will fall away. PETER says he will not fall away. Other DISCIPLES say the same thing.

ACT XIV, SCENE 5
(14:32–42)

Gethsemane. JESUS and DISCIPLES walk a few steps to the garden/tomb area. JESUS calls to PETER, JAMES, and JOHN, who follow him. The other DISCIPLES exit or wait to the side.[*]

JESUS prays and interacts with the THREE. They sleep. JESUS announces, "See, my betrayer is at hand" (14:42).

ACT XIV, SCENE 6
(14:43–52)

Gethsemane. Actors carrying swords, clubs, and torches enter from the parodos Stage Left and cross the orchestra, then climb the center stairs to the stage and go towards JESUS. The group includes JUDAS, GUARDS, and SLAVES. JUDAS kisses JESUS; the GUARDS seize him. *[PETER]* grabs a sword, and strikes at the conspicuous SLAVE OF THE HIGH PRIEST. *[GUARDS seize PETER.]* The other DISCIPLES flee out of the theater through the parodos Stage Right. *[On their way, they meet the healed DEMONIAC, wearing a himation and loincloth.]*

The DEMONIAC enters the stage and tries to follow JESUS.[†] *[The DEMONIAC loses his himation.]* A GUARD grabs his loincloth. The

---

because they are following the disciples who have interacted with the house owner Stage Left and ascended the stairs there. The group eats the Last Supper Stage Center. Then they descend the stairs Stage Right to the mountain. This crossing is possible because the center of the upper stage is the "upper room" and under the house owner's control; it is no longer the Temple and not yet the praetorium.

[*] It is not clear if the other DISCIPLES exit now or remain to the side, then flee with JAMES and JOHN when JESUS is arrested. There is no room for them in the garden set, so they would have to wait in the parodos. Their presence might visually distract the audience during the Gethsemane scene. But on the other hand, "All of them deserted him and fled" (14:50) seems to imply more than two. Alternatively, if the Olivet Discourse was staged after the Last Supper, then JESUS had dismissed the nine follower DISCIPLES after the meal and they have already exited.

[†] The DEMONIAC's stage action is not clear. Does he, like PETER, attempt to interfere with the arrest? I suspect his behavior was familiar from comedy or mime situations involving slaves and masters.

DEMONIAC flees through the audience and out the back. During this distraction, the set in front of the royal door is changed to the praetorium, and on the lower stage Stage Center, benches are brought out for the trial. The HIGH PRIEST, CHIEF PRIESTS, ELDERS, and SCRIBES enter from the parodos Stage Left and seat themselves.

ACT XIV, SCENE 7
(14:53–65)
Jerusalem, house of the high priest. JESUS is led before the COUNCIL. Lit torches indicate "night." The SLAVES OF THE HIGH PRIEST bring *[PETER (in custody) and]* a small brazier into the "courtyard" in the orchestra.

The HIGH PRIEST and COUNCIL try to get witnesses to give testimony that will condemn Jesus. (The logical choices for witnesses are JUDAS, PHARISEES, and SCRIBES, but possibly also MULTITUDES.)

Some witnesses state that JESUS said, "I will destroy this temple that is made with hands, and in three days I will build another, not made with hands" (14:58). The HIGH PRIEST questions JESUS, but he does not answer. The HIGH PRIEST asks JESUS if he is the Christ. JESUS answers that he is.

The HIGH PRIEST tears his clothes and says that JESUS has blasphemed. The COUNCIL declares that he deserves death. The members of the COUNCIL spit on JESUS, blindfold him, and strike him; and GUARDS hit him.

ACT XIV, SCENE 8
(14:66–72)
Courtyard of the house of the high priest. *[The fire in the brazier is revealed, drawing the audience's attention to this scene.]* BYSTANDERS are present. The MAIDSERVANT OF THE HIGH PRIEST says that PETER was with JESUS. PETER denies it. A cock crows. PETER continues to deny JESUS. The cock crows again. PETER changes demeanor and weeps.*

---

* PETER's weeping implies that the second cock crow has "awakened" him, i.e., SATAN's spell has been broken. SATAN may now be visible on the scene building; if so, he reacts to PETER's return to sanity. The audience will henceforth watch both SATAN and PETER.

ACT XV, SCENE 1

(15:1–15)

Praetorium. Day. The *[torches and the]* fire in the brazier have been extinguished. PILATE and SOLDIERS emerge from the royal door. The COUNCIL orders GUARDS to put JESUS in chains. The GUARDS and CHIEF PRIESTS take him to the upper level, or onto the stairs, within speaking distance of PILATE, who is in front of the royal door. Below, BARABBAS is held by SOLDIERS, and MULTITUDES observe.

PILATE asks JESUS if he is the king of the Jews. JESUS answers. The CHIEF PRIESTS list the charges. PILATE asks JESUS to reply. JESUS is silent.

The MULTITUDES ask PILATE to follow his custom of releasing a prisoner. The CHIEF PRIESTS incite the MULTITUDES to demand the release of "Barabbas." Eventually PILATE complies. Then he (or a SOLDIER) scourges JESUS.

ACT XV, SCENE 2

(15:16–20)

"Courtyard" of the praetorium. SOLDIERS take JESUS into the orchestra, Stage Left.* More SOLDIERS enter.† They remove JESUS's now-bloodstained white himation and give him a purple himation. They seat him, twist a crown of thorns, crown him, and salute him.

The SOLDIERS strike JESUS's head with a reed, spit on him, and bow down to him. Then they take off the purple himation, and reclothe him in the white himation.

ACT XV, SCENE 3

(15:21–22)

The SOLDIERS give JESUS the cross beam to carry, then force him to cross the orchestra to Stage Right. *[Weakened by the beating, JESUS collapses.]*

---

* This "mocking" scene holds the audience's attention while the benches are removed from Stage Center. Therefore, the mocking occurs away from the stage. The location specified, "courtyard of the praetorium," implies that it is similar to the "courtyard of the house of the high priest," and is therefore probably in the orchestra. The mocking should be Stage Left to give maximum dramatic extensivity to JESUS's walk towards the cross (Stage Right, offstage).

† These SOLDIERS bring in the purple himation, thorns, seat, cross beam, and any other necessary props.

The MAN WITH A PITCHER* is present. The SOLDIERS force him to carry the cross beam. *[JESUS stands up.]* The SOLDIERS lead/push them out of the performance area through the parodos Stage Right.

ACT XV, SCENE 4
(15:23–32)
The audience hears the sounds of crucifixion offstage Stage Right.† The audience hears the SOLDIERS offer drugged wine and JESUS's refusal (or this is reported). SOLDIERS return with JESUS's bloodstained white clothes. They gamble for the clothes. MULTITUDES, CHIEF PRIESTS, and SCRIBES gather to observe the crucifixion, and speak mockingly. The audience hears the other crucified men insult JESUS.

ACT XV, SCENE 5
(15:33–40a, 15:41b)
"Darkness." Actors onstage indicate "darkness" by stumbling, etc. Offstage, JESUS cries out *[in words that the audience "hears" as "Thou sun, thou sun, why have you forsaken me?"]*. A BYSTANDER says that JESUS is calling for Elijah. The actors change their behavior to indicate some return of light. *[The POISONER (a female OUTCAST) mixes poison into some wine.]* A BYSTANDER takes the wine and a sponge on a rod, and exits through the parodos Stage Right.

JESUS cries out and dies. With a loud sound, the curtains above the stage tear apart. Possibly there are lightning flashes or other visual effects. Possibly an earthquake occurs. The CENTURION says, "Truly this man was God's Son!" (15:39).

ACT XV, SCENE 6
(15:42–46)
Evening. JOSEPH enters from Stage Left, then goes to the upper stage to PILATE and SOLDIERS. JOSEPH introduces himself, and asks for the

---

* In the received text of GMark, PILATE does not wash his hands. But he does in Mt 27:24. Possibly in the performance of GMark PILATE did wash his hands.

† The crucifixion occurred *entirely* offstage. Why? There is no room *on the stage* behind the garden/tomb set for three crosses. Even if there was room, the many actors onstage would block the audience's view. Even if there was a view, the cross tops would be squashed into the far corner of the stage. And such an important scene would not be staged the parodos. I note that Mark is interested less in JESUS's experience than in the reaction of the actors onstage to his suffering and death.

body of JESUS. PILATE calls for the CENTURION, who is brought over; they converse. PILATE gives JOSEPH permission. JOSEPH goes downstairs, then offstage through the parodos Stage Right. He returns carrying a "corpse" wrapped in linen. A BYSTANDER rolls away the rock disc in front of the tomb. JOSEPH places the "corpse" inside. The audience sees JOHN THE BAPTIST's headless body. JOSEPH rolls the rock disc to close the tomb, then exits.

ACT XVI, SCENE 1
[The original ascension scene.
The entire stage and orchestra.
PILATE and SOLDIERS are on the upper level of the stage in front of the royal door. The HIGH PRIEST and COUNCIL (and PHARISEES?) are Stage Center. MULTITUDES are on the wing Stage Left. PETER and SLAVES OF THE HIGH PRIEST are in the orchestra. SATAN is present on his perch near the top of the scene building.

On the stage crane, an ANGEL in a white robe descends to the tomb. He rolls away the rock disc. The JESUS actor is alive inside the tomb, probably dressed in a white robe. (The wrapped, headless corpse of JOHN THE BAPTIST is still inside and visible to the audience.) The ANGEL leads (assists?) JESUS into the bucket of the stage crane (or a second stage crane). They ascend, then pause above the scene building. Only SATAN sees them.

The open tomb faces the audience and the actors in the orchestra.

PETER notices that the SLAVE OF THE HIGH PRIEST has a damaged ear. PETER points at it and exclaims, "His ear! It is bleeding! Look!"

The SLAVE OF THE HIGH PRIEST feels his ear, looks stricken. The other SLAVES are shocked. The HIGH PRIEST and COUNCIL look and see the blood. Horrified by having participated in a trial conducted by an impure high priest* and by his pollution of the Temple, they flee. So do the SLAVES OF THE HIGH PRIEST and some of the MULTITUDES.

PETER, pointing at the tomb, shouts excitedly, "Look, Jesus's body is not in the tomb!" He pauses. Then, "He has risen! Just as he said he would! (pause) Glory to Jesus the Son of God, who has risen and sits at his Father's right hand! Glory to God who is served by the true high priest in the Temple made without hands!"†

---

* I assume that THE SLAVE OF THE HIGH PRIEST was the HIGH PRIEST's personal representative, and therefore required to be, like the HIGH PRIEST, a perfect physical specimen. But I do not have any reference for this assumption.

† Obviously, Peter pronounces doctrine. I am just approximating it.

Appendix E - A Partial Reconstruction of the Play

Some of the MULTITUDES run towards the tomb to see for themselves. Some flee through the parodoi. Others are jubilant. For PILATE and (all?) SOLDIERS, this is just another day in the provinces: they exit quietly through the royal door and close it behind them. PETER leads the jubilant MULTITUDES out of the theater.* JESUS and the ANGEL continue their ascent and disappear into the heavens. SATAN reacts, then withdraws. The stage and orchestra are now empty.]

THE END

---

* PETER, who had been "rocky ground," is now "the rock of the church," as Matthew noticed ("on this rock I will build my church" [Mt 16:18]). As they exit, perhaps PETER and the MULTITUDES sing, emulating the exit song of a tragic chorus.

Notes

1. In particular, see Part Two, "A Life in Eclipse," in Earl Doherty, *The Jesus Puzzle* (Ottawa: Age of Reason Publications, 2005), 55–76. I should mention that although I think Doherty makes a persuasive case against a historical human Jesus, I do not accept much of Doherty's proposed history of the Jesus movement/early Christianity.

2. Mary Ann Beavis reviews the scholarship and concludes, "while the weight of the evidence tips the balance in favor of Roman (or at least Western) provenance, it is not compelling enough to assign Mark to Rome or any other location, although the fact that most early Christian communities were founded in cities makes an urban setting likely." *Mark*, Paideia: Commentaries on the New Testament (Grand Rapids, MI: Baker Academic, 2011), 12.

3. Latin words are used (5:9, 12:15, 12:42, 15:16, 15:39), and Mark uses Roman time ("the fourth watch of the night" 6:48; "the sixth hour" 15:33). Mark or an editor explained that "Golgotha" (15:22) means "place of a skull," which was meaningful to an audience in Rome: the Capitoline Hill was the Roman equivalent of the Jerusalem Temple Mount, and "Capitoline" comes from the *caput* (skull) supposedly found there when workmen were digging the foundations of the Temple of Jupiter.

4. See Timothy Michael Law and Charles Halton, eds., "Jew and Judean: A MARGINALIA Forum on Politics and Historiography in the Translation of Ancient Texts," *Marginalia Review of Books* (August 26, 2014), http://marginalia.lareviewofbooks.org/jew-judean-forum/.

5. "From the early third century, things begin to change dramatically among Christian writers. To the church fathers...we owe a new use of 'Ιουδαϊσμός and Iudaismus, now indeed to indicate the whole belief system and regimen of the Ioudaioi: a true '-ism,' abstracted from concrete conditions in a living state and portrayed with hostility." Steve Mason, "Jews, Judaeans, Judaizing, Judaism: Problems of Categorization in Ancient History," *Journal for the Study of Judaism* 38 (September 2007): 460, doi .org/10.1163/156851507X193108. Mason locates the changeover in the Latin-speaking Tertullian, in whose writing "every occurrence of Christianismus is paired with Iudaismus," 472. The only second-century instances of "Christianizing" cited by Mason (469–71) are in the Letters of Ignatius of Antioch and the Letters of Paul. Both collections have been heavily edited and contain material of various dates.

6. Beavis, *Mark*, 14–17.

7. Some "Biblical Performance Critics" have treated the Gospel as written for dramatic reading. For GMark, see Whitney Shiner, *Proclaiming the Gospel: First-Century Performance of Mark* (Harrisburg, PA: Trinity Press International, 2003). Dramatic readings are available on video, e.g., "Whitney Shiner Performs Mark 7:1-30," July 19, 2011, www.youtube.com/watch?v=kBxwqKozFpk.

8. Ernest W. Burch has proposed that the Gospel was a closet drama, "Tragic Action in the Second Gospel: A Study in the Narrative of Mark," *Journal of Religion* 11, no. 3 (July 1931): 346, www.jstor.org/stable/1196612. Gilbert Bilezikian says that Mark "adapt[ed] some of the formal features of tragedy to meet the exigencies of his

own story" about Jesus of Nazareth, *The Liberated Gospel: A Comparison of the Gospel of Mark and Greek Tragedy*. (1977; repr., Eugene, Oregon: Wipf & Stock, 2010), 29. But Bilezikian believes that the Gospel was written for oral delivery, 119. Stephen H. Smith writes in "A Divine Tragedy: Some Observations on the Dramatic Structure of Mark's Gospel," *Novum Testamentum* 37, no. 3 (July 1995): 209–31, www.jstor.org/stable/1561221, "Mark's Gospel is *not* a play, and was never written for performance by actors," 222. Instead, "he intended it to be presented to a specific audience in the manner of a closet drama," 229.

9. For a brief review of scholars' views on the performability of Seneca's plays, see Eric Dodson-Robinson, "ADIP 1—Performing the 'Unperformable' Extispicy Scene in Seneca's *Oedipus Rex*," *Didaskalia* 8 (2011) 27, 179–84, www.didaskalia.net/issues/8/27/.

10. *Encyclopaedia Britannica Online*, s.v. "Senecan tragedy," accessed May 24, 2018, www.britannica.com/art/Senecan-tragedy.

11. J. M. Robertson, *Pagan Christs: Studies in Comparative Hierology*, 2nd ed. (London: Watts, 1911). Compression, 197. Main argument, 197–201. The Passion "is an addition to a previously existing document," 201. Earlier scenes in the gospel story may have been presented dramatically, 203–4.

12. Livio C. Stecchini and Jan Sammer, introduction to *The Gospel According to Seneca* (N.p.: Monica Stecchini, Steven Stecchini, and Jan Sammer, 1996).

13. Michael Bryant, *The Drama of Calvary* (Bloomington, IN: AuthorHouse, 2011), 110.

14. Bryant, *Drama of Calvary*, 98–99.

15. Michael Turton suggests that GMark was performed on a stage: "the writer's vague geography and lack of geographical description and detail may reflect the expectation that those items would be presented visually." "Chapter 9: Excursus," *Michael A. Turton's Historical Commentary on the Gospel of Mark*, last modified December 31, 2004, www.michaelturton.com/Mark/GMark09.html.

16. Robert M. Price, *The Incredible Shrinking Son of Man* (Amherst, NY: Prometheus Books, 2003), 149.

17. Turton, "Chapter 1: Excursus: Chiastic Structures in Mark," *Historical Commentary*, www.michaelturton.com/Mark/GMark01.html, and an annotated version at "Chiastic Structure of Mark," *Historical Commentary*, www.michaelturton.com/Mark/GMark_chiasm.html. Turton's methodology is reviewed by Jacob Aliet, "Review of Michael Turton's *Historical Commentary on the Gospel of Mark*" (December 2005), *Historical Commentary*, www.michaelturton.com/Mark/GMark_review01.html. In a critique of Turton's website, Ben C. Smith points out that "chiasm" is not the right term for the structures Mark uses for his scenes. Ben C. Smith, "Michael Turton on Marcan chiasms," *Text Excavation* (blog), last modified May 23, 2007, accessed June 29, 2018, www.textexcavation.com/turtonchiasms.html. Turton agrees that a different term is needed, in Michael Turton, "Ben C. Smith on the Original Structure of Mark," *The Sword* (blog), October 22, 2005, http://michaelturton2.blogspot.com/2005/10/ben-c-smith-on-original-structure-of.html. I want to clarify here that Turton has arranged the received text of GMark in chiasms, noting where he found structural deficiencies that implied the hand of an editor. Although I often take issue with Turton's structures—the received text that he uses includes much nonoriginal material—I think his basic concept is sound.

18. Turton, "Chapter 3," *Historical Commentary*, www.michaelturton.com/Mark/GMark03.html. Here, as usual, the A' bracket begins the next scene.

19. "The writer's A brackets are typically geographical movements." Turton, "Chapter 11," *Historical Commentary*, www.michaelturton.com/Mark/GMark11.html.

20. "In Markan centers one bracket typically summarizes and comments on or explains the other, with one bracket often much longer." Turton, "Chapter 6: Excursus: Mark without Bethsaida," *Historical Commentary*, www.michaelturton.com/Mark/GMark06.html.

21. Howard Jacobson, "Two Studies on Ezekiel the Tragedian," *Greek, Roman, and Byzantine Studies* 22, no. 2 (May 1981): 167n2, http://grbs.library.duke.edu/article/view/6621.

22. Thomas D. Kohn, "The Tragedies of Ezekiel," *Greek, Roman, and Byzantine Studies* 43 (2002/3): 12. "This division into four plays fulfills a number of functions. First, it explains why Polyhistor and Clement refer to Ezekiel as the 'maker of [plural] tragedies.' Second, it divides the story of the Exodus into discrete actions. Third, it alleviates the objectionable violations of Time and Space....Fourth, it allows for the leisurely development of stories, characters, and ideas, as well as giving room for choral passages, none of which would fit comfortably in the rapid shifts across times and places required if all the fragments came from one play."

23. Jacobson, "Two Studies," 170–71.

24. Eric Csapo states, "If mime was the successor to comedy, pantomime was the natural successor to tragedy." Eric Csapo and William J. Slater, eds., *The Context of Ancient Drama* (Ann Arbor: University of Michigan Press, 1995), 372. Csapo notes there is "literary and textual evidence for performances of mime or pantomime which continue on both the public and private stage until at least the sixth century AD." *Actors and Icons of the Ancient Theater* (Chichester, UK: Wiley-Blackwell, 2014), 154.

25. "Petronian studies that touch upon the subject agree almost unanimously that Roman popular theatre, especially mime, and its tastes, techniques, and concerns have left many recognizable traces throughout the *Satyricon*." Gerald N. Sandy, "Scaenica Petroniana," *Transactions of the American Philological Association (1974-)* 104 (1974): 329, doi.org/10.2307/2936096.

26. R. Elaine Fantham, "Mime: The Missing Link in Roman Literary History," *Classical World* 82, no. 3 (January–February 1989): 155, doi.org/10.2307/4350348.

27. Stavros Tsitsiridis, "Greek Mime in the Roman Empire (P.Oxy. 413: *Chariton* and *Moicheutria*)," *Logeion* 1 (2011): 184, www.logeion.upatras.gr/node/145.

28. For time span, see note 24. Csapo, *Actors and Icons*, 178, writes that Ptolemy II Philadelphus (308/9–246 BCE) "kept mimes and pantomimes, long before we have evidence for their appearance in any public theater" and that "Antiochus II of Syria, rival and son-in-law of Ptolemy Philadelphus, seems to have shared his fondness for pantomimes and mimes."

29. "With the exception of literary mimes (Theocritus, Herodas) and some scattered references, the evidence for mimes is limited to a few fragments mainly from papyri (generally short and occasionally questionable) and even fewer archaeological testimonies." Tsitsiridis, "Greek Mime," 184. Sandy suggests that the overblown verses in *Satyricon* 55 were written by the mime writer Publilius Syrus, "Scaenica Petroniana," 337.

30. Tsitsiridis, "Greek Mime," 218.

31. Fantham, "Mime," 154.

32. Tsitsiridis, "Greek Mime," 220.

33. Sandy, "Scaenica Petroniana," 331, based on 331n4, which cites Cicero *Pro Caelio* 65, "This is rather the end of a farce [mime] than a regular comedy; in which, when a regular end cannot be invented for it some one escapes out of some one else's hands, the whistle sounds, and the curtain drops." I note that as Cicero contrasts mime with comedy, his remark refers to mime *plays* rather than the street-corner variety-show type of mime performance. I also note that Mark has retained the mime motif of "escapee" but changed the character into a *willing* follower of Jesus rather than an unwilling captive.

34. Bilezikian, *Liberated Gospel*, 115–16.

35. Bernard Grebanier, *Playwriting: How to Write for the Theater* (1961; repr., New York: Barnes & Noble, 1979), 85.

36. Grebanier, *Playwriting*, 86.

37. "*Since the persecution of the Saviour is intelligible only in the light of His work as teacher*, this part of the life of Christ was also added, while some authors of these plays went back to the Old Testament for symbolical scenes, which they added to the Passion Plays as 'prefigurations'; or the plays begin with the Creation, the sin of Adam and Eve, and the fall of the Angels" (emphasis added), *The Catholic Encyclopedia*, vol. 11, s.v. "Passion Plays," by Anselm Salzer (New York: Robert Appleton, 1911), www.newadvent.org/cathen/11531a.htm.

38. "Scholars have identified some of the problematical historical issues with the Sanhedrin Trial as (1) capital trials can only take place in daylight; (2) court proceedings may not take place on the sabbath, on festivals, and the corresponding days of rest; (3) a death sentence may not be passed on the first day of a trial, but can only in a new session on the following day; (4) blasphemy consists solely of speaking the name of YHWH, which Jesus does not do in Mark; and, (5) the regular place of assembly is a hall within the Temple (the writer is usually seen to imply that the Sanhedrin met at the house of the High Priest). The Temple gates are closed at night. Other scholars take issue with all these points, however." Turton, "Chapter 14," *Historical Commentary*, www.michaelturton.com/Mark/GMark14.html. I add that although some of the problematic issues went by too fast in performance for all audience members to grasp, they were salient to the Scripturally-educated reader of the polished text, e.g., the high priest tears his robe whereas Lv 10:6 and Lv 21:10 prohibit a high priest from tearing his clothes.

39. The story of Christians martyred after the Fire is found in Tacitus, *Annals* 15:44. Pliny the Younger wrote from Asia in the 110s to the Emperor Trajan asking how to deal with Christians there, as Pliny did not know of any precedents (Pliny, *Letters* 10.96). Both Pliny and Trajan had been senators in Rome at a time when the Fire was still being commemorated. If Christians had been martyred after the fire, Pliny would have already been familiar with Christians and Christian beliefs.

40. Jérôme Carcopino discusses the fad for public recitations in *Daily Life in Ancient Rome: The People and the City at the Height of the Empire*, ed. Henry T. Rowell, trans. E. O. Lorimer (New Haven: Yale University Press, 1940), 195–201.

41. The convention is mentioned by the second-century scholar and rhetorician, Julius Pollux (*Onomasticon* 4.126.15), who uses "left" and "right" from the actors' standpoint. Kelley Rees, "The Significance of the Parodoi in the Greek Theater," *American Journal of Philology* 32:4 (1911): 379, doi:10.2307/288639.

42. Rees, "Significance," 380.

43. Rees, "Significance," 402. "It cannot be doubted that in the stereotyped scene of the New Comedy the side-entrances had come to have the conventional significance which Pollux is, apparently, endeavoring to describe."

44. Stecchini and Sammer get the details of the set from Jn 19:41. "Now there was a garden in the place where he was crucified, and in the garden there was a new tomb in which no one had ever been laid" (Jn 19:41 NRSV). "A Tomb Cut in the Rock," *Gospel According to Seneca*. I cannot say why the author of GJohn placed the tomb in a garden (the synoptic authors do not). Perhaps the author of GJohn was visualizing the entombment of Jesus enacted on a stage, and assumed that a tomb would be outside the city and therefore on the side of the stage that represented the "country."

45. "The skene was now typically two stories high. Projecting out from its first story, at about 10 feet (3 metres) above the orchestra, was the raised stage, supported by a row of columns along its front edge. Backgrounds for the raised stage were provided by the second story of the skene, which seems to have had a number of large openings that could be used as entrances." *Encyclopaedia Britannica Online*, s.v. "Theatre Design," by Franklin J. Hildy, last modified November 28, 2018, www.britannica.com/art/theatre-design/History.

46. *Encyclopaedia Britannica Online*, s.v. "Theatre of Dionysus," accessed May 15, 2018, www.britannica.com/topic/Theatre-of-Dionysus.

47. The four tombs with disc-shaped stone doors that have been discovered belonged to wealthy or royal families, according to Megan Sauter, "How Was Jesus' Tomb Sealed?" *Bible History Daily* (March 23, 2018), www.biblicalarchaeology.org/daily/biblical-sites-places/jerusalem/how-was-jesus-tomb-sealed/. The article includes a photograph of a disc door, captioned, "Measuring 4.5-feet tall, the disk-shaped stone at the so-called Tomb of Herod's Family could be rolled to cover the entryway of the tomb or rolled back into a niche to open it, thereby permitting new burials to be added to the family tomb."

48. Leonhard Schmitz, "*Theatrum*," in William Smith, *A Dictionary of Greek and Roman Antiquities* (London: John Murray, 1875), 1122, http://penelope.uchicago.edu/Thayer/E/Roman/Texts/secondary/SMIGRA*/Theatrum.html.

49. "Mark 1-6 contains a programmatic statement of Jesus' claim to a high priestly identity as the 'holy one of God' (1.24), with a high priestly contagious holiness (1.40-45; 5.25-34; 5.35-43), freedom to forgive sins (2.1-12) and the embodiment of divine presence in a Galilean cornfield (2.23-28). As true high priest he makes divine presence 'draw near' to God's people (1.15), where before they had to 'draw near' to the Jerusalem temple." Crispin H. T. Fletcher-Louis, "Jesus as the High Priestly Messiah," pt 2, Abstract, *Journal for the Study of the Historical Jesus* 5, no. 1 (2007), doi.org/10.1177/1476869006074936.

50. Emil G. Hirsch et al., "Demonology," *The Jewish Encyclopedia* vol. 4 (New York: Funk & Wagnalls, 1903), 517, www.jewishencyclopedia.com/articles/5085-demonology. I note that in the play (Mk 3:22–23), Satan is conflated with Beelzebul, originally a Philistine god that some Judeans saw as prince of demons.

51. In the first century, in the great theaters of Rome, "a scented saffron spray cooled the air." Richard C. Beacham, *Spectacle Entertainments of Early Imperial Rome* (New Haven: Yale University Press, 1999), 128. When Nero returned to Rome from

his "actor's triumph" in (approximately) January 68, the streets of Rome were sprinkled with perfume (Suetonius, *Nero* 25.2). Scent was used at elite dinners: the dining rooms of Nero's palace had pipes in the ceiling to sprinkle the guests with perfumes (*Nero* 31.2).

52. Bryant, *Drama of Calvary*, 85–86.

53. Bryant, *Drama of Calvary*, 83–86. He adds, "Κυρηναιος is similar to *aquarinus*, especially if prefixed with the definite article, ό," 83. "The recorded form of this word lacks the -*n*-, but the form with -*n*- is possible: I favour it, partly because the form without *n* might be misinterpreted as the Aquarius of Greek mythology, and because it gives a long -*i*- as well as the *n*. Both forms would fit into a pentameter, and Mark's skill at disguising the originals could produce his Greek form from either," 83n42.

54. Bryant, *Drama of Calvary*, 86.

55. Bryant, *Drama of Calvary*, 84.

56. Bryant, *Drama of Calvary*. Mary a dealer, 86. Provided the cyanide, 95. I note that cyanide is made from bitter almonds, a variety of the Mediterranean native almond, *Prunus dulcis*, and the pits of apricots and peaches. Their toxic properties must have already been well-known.

57. John W. Crossan, *The Birth of Christianity: Discovering What Happened in the Years Immediately After the Execution of Jesus* (San Francisco: HarperSanFrancisco, 1998), 554.

58. Shiner, *Proclaiming the Gospel*, 96–97. He adds, "It is easy to play the disciples for comic effect from Chapter 4 through the recognition scene in Chapter 8," 96.

59. Grebanier, *Playwriting*, 190.

60. Grebanier, *Playwriting*, 158.

61. *Merriam-Webster*, s.v. "dramaturgy," accessed August 4, 2018, www.merriam-webster.com/dictionary/dramaturgy.

62. Turton, "Chapter 6," *Historical Commentary*.

63. Turton writes of this passage, "Note the phrase 'and as many as touched it were made well.' In Mark such phrases, where immediately prior action is summarized and commented on, typically represent the second half of a center bracket, not the conclusion of a B′ bracket. It seems that a verse has been removed to make room for the interpolation." "Chapter 6," *Historical Commentary*.

64. Turton, "Chapter 8," *Historical Commentary*, www.michaelturton.com/Mark/GMark08.html.

65. Turton says, "The center is so wordy that it strikes me as unMarkan. Markan centers typically balance a prolix comment with a pithy one to produce a satisfying rhythmic effect." "Chapter 7," *Historical Commentary*, www.michaelturton.com/Mark/GMark07.html.

66. Turton, "Chapter 8," *Historical Commentary*. However, Turton notes that other scholars have mentioned the scene's "high concentration of unique vocabulary" and its parallel structure to the next scene, the Recognition. I note that an editor of a play or novel can make small changes to dialogue without affecting the action of a scene. Here, the remark about people who look like trees may not be original.

67. M. R. Niehoff, "Did the *Timaeus* create a textual community?" *Greek, Roman, and Byzantine Studies* 47, no. 2 (2007): 177. Niehoff reaches this conclusion because five of Plutarch's "Platonic Questions" in the *Table-talk* deal with the *Timaeus* (1012–1013).

68. The universe is "the product of rational, purposive, and beneficent agency. It is the handiwork of a divine Craftsman…who, imitating an unchanging and eternal model,

imposes mathematical order on a preexistent chaos to generate the ordered universe." Donald Zeyl, "Plato's *Timaeus*," *The Stanford Encyclopedia of Philosophy*, ed. Edward N. Zalta, (Spring 2014 ed.), http://plato.stanford.edu/archives/spr2014/entries/plato-timaeus.

69. Turton, "Chapter 10," *Historical Commentary*, www.michaelturton.com/Mark/GMark10.html.

70. For why the Olivet Discourse is not an apocalypse, see Bruce J. Malina, "Exegetical Eschatology, the Peasant Present and the Final Discourse Genre: The Case of Mark 13," *Biblical Theology Bulletin* 32 (May 2002): 49–59, doi.org/10.1177/014610790203200204.

71. Grebanier, *Playwriting*, 256.

72. "Jesus' forecast of the destruction of Jerusalem in Mark 13 belongs to the category of final words rooted in that type of Altered State of Consciousness that befalls a person aware of impending death." Malina, "Exegetical Eschatology," 57. Malina provides some famous "final words" from antiquity, 54.

73. Raymond E. Brown writes that Codex Bobiensis of North Africa (fourth or fifth century) has in Mark 15:34–36 "Jesus praying 'Heli, Helianm' [*sic*] (= Greek Ēli, Ēli: '*My God*'), and the bystanders referring to 'Helion...Helias' (= Greek *Ēlian...Ēlias:* 'Elijah'). Was there a moment in the Western Latin interpretation of Jesus' prayer that he was thought to have addressed a reproach to the sun for having forsaken him or reviled him? That would make perfect sense immediately following the verse about darkness having covered the whole earth!" *The Death of the Messiah*, vol. 2 (New York: Doubleday, 1994), 1055–56.

74. "Apollo's appearance at the end brings the play to the most spectacular climax in all Greek tragedy. Standing on a platform, the god addresses Orestes on the roof and Menelaos onstage. At ground level, in the orchestra, the chorus watches, silent till it speaks the closing formula. All four available regions of space are occupied: the ground, the stage, the roof, the sky." John Peck and Frank Nisetich, trans., *Euripides: Orestes* (New York: Oxford University Press, 1995), 16.

75. Schmitz, "*Theatrum*," 1122.

76. Grebanier, *Playwriting*, 51.

77. The Church Father Augustine explains the miracle, "By the five loaves are understood the five books of Moses," "Tractate 24 (John 6:1–14)," section 5, trans. John Gibb and James Inness, *Nicene and Post-Nicene Fathers*, 1st ser., vol. 7, ed. Philip Schaff (Buffalo, NY: Christian Literature Publishing, 1888; Peabody, MA: Hendrickson Publishers, 1995). Arguably, the theme of bread in GMark implies the similes of "bread = Scripture" and "nourishment = exegesis."

78. "In Talmudic sayings the Aramaic noun denoting carpenter or craftsman (*naggar*) stands for a 'scholar' or a 'learned man.'" Géza Vermes, *Jesus the Jew: A Historian's Reading of the Gospels* (Minneapolis: Fortress, 1981), 22. *Tektōn* is the Greek equivalent of *naggar*.

79. Almost all the men with Latin names were members of one synagogue, the Synagogue of Elaias. Jona Lendering, "Jewish Rome," Livius.org (website), last modified November 23, 2018, www.livius.org/articles/concept/diaspora/jewish-rome/.

80. "Modern research often proposes as the author an unknown Hellenistic Jewish Christian, possibly in Syria, and perhaps shortly after the year 70." "Introduction—Mark," *The New American Bible, Revised Edition (NABRE)* (Washington, DC: United States Conference of Catholic Bishops, 2011), www.usccb.org/bible/mark/0.

81. "Because upper-class women participated in the Roman status structure and could manage their own wealth (including freeing slaves), they could serve as both public and personal patrons. Inscriptions throughout Italy and the provinces commemorate women as public patrons." Barbara F. McManus, "Social Class and Public Display," VRoma (website), January 2009, www.vroma.org/~bmcmanus/socialclass.html.

82. "An eminent senator, a son of Titus' sister, and hence Domitian's nephew, is said to have adopted Judaism; even traces of the name 'Clemens' are visible in the account (Giṭ. 56b)." Richard Gottheil and Samuel Krauss, "Flavia Domitilla," *The Jewish Encyclopedia*, vol. 5 (New York: Funk & Wagnalls, 1903), 406, www.jewishencyclopedia.com/articles/5269-domitilla-flavia. The term "Judaism" is from the point of view of the Talmud writer, not necessarily from the point of view of Clemens.

83. Benjamin Jowett, "Coena," in Smith, *Dictionary*, 308, http://penelope.uchicago.edu/Thayer/E/Roman/Texts/secondary/SMIGRA*/Coena.html. Remember that the ancients did not observe Daylight Savings Time.

84. Two examples from the first century are the rose dinner the emperor Nero required his friend to host (Suetonius, *Nero* 27) and the all-black dinner hosted by the Emperor Domitian for senators and equestrians (Cassius Dio, *Roman History* 67.9). John H. D'Arms adds two examples where elite guests were commandeered to provide entertainment: Octavian hosted a dinner where the guests played the twelve gods and performed under the direction of a *choragos*, and Nero hosted a dinner where the guests were required to wear special headgear. "Performing Culture: Roman Spectacle and the Banquets of the Powerful," *Studies in the History of Art* 56 (1999): 306, www.jstor.org/stable/42622247. Obviously at least the first three of these dinners required a great deal of planning and stage management.

85. New Comedy "is so bound up with symposia that you could more easily regulate the drinking without wine than without Menander" (Plutarch, *Symposiacs* 7.8.3).

86. Csapo, *Actors and Icons*, 182.

87. At Hadrian's Villa, the north (Greek) theater's large size and distance from the residential area (with its dining areas) make it "a likely candidate for staff and all-Villa entertainment." William L. Macdonald and John A. Pinto, *Hadrian's Villa and Its Legacy* (New Haven: Yale University Press, 1995), 185.

88. Re Mk 10:26, Turton points out, "In many places in the OT wealth and material goods are considered a sign of God's favor (Job 1:10; Psalm 128:1-2; Isaiah 3:10). That is why the disciples are so astonished that the wealthy cannot enter the Kingdom." "Chapter 10," *Historical Commentary*.

89. "Women, slaves, and minors were not required to pay the tax, though their money was accepted if they offered it." Wilhelm Bacher and Jacob Zallel Lauterbach, "Sheḳalim," *The Jewish Encyclopedia*, vol. 11 (New York: Funk & Wagnalls, 1905), 256, www.jewishencyclopedia.com/articles/13534-shekalim.

90. Pat Southern, *Domitian: Tragic Tyrant* (London: Routledge, 1997), 116.

91. Csapo, *Actors and Icons*, 189.

92. Southern, *Domitian*, 123. I suggest that Domitian's mistrust hid insecurity, for which he overcompensated by demanding (or accepting) the titles *Dominus et Deus* ("Lord and God").

93. "Because there was extensive similarity between the situation of the Hellenized Jews of New Testament times and that of nineteenth-century emancipated Jews, we can expect something analogous to the Reform movement to have attracted the Hellenized Jews." Rodney Stark, *The Rise of Christianity: A Sociologist Reconsiders History* (Princeton: Princeton University Press, 1996), 57. "Christianity offered twice as much cultural continuity to the Hellenized Jews as to Gentiles. If we examine the marginality of the Hellenized Jews, torn between two cultures, we may note how Christianity offered to retain much of the religious content of *both* cultures and to resolve the contradictions between them." Stark, *Rise of Christianity*, 59.

94. Rodolfo Lanciani, *Pagan and Christian Rome* (Boston: Houghton, Mifflin, 1892), 315–16, http://penelope.uchicago.edu/Thayer/E/Gazetteer/Places/Europe/Italy/Lazio/Roma/Rome/_Texts/Lanciani/LANPAC/7*.html. I have not found any other descriptions in English of the decorations of the vestibule of the Crypt of the Flavians.

95. "In the first century they seem to be subjects taken from nature, such as were common in contemporary pagan art, and used largely for decorative purposes. The list includes dolphins, vine and flower designs, cupids, peacocks and other birds, animal forms, a sea monster, ideal forms, landscape genre pictures, a fishing scene, and various decorative designs. Regarding these first century pictures it must be remembered that they are found exclusively in the catacomb of Domitilla in the hypogeum of the Flavian family, and in a room known as the 'oldest cubiculum,' and in the catacomb of Priscilla in the hypogeum of the well known Acilian family. So they are not widely distributed, and exist in only one or two each.... There are...several pictures from Biblical sources in this collection, Daniel between the Lions, Noah, and the Good Shepherd. Cupid is also represented as the Good Shepherd, in the type of the Pasturing Shepherd." Clark D. Lamberton, "The Development of Christian Symbolism as Illustrated in Roman Catacomb Painting," *American Journal of Archaeology* 15, no. 4 (October–December, 1911): 510–11, doi.org/10.2307/497187. Lamberton is using Joseph Wilpert's compendium *Le pitture delle catacombe romane* (Rome: Desclée, Lefebvre, 1903). Wilpert's chronology "is founded on scientific criteria, such as the quality and number of layers of stucco, the technical execution of the paintings," etc., not the content of the pictures. Lamberton, "Development," 510.

96. Lamberton's list of the second-century catacomb decorations contains 20 instances of themes from Scripture (Moses Striking the Rock, Babylonian Children, Jonah, Susannah, Sacrifice of Isaac, Daniel, Noah) and 16 instances from the four-gospel narrative (Baskets of Bread, Annunciation, Raising of Lazarus, Paralytic Healed, Multiplication of Loaves, Virgin and Child, Woman of Samaria, Woman with Issue of Blood). There are 96 instances of nonspecific decorative themes or of Jesus movement themes (e.g., fish, Christ as Judge) that do not refer to the four-gospel story. Lamberton, "Development," 518–20.

97. Matthias Klinghardt, "The Marcionite Gospel and the Synoptic Problem: A New Suggestion," *Novum Testamentum* 50, no. 1 (2008): 1–27, www.jstor.org/stable/25442581.

98. In *First Apology* 46, Justin Martyr denies that Jesus was a human being, "But lest some should, without reason, and for the perversion of what we teach, maintain that we say that Christ was born one hundred and fifty years ago under Cyrenius, and subsequently, in the time of Pontius Pilate, taught what we say He taught; and should cry out against us as

though all men who were born before Him were irresponsible—let us anticipate and solve the difficulty." Justin instead affirms a divine intermediary, like that of Philo, "We have been taught that Christ is the first-born of God, and we have declared above that He is the Word." We can see evolution in the Jesus movement towards orthodoxy: Justin knows the canonical gospel story but does not see Jesus as a human being.

99. David Trobisch presents a brief version of his argument that Polycarp was the publisher of the New Testament in "Who Published the New Testament?" *Free Inquiry* 28, no. 1 (December 2007/January 2008): 30–33.

100. "Hans von Campenhausen noticed the strong similarity between the Pastorals and the second-century epistle of Polycarp, thereby nominating Polycarp author of the Pastorals. From here, Stephan Hermann Huller (*Against Polycarp: In Defense of "Marcion"*) has connected the dots, suggesting there is no better candidate than Polycarp as redactor of Ur-Lukas and author of Acts. It would certainly fit our information that Polycarp had publicly denounced Marcion as the first-born of Satan. He was someone with opportunity and motive to undo Marcion's work by co-opting his scriptures for the benefit of Catholicism." Robert M. Price, *The Pre-Nicene New Testament* (Salt Lake City: Signature Books, 2006), 498.

101. Walter Bauer, "Edessa," trans. John E. Steely and Robert A. Kraft, in *Orthodoxy and Heresy in Earliest Christianity* (2nd ed. Tübingen: J. C. B. Mohr, 1934, 1964), 35 (page number of the electronic English edition), http://web.archive.org/web/20101216204534/http://jewishchristianlit.com/Resources/Bauer/bauer01.htm. See Bibliography for additional details of publication.

102. Joseph Woods, "The Church of Alexandria." *The Catholic Encyclopedia*, vol. 1 (New York: Robert Appleton Company, 1907), www.newadvent.org/cathen/01300b.htm. Walter Bauer says, "We first catch sight of something like 'ecclesiastical' Christianity in Demetrius, the bishop of Alexandria from 189 to 231. Certainly there had already been orthodox believers there prior to that time, and their community possessed a leader. But we can see how small their number must have been from the fact that when Demetrius assumed his office he was the *only* Egyptian 'bishop'" (italics in original). "Egypt," *Orthodoxy and Heresy*, 53 (page number of the electronic English version), http://web.archive.org/web/20101216204724/http://jewishchristianlit.com/Resources/Bauer/bauer02.htm. See Bibliography for additional details of publication.

103. "Full weight must be given to the fact, that the Alexandrian fathers Clement and Origen make no reference to any sojourn or work of the evangelist [Mark] in the metropolis. Their silence, it is said, cannot but throw suspicion on a tradition about which they may reasonably be expected to have some knowledge. This argument from silence, is, however, not quite conclusive, as St. Mark was a relatively obscure person in the early Church." L. W. Barnard, "St. Mark and Alexandria," *The Harvard Theological Review* 57, no. 2 (April 1964): 146, www.jstor.org/stable/1508784. I note that Clement of Alexandria adopted the name "Titus Flavius Clemens," which shows that Flavia's husband was still remembered and respected as an early member of the orthodox sect.

104. Bauer, "Egypt," *Orthodoxy and Heresy*, 60 (page number in English translation).

105. Stecchini and Sammer, "From Tragedy to Gospel," *Gospel According to Seneca*.

106. Stecchini and Sammer, "The Verdict," *Gospel According to Seneca*.

107. Stecchini and Sammer, "The Arrival of the Chorus," *Gospel According to Seneca*. I note that torches are useful in the next scene, the trial in the house of the high priest, to indicate that that scene too occurs at night.

108. Sammer writes, "This manuscript came to my attention only after [Stecchini's] death [in September 1979], through a mutual friend. Intrigued, I got in touch with his widow, and after some discussions she agreed that I should go through his papers and try to assemble the manuscript into a book. The manuscript, actually stacks of loose papers, was very fragmentary, with many overlapping drafts, and basically missing the earlier chapters. I suspect some parts were written but lost before I got to them. The division into acts was also not finalized. I found that two acts were merged into one and the first act was missing. For the above-stated reasons co-authorship is not the traditional type.… The only major deviation from his scheme was the division into acts. The missing chapters are only partially written. I think they are necessary to support the thesis of the book." Jan Sammer, email to Danila Oder, February 12, 2018. Stecchini was a professor of ancient history; he specialized in the history of science; ancient weights and measures; and the history of cartography in antiquity.

109. Stecchini and Sammer, "From Tragedy to Gospel," *Gospel According to Seneca*.

110. "I think the identification of Seneca as the author is too specific and unnecessary for establishing the general thesis." Jan Sammer, email to Danila Oder, February 12, 2018.

111. Stecchini and Sammer, "Prologue," *Gospel According to Seneca*.

112. Stecchini and Sammer, "From Tragedy to Gospel," *Gospel According to Seneca*.

113. Dennis E. Smith and Joseph B. Tyson, eds., *Acts and Christian Beginnings: The Acts Seminar Report* (Salem, OR: Polebridge Press, 2013), 3.

114. "An increasing number of scholars situate the Gospel of Mark within the Pauline sphere of influence." Michael Kok, "Does Mark Narrate the Pauline Kerygma of 'Christ Crucified'? Challenging an Emerging Consensus on Mark as a Pauline Gospel," Abstract, *Journal for the Study of the New Testament* 37, no. 2 (November 25, 2014), doi.org/10.1177/0142064X14558021.

115. The letters of Paul are "collections of fragments and pericopae contributed and fabricated by authors and communities of very different theological leanings." Robert M. Price, *The Amazing Colossal Apostle: The Search for the Historical Paul* (Salt Lake City: Signature Books, 2012), viii.

116. I used the drawing of the ground plan of the Greek theater at Hadrian's Villa. The drawing is Figure 1 in Rafael Hidalgo Prieto, "El Teatro Greco y su entorno (campañas 2003–2010)," *Lazio e Sabina 8* (Atti del Convegno. Roma 30–31 marzo, 1 aprile 2011) (2012): 152.

117. The birds were probably attached to strings and retrieved by stagehands. "At the procession of the Ptolemaieia [spectators] caught the pigeons, ring-doves, and turtle-doves which flew forth from a cart and were equipped with nooses tied to their feet so that they could be easily caught by the spectators." Jens Koehler, "Pompai. Untersuchungen zur hellenistischen Festkultur," (Ph.D. diss., Frankfurt: Peter Lang, 1996): 150, cited in Angelos Chaniotis, "Theatricality beyond the Theater. Staging Public Life in the Hellenistic World," *Pallas* 47 (1997): 247, www.jstor.org/stable/43685038.

Selected Bibliography

These works directly pertain to my assumptions about Mark; Mark's social, religious, and artistic contexts; or the proposals presented in this book.

Bacon, Benjamin W. *Is Mark a Roman Gospel?* Cambridge, MA: Harvard University Press, 1919. archive.org/details/ismarkromangospe07baco.

Bauer, Walter. *Orthodoxy and Heresy in Earliest Christianity.* 2nd ed. Tübingen: J. C. B. Mohr, 1934, 1964. English translation edited and supplemented by Robert A. Kraft and Gerhard Kroedel with a team from the Philadelphia Seminar on Christian Origins. Philadelphia: Fortress Press, 1971. Updated electronic English edition by Robert A. Kraft, February 25, 1991. http://web.archive.org/web/20110109095956/http://jewishchristianlit.com:80/Resources/Bauer/.

Beacham, Richard C. *The Roman Theatre and Its Audience.* Cambridge, MA: Harvard University Press, 1992.

Beacham, Richard C. *Spectacle Entertainments of Early Imperial Rome.* New Haven: Yale University Press, 2011.

Beare, W. *The Roman Stage.* Cambridge, MA: Harvard University Press, 1951.

Beavis, Mary Ann. *Mark.* Paideia Commentaries on the New Testament. Grand Rapids, MI: Baker Academic Press, 2011.

Bilezikian, Gilbert. *The Liberated Gospel: A Comparison of the Gospel of Mark and Greek Tragedy.* Eugene, OR: Wipf & Stock, 2010. First published 1977 by Baker Books.

Bonner, Stanley F. *Education in Ancient Rome: From the Elder Cato to the Younger Pliny.* Berkeley: University of California Press, 1977.

Boomershine, Thomas E. "Audience Address and Purpose in the Performance of Mark." In *Mark as Story: Retrospect and Prospect*, edited by Kelly R. Iverson and Christopher W. Skinner, 115–42. Atlanta: Society of Biblical Literature, 2011.

Brant, Jo-Ann A. *Dialogue and Drama: Elements of Greek Tragedy in the Fourth Gospel.* Peabody, MA: Hendrickson Publishers, 2004.

Brodie, Thomas L. *The Crucial Bridge: The Elijah-Elisha Narrative as an Interpretive Synthesis of Genesis-Kings and a Literary Model for the Gospels.* Collegeville, MN: Liturgical Press, 2000.

Bryant, Michael. *The Drama of Calvary*. Bloomington, IN: AuthorHouse, 2011. Bryant's biography on the book cover is: "Michael Bryant graduated in ancient languages in 1962, in the University of Durham. He also holds the Postgraduate Diploma in Theology. He held a succession of posts in parishes, cathedrals and schools of the Church of England. In retirement he has translated the Psalms into modern and inclusive language, and produced contemporary translations of many Latin hymns."

Burch, Ernest W. "Tragic Action in the Second Gospel: A Study in the Narrative of Mark." *Journal of Religion* 11, no. 3 (July 1931): 346–58. www.jstor.org/stable/1196612.

Carcopino, Jérôme. *Daily Life in Ancient Rome: The People and the City at the Height of the Empire*. Edited by Henry T. Rowell. Translated by E. O. Lorimer. New Haven: Yale University Press, 1940.

Carrier, Richard C. *Proving History: Bayes's Theorem and the Quest for the Historical Jesus*. Amherst, NY: Prometheus Books, 2012.

Cassels, Walter R. *The Gospel According to Peter: A Study*. London: Longmans, Green, 1894.

Chaniotis, Angelos. "Theatricality beyond the Theater. Staging Public Life in the Hellenistic World." *Pallas*, no. 47 (1997): 219–59. www.jstor.org/stable/43685038.

Chickering, Edward Conner. *An Introduction to* Octavia Praetexta. Jamaica, NY: Marion Press, 1910. www.archive.org/details/cu31924026554257.

Cohen, Shaye J. D. *The Beginnings of Jewishness: Boundaries, Varieties, Uncertainties*. Berkeley: University of California Press, 1999.

Cromhout, Markus. "Were the Galileans 'Religious Jews' or 'Ethnic Judeans'?" *HTS Theological Studies* 64, no. 3 (2008): 1279–97. doi.org/10.4102/hts.v64i3.68.

Crossan, John Dominic. *The Cross That Spoke: The Origins of the Passion Narrative*. San Francisco: Harper & Row, 1988.

Csapo, Eric. *Actors and Icons of the Ancient Theater*. Chichester, UK: Wiley-Blackwell, 2014.

Csapo, Eric, and William J. Slater, eds. *The Context of Ancient Drama*. Ann Arbor: University of Michigan Press, 1995.

D'Arms, John H. "Performing Culture: Roman Spectacle and the Banquets of the Powerful." *Studies in the History of Art* 56 (1999): 300–319. www.jstor.org/stable/42622247.

Doherty, Earl. *The Jesus Puzzle*. Ottawa: Age of Reason Publications, 2005.

Doherty, Earl. Review of *Jesus—One Hundred Years Before Christ: A Study in Creative Mythology*, by Alvar Ellegård. Jesus Puzzle (website). Accessed December 3, 2018. www.jesuspuzzle.com/jesuspuzzle/BkrvEll.htm.

Doherty, Earl. "Supplementary Articles: Adding Pieces to the Jesus Puzzle." Jesus Puzzle (website). Accessed December 3, 2018. www.jesuspuzzle.com/jesuspuzzle/mainarticles-1.html#suppl.

Domeris, W. R. "The Johannine Drama." *Journal of Theology for Southern Africa* 42 (March 1983): 29–35.

Downing, F. Gerald. "Cosmic Eschatology in the First Century: 'Pagan', Jewish and Christian." *L'Antiquité Classique* 64, no. 1 (1995): 99–109. www.persee.fr/doc/antiq_0770-2817_1995_num_64_1_1219.

Ellegård, Alvar. *Jesus—One Hundred Years Before Christ: A Study in Creative Mythology.* Woodstock, NY: Overlook Press, 1999.

Fantham, R. Elaine. "Mime: The Missing Link in Roman Literary History." *Classical World* 82, no. 3 (1989): 153–63. doi.org/10.2307/4350348.

Flickinger, Roy C. *The Greek Theater and Its Drama.* Chicago: University of Chicago Press, 1918. https://archive.org/details/greektheaterand04flicgoog.

Godfrey, Neil, and Tim Widowfield, eds. *Vridar* (blog). http://vridar.org/.

Grebanier, Bernard. *Playwriting: How to Write for the Theater.* New York: Barnes & Noble Books, 1979. First published 1961 by Harper & Row.

Hadas, Moses. *Hellenistic Culture: Fusion and Diffusion.* New York: Columbia University Press, 1959.

Herington, C. J. "*Octavia Praetexta:* A Survey." *Classical Quarterly* 11, no. 1 (1961): 18–30. www.jstor.org/stable/637743.

Hoxby, Blair. "The Baroque Tragedy of the Roman Jesuits: Flavia and Beyond," in *Politics and Aesthetics in European Baroque and Classicist Tragedy*, edited by Jan Bloemendal and Nigel Smith, 182–217. Leiden: Brill, 2016. doi.org/10.1163/9789004323421_008.

Jacobson, Howard. "Two Studies on Ezekiel the Tragedian." *Greek, Roman and Byzantine Studies* 22, no. 2 (1981): 167–78. http://grbs.library.duke.edu/article/view/6621.

Jensen, Robin M. "Dining in Heaven." *Bible Review* 14, no. 5 (October 1998): 32. https://members.bib-arch.org/bible-review/14/5/17.

Jones, Christopher P. "Dinner Theater." In *Dining in a Classical Context*, edited by William J. Slater, 185–98. Ann Arbor: University of Michigan Press, 1991.

La Piana, George. "The Jews in Rome; Jewish Districts; Synagogues and Cemeteries." Section 6 in "Foreign Groups in Rome during the First Centuries of the Empire." *Harvard Theological Review* 20, no. 4 (October 1927): 341–71. www.jstor.org/stable/1507743.

Lamberton, Clark D. "The Development of Christian Symbolism as Illustrated in Roman Catacomb Painting." *American Journal of Archaeology* 15, no. 4 (October–December, 1911): 507–22. doi.org/10.2307/497187.

Leprohon, Ronald J. "Ritual Drama in Ancient Egypt." In *The Origins of Theater in Ancient Greece and Beyond: From Ritual to Drama,* edited by Eric Csapo and Margaret C. Miller, 259–92. Cambridge: Cambridge University Press, 2007.

MacDonald, Dennis Ronald. *The Homeric Epics and the Gospel of Mark.* New Haven: Yale University Press, 2000.

Malina, Bruce J. "Exegetical Eschatology, the Peasant Present and the Final Discourse Genre: The Case of Mark 13." *Biblical Theology Bulletin* 32, no. 2 (May 2002): 49–59. doi.org/10.1177/014610790203200204.

Mason, Steve. *A History of the Jewish War (AD 66–74).* New York: Cambridge University Press, 2016.

Mason, Steve. "Jews, Judaeans, Judaizing, Judaism: Problems of Categorization in Ancient History." *Journal for the Study of Judaism* 38, no. 4 (September 2007): 457–512. doi.org/10.1163/156851507X193108.

Mason, Steve. *Josephus and the New Testament.* 2nd ed. Peabody, MA: Hendrickson Publishers, 2003.

Platts, Hannah. "Keeping Up with the Joneses: Competitive Display within the Roman Villa Landscape, 100BC–AD200." In *Competition in the Ancient World*, edited by Nick Fisher and Hans van Wees, 239–77. Swansea: Classical Press of Wales, 2010. www.academia.edu/3408034/Keeping_up_with_the_Joneses_Competitive_Display_within_the_Roman_Villa_Landscape_100BC-AD200.

Price, Robert M. *The Amazing Colossal Apostle: The Search for the Historical Paul.* Salt Lake City: Signature Books, 2012.

Price, Robert M. "Christianity, Diaspora Judaism, and Roman Crisis." Robert M. Price's website. 2007. www.robertmprice.mindvendor.com/art_diaspora.htm.

Price, Robert M. *The Pre-Nicene New Testament.* Salt Lake City: Signature Books, 2006.

Rees, Kelley. "The Significance of the Parodoi in the Greek Theater." *The American Journal of Philology* 32, no. 4 (1911): 377–402. doi:10.2307/288639.

Rist, Martin. "Caesar or God (Mark 12:13–17)? A Study in 'Formgeschichte.'" *Journal of Religion* 16, no. 3 (July 1936): 317–31. www.jstor.org/stable/1196449.

Robertson, J. M. *The Jesus Problem: A Restatement of the Myth Theory.* London: Watts, 1917.

Robertson, J. M. *Pagan Christs: Studies in Comparative Hierology.* London: Watts, 1911.

Rutgers, Leonard Victor. "Roman Policy towards the Jews: Expulsions from the City of Rome during the First Century C.E." *Classical Antiquity* 13, no. 1 (April 1994): 56–74. doi.org/10.2307/25011005.
Sandy, Gerald N. "Scaenica Petroniana." *Transactions of the American Philological Association (1974–)* 104 (1974): 329–46. doi.org/10.2307/2936096.
Scobie, Alex. "Storytellers, Storytelling, and the Novel in Graeco-Roman Antiquity." *Rheinisches Museum für Philologie* 122, no. 3/4 (1979): 229–59. www.jstor.org/stable/41244988.
Shiner, Whitney Taylor. *Proclaiming the Gospel: First-Century Performance of Mark*. Harrisburg, PA: Trinity Press International, 2003.
Shiner, Whitney Taylor. "Sounding the Eschatological Alarm: Chapter Thirteen in the Performance of *Mark*." Paper presented at the Annual Meeting of the Society of Biblical Literature, Atlanta, GA, November 23, 2003. www.sbl-site.org/assets/pdfs/Shiner.pdf.
Smallwood, E. Mary. "Domitian's Attitude toward the Jews and Judaism." *Classical Philology* 51, no. 1 (January 1956): 1–13. www.jstor.org/stable/266380.
Smith, Dennis E., and Joseph B. Tyson, eds. *Acts and Christian Beginnings: The Acts Seminar Report*. Salem, OR: Polebridge Press, 2013.
Smith, Stephen H. "A Divine Tragedy: Some Observations on the Dramatic Structure of Mark's Gospel." *Novum Testamentum* 37, no. 3 (July 1995): 209–31. www.jstor.org/stable/1561221.
Southern, Pat. *Domitian: Tragic Tyrant*. London: Routledge, 1997.
Stecchini, Livio C., and Jan Sammer. *The Gospel According to Seneca*. N.p.: Monica Stecchini, Steven Stecchini, and Jan Sammer, 1996. www.nazarenus.com/0-1-contents.htm (site discontinued).
Trobisch, David. *The First Edition of the New Testament*. New York: Oxford University Press, 2000.
Trobisch, David. "Who Published the New Testament?" *Free Inquiry* 28, no. 1 (December 2007/January 2008): 30–33. https://secularhumanism.org/2008/01/cont-who-published-the-new-testament/.
Tsitsiridis, Stavros. "Greek Mime in the Roman Empire (P.Oxy. 413: *Charition* and *Moicheutria*)." *Logeion* 1 (2011): 184–232. www.logeion.upatras.gr/node/145.
Turton, Michael A. *Michael A. Turton's Historical Commentary on the Gospel of Mark*. Last modified December 31, 2004. www.michaelturton.com/Mark/GMark_index.html.
Tyson, Joseph B. *Marcion and Luke-Acts: A Defining Struggle*. Columbia, SC: University of South Carolina Press, 2006.

Wells, G. A. "Earliest Christianity." *New Humanist* 114, no. 3 (September 1999): 13–18. Electronic version published by Internet Infidels, Inc., 2000. http://infidels.org/library/modern/g_a_wells/earliest.html.

Winn, Adam. *Mark and the Elijah-Elisha Narrative: Considering the Practice of Greco-Roman Imitation in the Search for Markan Source Material.* Eugene, OR: Pickwick Publications, 2010. Adobe Digital Editions EPUB.

Wiseman, Timothy Peter. "*Praetextae, Togatae* and Other Unhelpful Categories." Chap. 11 in *Unwritten Rome,* 194–99. Liverpool: Liverpool University Press, 2008. www.jstor.org/stable/j.ctt5vjn65.

Wright, Adam Z. "Recognizing Jesus: A Study of Recognition Scenes in the Gospel of Mark." *Journal of Greco-Roman Christianity and Judaism* 10 (2014): 174–93. www.jgrchj.net/volume10/JGRChJ10-8_Wright.pdf.

Index

Note: The only element of Appendix E that is indexed is the footnotes.

1

1 Clement, 138
1 Peter, 147

A

acting, 30, 80
  healing of diseases, 64
actors. *See also under* roles; *See also* name of role
  female, 65
  Mark as Jesus, 66
  number of, 134
Acts of the Apostles, 144, 146, 152
Age of Pisces, 77
Andrew, 67n, 68–69
anointing woman in Bethany, 130, 136
Appendix E, introduction to, 116–118
Aristotelian unities, 44
arrest scene, 74–75, 112n
ascension scene
  predictions of, 110
  reconstructed, 111–113
assumptions of this book, xvii
  about Mark, xvii
  about Mark's Jesus, xvii
  about the Jesus movement, xvii
  about the Letters of Paul, xviii
  about the performance, xvii
  a play was performed, xvii
atrium, as possible venue, 50
audience
  description of, 139
  experience at the performance, 121–122
  Mark's sisters in, 126
  participation of, 65, 82, 130, 133, 178n
auditorium, as possible venue, 50

B

baptism scene, staging, 55, 116, 167n
Barabbas, 75–76
Bauer, Walter, 145, 148
Beacham, Richard, xvii
Beelzebul, 39n
benefaction. *See under* Flavia Domitilla
Bethany, dinner in, 129–130
Bethsaida, 56
  and Clemens, 136–137
  blind man of, 136–137
  name, 57
Bethsaida section
  analysis of scenes in, 89–98
  chiasm of reconstructed, 92
Boanerges, 71
boat trips
  number of, 55
  number of actors, 55
Bryant, Michael, 74, 76, 77

C

Caesarea Philippi, 30, 56
calling of Levi, 103, 123
calling of the fishermen, 69, 115, 116
calling of the Twelve, 68
cantilevers, xx
Capernaum, 30, 57n
carpenter, meanings of, 126
cast. *See under* roles; *See* Chorus
Catacombs of Domitilla, 141, 142
central door of scene building. *See* royal door of scene building
Charition, 36
chiasms
  Michael Turton on, 31
  play-level, 32, 69n, 92, 170n
  scene-level, 31, 32
  sentence-level, 31
chief priests, xxii, 43, 73, 74, 76, 178n
Chorus
  allegiance of, 119n
  doubling of, 65, 134
  entry of, 114, 116
  in the Passion, 45

Chorus (*continued*)
   in the subplot, 42, 65
   waiting area, 51
Christ, 41, 64, 143
Christian mythos, 145
church, defined, xxiii
Clemens
   and Clement I, 131
   biography, 130–131
   death, 138
   participation in the performance, 136–137
Clemens, Titus Flavius. *See* Clemens
Clement I, 131, 138n, 142
climax
   defined, 38–39
   of *Hamlet*, 38
   of the Passion, 44
   of the plot of GMark, 40, 106
   of the subplot of GMark, 43. *See also* Temple Incident
contagious holiness, 63
Coptic Orthodox Church, 147
costumes, 63, 75, 170n
Council
   allied with Pharisees, xxii
   defined, xxii
   in subplot of GMark, 42–43
   members of, 73
   onstage location of, 58
crucifixion, staging, 183n
Csapo, Eric, xvii, 132

D

Dalmanutha, 56, 96, 100
dancer, 72–73
date of performance, 127–128
Decapolis, 59
deserted places, 59–60
dialogue
   as pointers to Mark's sources, 30
   cannot be reconstructed, 117
   in Appendix E, 117
   in polished text
     and narration, 26, 29
     not evenly condensed, 32
     preserves key lines, 32
   of mime plays, 35

dinner in Bethany, staging, 71, 129–130
dinner parties
   as venues of social competition, 132
   entertainment at, 131–132
dinner party, defined, 49n
dinner with outcasts, staging, 53–54
Dionysus, 120
disciples
   exit of, 43, 180
   "follower", 70–71, 72
   ignorance of, 41, 115
   in received text, 67
   mission trip of, 93, 95
   names, 71, 81
doctrine, why ignored here, xviii–xix
Doherty, Earl, xvi
Domitian
   and Flavia's sons, 131, 138
   death, 139
   personality, 139
   purge by, 138n
dramatic reading, 27
Dramaturgical Criterion, 86

E

early editors of the polished text, 122–123, 139
earthly story, as subplot of the play, 42
editing, criteria to identify
   Dramaturgical Criterion, 86
   limits of, 86
   Performability Criterion, 85
elders, 73
"*Eloi, Eloi*", 109
empty tomb scene
   origin, 113
   problems with, 110
entry of Jesus, staging, 114
entry to Jerusalem, staging, 56
Esther, 27, 89
Euripides, 112
Eusebius, 146
evening event, defined, 49n
evening events, plays at, 132
Ezekiel the Tragedian, 34

F

First Feeding Miracle
  addition of, 122, 141
  staging problems with, 93
fishermen, as comic characters, 80
Flavia Domitilla
  as anointing woman in Bethany, 136
  as producer of the play, 129, 133
  benefaction
    and Mark's writing, 134
    Catacombs of Domitilla, 142
    Clement I as evidence of, 131
    compatible with the play, 135–137
    historical importance of, 149
    political effect of, 138
    shaping of the performance, 134
  biography, 130
  death, 138
  honored in the play, 133
Flavius Josephus. *See* Josephus

G

Gennesaret, healings at, 94
Gentiles, welcomed in the play, 128, 137
Gerasa scene
  disciples in, 55
  staging, 33, 51, 61, 72, 75
Gerasene demoniac, 72
  as naked young man, 75
  exit of, 59
Gethsemane scene, foreshadowing of, 109
gifts to the audience
  at Second Feeding Miracle, 99
  at Temple Incident, 65
God, defined, xxii
Gospel According to Seneca. See Stecchini and Sammer
Gospel of John, xix, 144, 151n
Gospel of Luke, 151n
  and Gospel of Marcion, 143, 144
Gospel of Mark
  as drama not history, 81
  as source for Marcion, 143
  emotional power of, 46–47

Gospel of Mark (*continued*)
  five-act structure, 46
  in the second century, 148
  not an x-ray of doctrine, 121
  sources of, 30
Gospel of Matthew, 151n
  date of, 144
  Temptation in, 103–105
Gospel of Peter, xixn, 29n
Grebanier, Bernard, 37–39, 42, 81, 107, 117

H

Hadrian, as host, 132
Hadrian's Villa, Greek theater at, 132, 158
Hamlet
  climax of, 38
  Proposition of, 38
healings
  at Gennesaret, 94, 122
  blind Bartimaeus, 101–102, 122
  blind man of Bethsaida, 59, 100–101, 136–137
  deaf-mute, 100
  epileptic boy, 56, 70
  Jairus's daughter, 119, 171n
  leper, 114, 116
  list of, 118
  man with withered hand, 115
  of conditions caused by possession, 64
  paralytic, 30, 54
  possessed man, 115
  Simon's mother-in-law, 115
  Syrophoenician woman's daughter, 94
  woman with hemorrhage, 119
heavenly story, as plot of GMark, 37, 40
Hebrews, 121
Herod Agrippa II, 89
Herodians, 73, 97
Herod scene, reconstruction of, 86–88

I

induction, xx
Irenaeus, xxiii, 144, 147
  and Jesus of Nazareth, 145
  on Mark and Peter, 147

J

James (role), 71
Jericho, 57
  original scene in, 102
Jesus figure
  as high priest, 42, 120, 143
  conversion into Jesus of Nazareth, 143–145
  defined, xxii
  early concepts of, 143
  identified as Christ, 41, 64, 143
Jesus movement, defined, xxii
Jesus of Nazareth
  defined, xxii
  in Gospel of Mark, 81
  origin of biography of, 148
  orthodox promotion of, 145
  timeline of creation of, 143–144
Jesus prays on a mountain, staging, 97
Jesus (role), 66
  age, 125
  as Cynic philosopher, 135
  as high priest, 55, 63
  attitude to wealth, 135
  compared to John the Baptist, 89
  in overlaid plot, subplot and Passion, 47
Jesus's death, staging, 62, 77, 109, 183n
Jesus's solitary prayer, staging, 41, 115
Jews, xxi. *See also* Judeans
John Barelycon, 33n
John Bully, 33n
John Doe names
  Marcus, 127
  Mary, 78
  Simon, 33
John (role), 71
John the Baptist, compared to Jesus, 88–89
John the Baptist (role), 55
Joseph of Arimathea, 33
  and Josephus, 78–79
Josephus, 79, 128
Judaism, xxi
Judas Iscariot, 69, 70, 74
Judeans
  as ethnic identity, xxi
  as Roman congregation's identity, 141
  term used in this book, xxi
Judean theater, 34
Justin Martyr, 76, 144

L

Last Supper
  as first scene of the Passion, 44
  staging, 52, 55, 76, 82, 179n
Law, defined, xxii
Legio X Fretensis, 61
Letter of Clement, 138
Levi, 54, 70, 103, 123
lighting, 61–62
Little Apocalypse. *See* Olivet Discourse

M

Marcion, 143–144, 149, 152
Mark
  age, 125
  and Egypt, 147
  and role of Jesus, 125
  and Venice, 148
  as amanuensis of Peter, 146–147
  as Judean, 126–127
  death of, 140
  name, 127
  sisters of, 126
Mark 1, reconstruction of, 114–116
Mary Magdalene, 77–78
mechane. *See* stage crane
mime features of the performed play
  audience participation, 82
  component mini-tragedy, 44
  female actors, 65
  informal entry of Chorus, 115
  nudity, 75
  raucous mêlée, 36, 113
  stupid second actor, 80
mime (genre)
  and diction of polished text, 36
  as genre of Mark's play, 25, 36, 120
  defined, 35–36
miniature theater
  single-level
    blocking of the play, 52
  two-level
    blocking of the play, 53
    dimensions of, 158–160

miniature theater
  two-level (*continued*)
    photograph of, 84
    sources of, 158
mocking of Jesus, 182n
Moicheutria, 36
music, 63
mystery plays, 28, 120

N

naked young man, 74–75
nard, 64
Narrator, 25–26
Nero, 125n
Nerva, 139

O

Olivet Discourse, 106–109
  ascension prediction in, 110
  does not date the play, 127
  editing of, 123
  reconstruction, 107–108
Orestes, 112
orthodoxy
  defined, xxiii
  Irenaeus as representative of, 144
  usefulness of Jesus of Nazareth to, 147
Osiris, 120
"other boats were with him", 55
outcasts, 54, 77
Oxyrhynchus, 36

P

papacy, and the Roman congregation, 142
Papias, 146
parable of the sower, 41
parables of Mk 4, 117
Passion
  as separate play
    by Mark, 44, 134
    not by Mark, xvi, 28, 45
  as tragedy, xvi, 44
  climax of, 44
  defined, xxiii
  potential reversals in, 45–46
  Proposition of, 44

Passion plays, 45
patronage. *See under* Flavia Domitilla, benefaction
Paul, 152
Performability Criterion, 85
performative reading, 27
performed play
  acting, 80
  and dinner, 133–134
  and mystery plays, 120
  assumption of performance of, xvii
  audience for, 49
  comic elements of, 80
  date of, 127–128
  deleted partial scenes
    boat trips to/from Dalmanutha, 96
    conversation about no bread, 96–97
    disciples' mission trip, 93, 95
    explanation of what defiles, 95–96
    Jesus prays on a mountain, 97
    list of, 95
    "other boats were with him", 55
    private teachings, 54
  deleted scenes
    calling of Levi, 103
    empty tomb scene, 110, 113
    First Feeding Miracle, 93–94
    healing of blind Bartimaeus, 101–102
    healing of deaf-mute, 100
    healing of possessed man, 115
    healing of Simon's mother-in-law, 115
    healings at Gennesaret, 94
    list of, 92
    Syrophoenician-woman scene, 94
    travel to a deserted place, 93
  did not present new doctrine, xix
  discovery of, 25
  duration of, 120
  Flavia's production of, 133
  genre, 25, 35, 120–121
  implications of benefaction for, 134
  locations in the theater
    Bethany, 165
    Bethsaida, 75
    Capernaum, 55
    courtyard, 61
    mapped to miniature theater, 84

performed play
   locations in the theater (*continued*)
      garden, 51
      Gerasa, 51, 75
      Gethsemane, 75
      harbor on Sea of Galilee, 51
      house, 53
      house of the high priest, 75
      Jordan River, 55
      mountain, 51
      names spoken, 57
      praetorium, 53, 55
      Sea of Galilee, 55, 57
      synagogue, 53, 55
      Temple Court, 53, 57
      Temple holy precincts, 55, 57
      the way, 56
      tomb, 51
      upper room, 53, 55
      villages, 58–59
      wilderness, 60
   missing scenes
      boat trip to Bethsaida, 98
      Jericho scene, 102
      Satan entrances Peter, 106
   not a "religious" event, 133
   pro-Gentile slant of, 128, 135, 137
   reconstruction, limits of, 116–118
   rehearsals of, 133
   reported scenes
      dinner with outcasts, 54
      Herod scene, 87–88
   scent in, 64
   single performance of, 135
   staging
      arrest scene, 74–75, 112n
      ascension, 111–112
      baptism scene, 55, 116, 167n
      blessing of children, 82
      boat trips, 55
      calling of the fishermen, 69, 115
      crossing of upper stage, 179n
      crucifixion, 183n
      dinner in Bethany, 64, 130, 136
      dinner with outcasts, 54
      earthquake, 64

performed play
   staging (*continued*)
      entombment of Jesus, 78
      entry of Jesus, 114
      entry of the Chorus, 114, 116
      entry to Jerusalem, 56, 102
      exit of demoniac from Gerasa, 59
      Gerasa scene, 51, 61, 72, 170n
      healing of blind man of Bethsaida, 59, 100–101, 136–137
      healing of epileptic boy, 70
      healing of Jairus's daughter, 171n
      healing of leper, 114, 116
      healing of paralytic, 30, 54
      indoor scenes, 53
      Jesus in the villages teaching, 58
      Jesus's death, 62, 77, 109–110, 183n
      Jesus's solitary prayer, 41, 115
      Judas's conspiring, 74
      Last Supper, 55, 82
      march to the cross, 76
      mocking of Jesus, 76
      mountain scenes, 60
      obtaining a colt, 58
      Peter in the courtyard, 61
      Pharisees demand a sign, 92
      Recognition, 105–106
      Second Feeding Miracle, 98–99
      stilling-of-the-storm scene, 99
      teaching from a boat, 55
      Temple Incident, 43, 52, 65, 82
      Transfiguration, 60
      trial before Pilate, 75, 76
      trial before the Council, 45, 117
      water-walk scene, 62, 99
   tableaux
      ascension scene, 112
      Last Supper, 55
      Recognition, 106
   technical elements
      costumes, 63, 75, 170n
      lighting, 61–62
      sound, 63
   time of day performed, 133–134
   venue, 49
Persephone, 120

Peter
    as stupid second actor, 80
    entrancement of, 174n, 181n
    in arrest scene, 112
    in ascension scene, 111–112
    in climax of plot, 41, 105–106
    name, 71, 112n
Pharisees
    allied with scribes, xxii, 73
    and the Second Feeding Miracle, 98
    concerns of, 73
    conspire with Judas, 69, 74
    demand a sign, 92, 100, 173n
    influence on Chorus, 65
    in reconstructed Bethsaida section, 92
    location onstage, 58
    yeast of, 97
pigs, 33, 61
Pilate, 45, 46, 75, 76
    historical Pontius, 127
play, defined, xxiii
Playwriting: How to Write for the Theater, 37. *See also* Grebanier, Bernard
plot of GMark
    as heavenly story, 37
    climax of, 40
    Proposition of, 40
    relationship to subplot, 40, 42, 44
    second-century erasure of, 148
poison, 77
polished text
    as a myth, 29, 121
    bias of, 137
    defined, 29
    early editors of, 122, 139, 143
    genre of is preserved play, xix, 28
    gift to Flavia Domitilla, 135
    in the second century, 148
    literary features
        chiasms, 31–32
        condensed dialogue, 117
        diction, 36
        key lines, 32
        names of characters and places, 30
        narrated speech and action, 29
        pointers to Mark's sources, 30

polished text
    literary features (*continued*)
        time lapses, 30
    Mark's expectation of survival, 135
    not didactic, xix
    pro-Judean edits to, 141
Polycarp of Smyrna, 144
precession of the equinoxes, 77n
preserved play
    genre of polished text, 28
    genre of received text, 27n
Price, Robert M., xvi, xviii
Price, William T., 37
Proposition
    defined, 37, 39
    of *Hamlet*, 38
    of the Passion, 44
    of the plot, 40
    of the subplot, 42
proto-orthodoxy, defined, xxiii
Psalm 22, 109–110, 121, 151

R

received text of GMark
    diction, 27
    playlike features, 34
    proposals for genre, 27–28
Recognition
    received staging, 33
    reconstructed staging, 106
    religious meaning of, 41
reconstruction, limits of, 116–118
Reform Judaism, 142
Robertson, J. M., xvi, 28
roles
    Andrew, 67n, 68–69
    anointing woman in Bethany, 129–130
    Barabbas, 75–76
    blind man of Bethsaida, 136–137
    chief priests, xxii, 43, 73, 74, 76, 178n
    Chorus, 65, 119n
        in the Passion, 45
    disciples, 67–72, 174n
    elders, 73
    enemies of Jesus, 73
    Gerasene demoniac, 72, 75

roles (*continued*)
  Herodians, 73
  James, 71
  Jesus, 66, 135
  John, 71
  John the Baptist, 55, 88–89
  Joseph of Arimathea, 78–79
  Judas Iscariot, 69, 70, 74
  leper, 116
  Levi, 54, 70
  Mary Magdalene, 77–78
  naked young man, 74–75
  names spoken in performance, 81–82
  outcasts, 54, 77
  Peter. *See* Peter
  Pharisees. *See* Pharisees
  Pilate, 45, 46
  Roman soldiers, 61, 78, 99
  Satan. *See* Satan (role)
  scribes, 43, 53, 73, 76
  Simon of Cyrene, 76–77
  Simon the Leper, 136
  the slave of the high priest, 111n, 184n
Roman church. *See* Roman congregation
Roman congregation
  in Mark's time, 128, 143
    ancestor of orthodox churches, 131
  in the second century, 146
    canon of, 144
    headquarters of orthodoxy, 142
    identity of, 141
Roman soldiers, 61, 78–79, 99
Rome, as site of the performance, xvii
Rostra, 56n
royal door of scene building
  area in front of, 55, 179
  closing of, 112
  opening of, 114

S

Sadducees, 178n
Sammer, Jan. *See* Stecchini and Sammer
Sanhedrin. *See* Council
Satanic spirits. *See also under* healings
  as agents of Satan, 39
  possession by, 64, 69n, 70n, 78

Satan (role)
  and Beelzebul, 39n
  antagonist in plot, 39–40
  blurred by editors, 41, 66
  entrancement of Peter, 106, 174n
  in the Recognition, 106
  in the Temptation, 103–105
  scenes. *See* name of scene; *See under* performed play, staging.
scribes, 43, 53, 73, 76
  as allies of Pharisees, 73
Scripture, defined, xxii
Seneca the Younger, 27, 151
Septuagint, xxii
Shiner, Whitney, 80
Simon, as John Doe name, 33
Simon of Cyrene, 33, 76–77
Simon Peter. *See* Peter
Simon the Cananaean, 33
Simon the Leper, 33, 136
S-Mark, 122, 139
sound effects, 63
sources of GMark, why not discussed, xviii–xix
Southern, Pat, 138, 139
spikenard, 64
stage crane, 64, 114
  in ascension scene, 111
  in the Temptation, 104
Stage Left, defined, 50
Stage Right, defined, 50
Stecchini and Sammer
  contributions of, 28, 51, 150
  limitations of work of, 150–151
Stecchini, Livio. *See* Stecchini and Sammer
stilling-of-the-storm scene, 99
subplot of GMark
  alternative antagonists for, 42
  as earthly story, 37
  Jesus-Council conflict as, 42
  Proposition of, 42
  relationship to plot, 40
  second-century treatment of, 148
  Temple Incident as climax of, 43–44
subplots, structural difference from plots, 42

Syrophoenician-woman scene, 122, 141
   problems with, 94

T

Temple Incident
   as climax of the subplot, 43
   coins as gifts at, 65, 82
   sets up disciples' exits, 43
   staging, 43, 52
   why Jesus not arrested at, 43
Temple veil, 58
Temptation
   exposition at, 39
   reconstruction, 103–105
Ten Towns, 59
Theater of Dionysus
   drawing of, 52, 83
   source for two-level miniature theater, 158
   source of staging conventions, 50
theater of the performance
   and locations of the play, 60
   seating in, 130, 132
theater, private, as possible venue, 50, 132
the slave of the high priest, 111, 112
thymele, 61
Transfiguration, staging, 60
trial by Pilate, 75, 76
trial by the Council
   ascension prediction in, 111
   illegality of, 45
triclinium, as possible venue, 49
Trimalchio, 35
Turton, Michael, xvi
   on chiasms in GMark, 31, 93, 97, 102
   on staging of GMark, 28

V

Venice, 148
Vridar (blog), xvi

W

water-walk scene, staging, 62, 99
way, the, stagings on, 56
we-have-no-bread scene, problems, 96–97
wilderness, 59–60

ABOUT THE AUTHOR

Danila Oder received a BA in history from the University of Chicago and studied at Spertus College of Judaica. She has studied playwriting and worked as an actor. She currently works as a freelance editor and proofreader. She lives in Los Angeles. This is her first book.

www.ingramcontent.com/pod-product-compliance
Lightning Source LLC
Chambersburg PA
CBHW021405290426
44108CB00010B/389